Computer Professional's Dictionary

Computer Professional's Dictionary

Allen L. Wyatt

Osborne McGraw-Hill

Berkeley   New York   St. Louis   San Francisco
Auckland   Bogotá   Hamburg   London   Madrid
Mexico City   Milan   Montreal   New Delhi   Panama City
Paris   São Paulo   Singapore   Sydney
Tokyo   Toronto

Osborne **McGraw-Hill**
2600 Tenth Street
Berkeley, California 94710
U.S.A.

Osborne **McGraw-Hill** offers software for sale. For information on software, translations, or book distributors outside of the U.S.A., please write to Osborne **McGraw-Hill** at the above address.

This book is printed on recycled paper.

Computer Professional's Dictionary

The manuscript for this book was prepared and submitted to Osborne **McGraw-Hill** in electronic form. The acquisitions editor for this project was Roger Stewart, the technical reviewer was Chuck Guzis, and the project editor was Laura Sackerman.

Text design by Judy Wohlfrom and Deborra Knotts, using Baskerville for text body and display. Graphics by Lance Ravella.

Color separation and cover supplier, Phoenix Color Corporation. Book printed and bound by R.R. Donnelley & Sons Company, Crawfordsville, Indiana.

1234567890 DOC 99876543210

ISBN 0-07-881705-6

Introduction

The world of computer technology seems to be ever-expanding. Computers permeate everyday life to a point unimagined just a decade or two ago. In this fast-changing world, it is easy to lose track of current terminology. This book has been developed as a reference to the use of terms in the computer field. It is not intended as a computer manual. Instead, it is a glossary of computer terminology, written not for the novice user, but for those who already have some familiarity with the industry. In it you will find many terms you know (or thought you knew), as well as many with which you are unfamiliar.

I have included terms from virtually every aspect of computing. There are terms from almost every discipline, language, and operating system. Some are arcane, others are faddish, and others you will run into in daily conversation.

That is not to say that this dictionary includes everything—on the contrary, there are several classifications of terms that have been purposely left out or limited in order to increase the conciseness and usefulness of the dictionary.

For instance, companies and application software products are not included, since names such as Apple Computer, IBM, Microsoft, and Hewlett-Packard are well-known to the general public. Likewise, anyone with even a rudimentary introduction to computers probably needs no definition for Lotus 1-2-3, WordPerfect, or MacWrite. Most computer-related associations have also been omitted.

Conventions Used in This Book

Before proceeding, let's take a look at a few conventions I have followed throughout this dictionary.

Presentation Order

Words are included in their absolute alphabetic order. This means that spaces, commas, periods, slashes, and hyphens that appear in a word are ignored. Terms are ordered as if the letters and numbers in them were all run together and all of the same case.

Terms beginning with numbers are grouped together at the beginning of the dictionary, before the As. They could have been placed in the dictionary as if the numbers had been spelled out (thus, 486 would have been placed after forward chaining and before fourth-generation language). I felt this would have been a little cumbersome to the reader, however.

Usage

Most words are used in only a single way—they are either nouns, verbs, adjectives, or some other part of speech. Once in a while, a term can be used in different ways. In these cases, the word is given two separate definitions. For instance, if a word can be used as both a noun and a verb, it is given two entries in the dictionary. The noun is the first definition, and it has an italic *n* to the right of the word. The verb form is the second definition, and it has an italic *v* to the right. For instance:

access *n*   The ability to read, write, execute, or otherwise use information stored in a computer system.

access *v*   To use a file or computer system, or the information stored therein.

In addition, there may be multiple definitions of a single term, as the term may have multiple meanings based on the context in which it is used. Many times a definition will vary depending on who is using it—the same word means different things to an electrical engineer than to a systems analyst.

In this dictionary, multiple definitions are shown in the following format:

accuracy   1. The exactness of a mathematical operation. 2.The correctness of information entered in a computer system.

There is one thing I would ask, however. Please send a written message. They are much easier to track, and there is less tendency to misunderstand what is written.

I hope you enjoy the dictionary and find it useful.

286   See *80286*.

287   See *80287*.

3270   An IBM terminal used with IBM mainframe computers.

386   See *80386*.

387   See *80387*.

3x box   In the OS/2 environment, the portion of the operating system that emulates an 8086-based PC running MS-DOS versions 2.*x* or 3.*x*.

486   See *80486*.

4GL   See *fourth-generation language*.

68000   See *MC68000*.

68020   See *MC68020*.

68030   See *MC68030*.

68881   See *MC68881*.

68882   See *MC68882*.

80286   A 16-bit microprocessor manufactured by Intel Corporation. It is formally called the iAPX 286, but commonly called simply the 286. This microprocessor is a second-generation of the earlier iAPX 86 (8086). It builds on the same instruction set as the 8086, but runs at a higher clock rate. It also introduced protected mode programming. This chip is used in second-generation IBM personal computers and clones beginning with the PC AT.

80287   A numeric processor extension manufactured by Intel Corporation; designed for use with 80286 and 80386 CPUs.

80386   A 32-bit microprocessor developed by Intel Corporation. It is formally called the iAPX 386, but commonly called the 386. It can address up to 4 gigabytes of physical memory, and up to 64 terabytes of virtual memory. The chip is downward-compatible with other members of the 80*x*86 family of processors, but through advances in architecture can operate at higher clock speeds (up to 33 MHz). Several new operating modes were introduced with the 386 that have yet to be effectively tapped by software. Versions of this chip are used in several members of the IBM PS/2 line and in many super PC AT clones. There are two versions of the 386: the 80386-SX and the 80386-DX. The SX is a scaled-down version of the full 32-bit 80386 (the 80386-DX).

80387   A numeric processor extension manufactured by Intel Corporation; designed to be used with the 80386 CPU.

80486   A 32-bit super microprocessor developed by Intel Corporation, commonly called the 486, but formally called the i486. This chip is downward-compatible with other members of the 80*x*86 family of processors, but through advances in architecture can operate at very high performance levels. In addition, the 486 includes an integrated numeric coprocessor equivalent to the 80387, so a separate specialized chip is not needed.

8086   A 16-bit microprocessor manufactured by Intel Corporation, formally called the iAPX 86. This microprocessor is closely related to the iAPX 88 (8088). The iAPX 86 and the iAPX 88 both understand the same instructions and have the same internal architecture. Their differences are minor: For instance, the 8086 uses a 16-bit external data bus and the 8088 uses an 8-bit data bus; where the pre-fetch queue of the 8086 fetches two instruction bytes at a time, the 8088 retrieves only one.

8087   A numeric processor extension manufactured by Intel Corporation; designed to be used with 8086/8088 CPUs.

8088   A 16-bit microprocessor manufactured by Intel Corporation, formally called the iAPX 88. This microprocessor is closely related to the iAPX 86 (8086). The iAPX 88 and the iAPX 86 both understand the same instructions and have the same internal architecture. Their differences are minor: For instance, the 8088 uses an 8-bit data bus and the 8086 uses a 16-bit external data bus; where the pre-fetch queue of the 8088 fetches only one instruction byte at a time, the 8086 retrieves two. This chip was used in the first-generation IBM personal computers and clones, as well as the PC XT and PCjr.

8088 memory model   See *tiny memory model*.

80x86   A reference to Intel Corporation's family of microprocessors. Includes the 8086, 8088, 80286, 80386, and 80486.

80x87   A reference to Intel Corporation's family of numeric processor extensions. Includes the 8087, 80287, and 80387.

86-DOS   A forerunner of MS-DOS. See also *MS-DOS*.

abbreviated addressing   A variation of direct addressing in which a portion of each address is assumed to be the same value. This allows quicker processing of the addresses since fewer bits must be manipulated.

abend   A contraction of abnormal end. This occurs when a program is presented with either commands or data it cannot process successfully. Typically, an abend is the result of hardware failure or faulty program logic.

abort *n*   A completely unrecoverable microprocessor exception; an interrupt that occurs when a processor cannot continue executing the current program. An example is an exception caused by division by zero.

abort *v*   To quit completely a process or program in an orderly, controlled manner. Some individuals use this term when they really mean abend. After aborting a process or program, the user's data is typically still intact and the system is still capable of processing other information.

ABS   A common name for a function that calculates absolute values. See also *absolute value*.

ABS frame   In the PICK operating system, one of the frames within the first group of frames of the operating system. This group of frames contains the PICK object code, and is known as the ABS section.

absolute address   The unique, explicit identification of a memory location, or a peripheral device or location within the device. Contrast with *relative address*.

absolute coding   When programming, using absolute addresses instead of symbolic addresses. While absolute coding often involves using numeric opcodes (machine language) instead of assembly language mnemonics, it is also possible to use absolute coding of an address within an otherwise symbolic program.

absolute coordinate   The absolute location (either two- or three-dimensional) of a point, with reference to a fixed origin point. The designation of such a point is controlled by the application software, but is commonly designated as a series of numeric values. Each value is separated from the next by a comma and represents an offset from the origin point along the x, y, or z axis. An example is 4.57,3.68,12.42.

absolute loader   A program routine that loads a program file from a disk drive or other peripheral storage into RAM, beginning at the absolute memory location specified as the origin when the program was first assembled. An absolute loader is typically a part of the operating system.

absolute pathname   In operating systems based on a hierarchical file structure system, the full path to a file, beginning at the root directory. In the MS-DOS operating system, the following is an absolute pathname:

```
C:\UTILITY\EDITOR\DATA\FRED.DOC
```

See also *path*.

absolute value   A number without its sign. For instance, the absolute value of both −846 and +846 is simply 846.

absolute vector   In computer graphics, a vector with its end point designated by absolute coordinates.

abstraction   The process of breaking a program into increasingly less specific components that are individually programmed. This modularization helps break programming tasks into manageable chunks and hides programming details from users.

accelerator board   A printed circuit board that increases the computing capacity of a computer. Typically, this is done by including a CPU on the accelerator board that is of a newer, faster generation than the one native to the computer the board is used with.

accelerator key   A special key combination that performs the same action as a menu selection. Commonly used on GUI systems such as the Macintosh and programs such as Microsoft Windows.

acceptance test   Final hardware and/or software testing done by a user after installation of a computer system.

ACCESS   The information retrieval language used in the PICK operating system.

access *n*   The ability to read, write, execute, or otherwise use information stored in a computer system.

access *v*   To use a file or computer system, or the information stored therein.

access arm   The mechanical device that holds, moves, and positions the read/write heads in a disk drive. An example of an access arm is shown here:

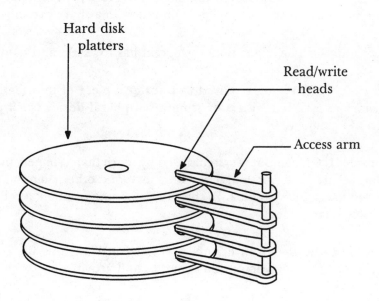

Hard disk
platters

Read/write
heads

Access arm

access channel control   In a network environment, the devices that manage the bidirectional transfer of information between the link stations and medium access control.

access code   A password or special series of characters or numbers that allows access to a computer system (hardware or software).

access control   A security systems feature that limits the number, type, or abilities of users. Access control can be implemented either as a part of the operating system (as in UNIX) or in application software.

access control byte   In a token-ring network, this is the byte following the start delimiter in a token or frame. It effectively controls access to the network. See also *access control*.

accessory   See *desk accessory* or *peripheral*.

access path   See *path*.

access priority   In a token-ring network, the priority level assigned to a token. This level controls the transmission of the token over the network.

access procedure   In LAN terminology, this is the procedure or protocol used by nodes on the network to gain access to a shared resource.

access rights   The rights that a program has to access and modify files.

access time   The time required to transfer a piece of information from memory to a CPU register, or from a peripheral device (such as a disk drive) to memory.

account   **1.** On computer systems used by more than one person, a logon name, security information, home directory, and other client information needed to use the system. **2.** In the PICK operating system, a collection of logically related files.

accounting audit file   In a LAN utilizing NetWare, this file contains a detailed record of all accounting charges and activities.

accumulator   A generic term for a CPU register that receives the results of an operation.

accuracy   **1.** The exactness of a mathematical operation. **2.** The correctness of information entered in a computer system.

ACD   See *automatic call distributor*.

ACK   See *acknowledge character*.

acknowledge character   In data communications, the acknowledgment code transmitted to signal that information has been received and that the receiver is again ready to accept information. The ASCII value for this character is 6, the EBCDIC value is 46, and the abbreviation is ACK. See also *negative acknowledge character*.

ACM   See *Association for Computing Machinery*.

acoustic coupler   A device used to connect a terminal or computer to a standard telephone handset. The handset's mouthpiece and receiver are cradled in the acoustic coupler so corresponding speakers and microphones in the coupler can transmit sounds to the computer's modem (see Figure A-1). The acoustic coupler often has a modem built into its housing.

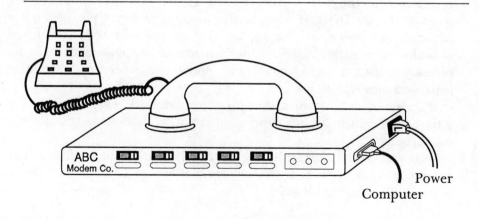

Figure A-1.   An acoustic coupler

AC signaling   In data communications, the use of alternating current signals or tones for the transmission of information or control signals.

action predicate   In Prolog, a predicate used for making a rule or goal.

active monitor   In network terminology, one node of the network functions as an active monitor to perform routine maintenance activities, such as starting token transmission and providing token error recovery.

active printer   The printer currently connected to a port and selected to receive output from a program.

active token monitor   In IBM's token-ring network, the computer that is responsible for network management.

active window   In a windowing environment, the window in which the user is currently working, or in which work is currently taking place.

ACU   See *Association of Computer Users* or *automatic calling unit*.

Ada   A high-level programming language developed by the Department of Defense in the 1970s. Ada is used as the standard programming language for the DOD. It is a language used for real-time processing (for instance, in embedded systems), and has its roots in both Pascal and Modula-2. It was designed for a broad spectrum of applications and ease of maintenance; as such, many programmers consider Ada difficult to learn and unwieldy to use.

Ada is modular in nature, thus programs can be developed one part at a time. It also includes object-oriented language extensions and permits concurrency.

Ada was named after Lady Augusta Ada Byron, one of the first female computer enthusiasts. Lady Byron was a friend of Charles Babbage, a pioneer in the computer field.

ADAPSO   See *Association of Data Processing Service Organizations*.

adapter   A device that allows one system to connect and work with another. In computers, an adapter usually refers to the printed circuit board that is responsible for communicating with an external peripheral. Sometimes referred to as a controller card.

adapter card   See *adapter*.

adapter support interface   In the IBM token-ring network environment, the software used to operate the network adapter cards and provide a common environment interface to application programs.

ADB   See *Apple desktop bus*.

ADC   An acronym for analog-to-digital converter.

ADCCP   See *advanced data communications control protocol*.

adder   A device designed to produce the sum of two numbers.

address   A unique numeric value assigned to a memory location for reference purposes. See also *logical address* or *physical address*.

addressable cursor   A cursor that can be moved (by a program) to any position on the screen.

address bus   An internal electrical channel between the CPU and memory, used to transmit memory addresses. These addresses can refer to data or code, and specify the location for storing information or fetching data needed by the CPU. Each line of an address bus carries one bit of an address, thus the number of lines limits the amount of memory that can be directly addressed.

addressing mode   The method used to derive an absolute memory address. Further information on addressing modes can be found under the various types:

   address register addressing
   base indexed addressing
   base relative addressing

data register addressing
direct addressing
direct indexed addressing
immediate addressing
indexed register indirect addressing
postincrement register indirect addressing
predecrement register indirect addressing
program counter indirect addressing with offset
program counter relative addressing
program counter relative addressing with index and offset
register addressing
register indirect addressing

address register   A register within the CPU that contains a pointer to a memory location. This location may be the next code instruction to be executed, or the next piece of data to be processed.

address register addressing   In the 680x0 (Motorola) family of microprocessors, a method of addressing in which the contents of an address register are used as an operand. See also *addressing mode*; *data register addressing*; *register addressing*.

address register direct   See *address register addressing*.

address-size prefix   A prefix for a programming instruction that explicitly specifies the size of address offsets.

address space   A range of memory locations (either physical or virtual) that may be accessed by a computer.

address translation   The process of changing from one memory addressing system to another and still maintaining a reference to the desired absolute memory location. In segmented memory systems (such as the Intel family of microprocessors), this is often done when using different segment and offset combinations to refer to the same memory location. In these systems, the process of going from one segment:offset combination to another is address translation.

ADF   See *application development facility*.

ADI   See *Apple desktop interface*.

ADP   An acronym for automatic data processing.

advanced BASIC   See *BASICA*.

advanced data communications control protocol   A data communications protocol certified by ANSI.

AdvanceNet   A Hewlett-Packard networking strategy incorporating the OSI and SNA architectures. AdvanceNet also supports MAP, Starlan 10, EtherNet, and X.25 packet switching networks.

AES   See *asynchronous event scheduler*.

AFIPS   See *American Federation of Information Processing Societies*.

AFP   See *AppleTalk filing protocol*.

aggregate function   In database terminology, a type of function that computes a single value based upon the collective values of a single column or field in all records of the database. For example, if a database has 100 records, an aggregate function may use the values in the third field of each of the 100 records to calculate a result.

AI   See *artificial intelligence*.

AIX   The IBM version of UNIX designed to run on 80386-series microcomputers, the IBM PC/RT, and IBM's System/370 mainframe series. AIX is a contraction of advanced interactive executive, and is based on AT&T's UNIX System V with Berkeley extensions.

alert box   In a GUI environment, a pop-up message box that is used to warn the user of an existing condition or the consequences of some impending action. The following is an example of an alert box.

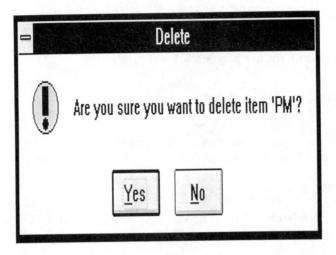

ALGOL   A high-level programming language developed in the early 1960s. ALGOL is a contraction of algorithmic language, and was intended as an international language allowing the expression of algorithms. There are two major versions of ALGOL: ALGOL 60 and ALGOL 68. ALGOL 60 is the earlier of the two, and was the first programming language to allow recursion. ALGOL 68 was developed later, and is a more comprehensive and difficult language.

algorithm   A formula, series of steps, or well-defined set of rules for solving a problem.

alias   An alternate name or label for another name or label.

aliasing   **1.** An undesirable effect of drawing a diagonal line on a low-resolution output device that uses dot-matrix technology. For example, close examination of diagonal lines created on a 300-dpi laser printer will reveal a "stairstep" effect that makes the lines appear choppy. Special hardware, software, or higher resolution is needed to overcome this condition. **2.** The process of creating an alias. See also *alias*.

align type   In the 80*x*86 (Intel) environment, an assembly language directive specifying how the start of the segment is to be aligned in memory. The align type is specified on the same line as the segment name and is accomplished with the ALIGN assembler directive.

allocate   To assign a computer resource (or a portion thereof) to a single process, user, or file. Such resources may include CPUs, CPU time, disk drives, printers, memory, or disk sectors.

allocation unit   See *cluster*.

all points addressable   A graphics mode in which each pixel on the screen can be accessed directly by a program. The common acronym is APA.

alphabetic   Information that contains only the letters of the alphabet, either upper- or lowercase.

alphameric   Same as *alphanumeric*.

alphanumeric   Information that contains both alphabetic characters and numeric digits.

alpha test   The first formal testing of new hardware or software. Alpha testing is typically done by and within the company that is developing the product. It is different from beta testing, which is done by individuals outside the company.

alternate track   A spare track on a hard disk that is used if a regular track is determined to be damaged or unusable.

Alt key   A specialized keyboard key that, when pressed with other keys, alters their meaning, function, or interpretation. It is similar in function to the Shift key. Alt is short for alternate, meaning the key provides alternate meanings for other keys on the keyboard.

ALU   See *arithmetic/logic unit*.

ambient conditions   The environment surrounding a computer, including light, temperature, and humidity.

ambient noise   Inherent interference always present in a communications line.

AMC   See *attribute mark count*.

American Federation of Information Processing Societies   An organization that serves as a voice for the computer industry. It was founded in 1961 and seeks to advance knowledge in the information-processing sciences. AFIPS can be contacted at:

American Federation of Information Processing Societies
1899 Preston White Drive
Reston, VA 22091
(703) 620-8900

American National Standards Institute   An organization devoted to the development of American industry standards (not just in the computer area). ANSI is supported by more than 1,000 companies, trade organizations, and professional societies. It represents the United States to the International Standards Organization (ISO) and the International Electrotechnical Commission (IEC). ANSI was founded in 1918 and can be contacted at:

American National Standards Institute
1430 Broadway
New York, NY 10018
(212) 354-3300

American standard code for information interchange   Commonly referred to by the acronym ASCII, this is the character coding system most commonly used by computer systems. It is used to convert numeric values to characters and digits that humans can understand, and vice-versa. ASCII defines 128 characters, each assigned a numeric value between 0 and 127, as shown in Table A-1.

Extended ASCII sets are used on many computers. In these supersets of ASCII, the numeric values between 128 and 255 are also assigned additional characters. There is no universally recognized standard for these additional characters. See also *extended character set*; *extended binary coded decimal interchange code*.

Decimal	Octal	Hex	Character	Comment
0	0	0	NUL	Null
1	1	1	SOH	Start of heading
2	2	2	STX	Start of text
3	3	3	ETX	Break/End of text
4	4	4	EOT	End of transmission
5	5	5	ENQ	Enquiry
6	6	6	ACK	Positive acknowledge
7	7	7	BEL	Bell
8	10	8	BS	Backspace
9	11	9	HT	Horizontal tab
10	12	A	LF	Line feed
11	13	B	VT	Vertical tab
12	14	C	FF	Form feed
13	15	D	CR	Carriage return
14	16	E	SO	Shift out
15	17	F	SI	Shift in/XON (resume output)
16	20	10	DLE	Data link escape
17	21	11	DC1	Device control character 1
18	22	12	DC2	Device control character 2
19	23	13	DC3	Device control character 3/XOFF (pause output)
20	24	14	DC4	Device control character 4
21	25	15	NAK	Negative acknowledge
22	26	16	SYN	Synchronous idle
23	27	17	ETB	End of transmission block
24	30	18	CAN	Cancel
25	31	19	EM	End of medium
26	32	1A	SUB	Substitute/End of file

Table A-1.   The ASCII Character Set

Decimal	Octal	Hex	Character	Comment
27	33	1B	ESC	Escape
28	34	1C	FS	File separator
29	35	1D	GS	Group separator
30	36	1E	RS	Record separator
31	37	1F	US	Unit separator
32	40	20	SP	Space
33	41	21	!	
34	42	22	"	
35	43	23	#	
36	44	24	$	
37	45	25	%	
38	46	26	&	
39	47	27	'	
40	50	28	(	
41	51	29	)	
42	52	2A	*	
43	53	2B	+	
44	54	2C	,	
45	55	2D	-	
46	56	2E	.	
47	57	2F	/	
48	60	30	0	
49	61	31	1	
50	62	32	2	
51	63	33	3	
52	64	34	4	
53	65	35	5	
54	66	36	6	
55	67	37	7	
56	70	38	8	
57	71	39	9	
58	72	3A	:	
59	73	3B	;	
60	74	3C	<	

Table A-1.   The ASCII Character Set (continued)

Decimal	Octal	Hex	Character	Comment
61	75	3D	=	
62	76	3E	>	
63	77	3F	?	
64	100	40	@	
65	101	41	A	
66	102	42	B	
67	103	43	C	
68	104	44	D	
69	105	45	E	
70	106	46	F	
71	107	47	G	
72	110	48	H	
73	111	49	I	
74	112	4A	J	
75	113	4B	K	
76	114	4C	L	
77	115	4D	M	
78	116	4E	N	
79	117	4F	O	
80	120	50	P	
81	121	51	Q	
82	122	52	R	
83	123	53	S	
84	124	54	T	
85	125	55	U	
86	126	56	V	
87	127	57	W	
88	130	58	X	
89	131	59	Y	
90	132	5A	Z	
91	133	5B	[	
92	134	5C	\	
93	135	5D	]	
94	136	5E	^	

Table A-1. The ASCII Character Set (continued)

Decimal	Octal	Hex	Character	Comment
95	137	5F	_	
96	140	60	`	
97	141	61	a	
98	142	62	b	
99	143	63	c	
100	144	64	d	
101	145	65	e	
102	146	66	f	
103	147	67	g	
104	150	68	h	
105	151	69	i	
106	152	6A	j	
107	153	6B	k	
108	154	6C	l	
109	155	6D	m	
110	156	6E	n	
111	157	6F	o	
112	160	70	p	
113	161	71	q	
114	162	72	r	
115	163	73	s	
116	164	74	t	
117	165	75	u	
118	166	76	v	
119	167	77	w	
120	170	78	x	
121	171	79	y	
122	172	7A	z	
123	173	7B	{	
124	174	7C			
125	175	7D	}	
126	176	7E	~	Tilde
127	177	7F	DEL	Delete

Table A-1.   The ASCII Character Set (continued)

amplifier A device that increases the power or amplitude of an analog electrical signal.

analog A method of data characterization represented by mechanical or physical means. Analog values can have an infinite number of values, whereas digital values are discrete and finite. Analog devices typically monitor real-world conditions (temperature, humidity, speed, movement, and so on) and convert them to an analogous representation. For example, the dial on an automobile speedometer moves as the speed of the car increases.

analog computer **1.** A computer that processes analog data; a device that constantly measures real-world conditions (such as temperature, speed, pressure, and so on) and converts them to quantities. **2.** A computer that uses analog signals to perform computations. Analog computers do not use logic gates or arrays (as do digital computers), but rely on the differential amplifier for processing signals.

analog-to-digital converter A hardware device that changes information from an analog format to digital. Once in digital format, the information can be used in modern computer systems. For example, a device that measures a real-world condition such as temperature must have its output translated to a digital format by an ADC before it can be used by a digital computer.

AND A Boolean operation that compares corresponding bit positions of two sets of equal-length data and sets the resulting bits based on the condition of the tested bits. If both corresponding bits are on, then the resulting bit is on. If either of the original bits is off, then the resulting bit is off. Sometimes referred to as a conjunction or intersection operation. The K-map for the AND operation using two variables is shown here:

	0	1
0	0	0
1	0	1

angstrom   A unit of measurement equal to one ten-thousandth of a micron.

animation   **1.** The illusion of motion created by showing a series of still pictures (frames) at a high speed. **2.** In the QuickBASIC environment, a debugging technique that highlights each program line as it is executed.

anisotropic mapping   In the Microsoft Windows environment, this is a mode in which logical coordinates are translated to physical coordinates without maintaining the relationship of the x and y axes. For example, a circle defined with logical coordinates could appear as an ellipse when mapped to physical coordinates.

anomaly   Something inconsistent, contradictory, or abnormal. Also a deviation from expected results: a mutation or variation.

anonymous pipe   In the OS/2 environment, a data storage buffer maintained in RAM by the operating system for use in interprocess communications.

anonymous variable   In Prolog, a variable used in place of a variable name in a clause whose specific value is of no interest. An underscore (_) symbolizes the anonymous variable.

ANSI   See *American National Standards Institute*.

ANSI compatible   If a product claims to be ANSI compatible, it must conform to standards devised by ANSI, the American National Standards Institute.

ANSI.SYS   In the MS-DOS environment, a device driver that allows display terminal control in compliance with guidelines developed by ANSI. ANSI.SYS is installed in the CONFIG.SYS file and is appended to the operating system when the machine is booted.

answer-back unit   See *callback unit*.

answer mode   The condition of a modem when it is set to answer and establish a connection with incoming calls.

answer-only modem   A modem that can only answer, not originate, calls.

antialiasing   Hardware or software designed to overcome aliasing. See also *aliasing*.

APA   See *all points addressable*.

APDA   See *Apple Programmers and Developers Association*.

aperture   In AutoCAD, a small box that encloses the intersection of the on-screen crosshairs. Figure A-2 shows an aperture.

API   See *application program interface*.

APL   A programming language popular in the 1960s that was used primarily in scientific applications because of its mathematic capabilities.

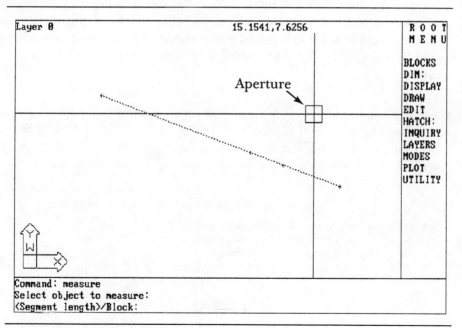

Figure A-2.   An aperture in AutoCAD

APL is an acronym for a programming language, and was developed by Ken Iverson. It is sometimes referred to as the Iverson Language, and is used primarily on mainframe computer systems. Because APL uses special symbols (such as Greek letters), it requires the use of a special terminal capable of displaying the characters. APL is well-suited to handling complex array operations.

APP   See *application portability profile*.

APPC   An acronym for advanced-program-to-program-communications software used in the IBM SNA environment.

append   To add to the end of something, particularly a file.

append mode   An output mode resulting in information being added to the end of a file.

Apple desktop bus   In the Macintosh environment, a connector on the back of the computer for connecting input devices such as a keyboard, mouse, trackball, or graphics tablet. The ADB port is available only on models of the Macintosh beginning with the Macintosh SE. It is capable of connecting up to 16 devices through the one port, and allows data transfer rates up to 4.5Kbps.

Apple desktop interface   A set of presentation and user interface protocols developed by Apple Computer, Inc. for use on the Macintosh line of computers. The ADI was developed so all applications running in the Macintosh environment could present a standard appearance to users.

apple key   On keyboards produced by Apple Computer, Inc., a special key with a picture of the Apple logo, as shown here:

This key is used by the operating system and certain applications to modify the function of other keys. It is analogous to the Ctrl or Alt key on other types of keyboards.

Apple Programmers and Developers Association   An organization sponsored by Apple Computer, Inc., whose membership includes companies and individuals developing products for Apple computers (including the Macintosh). The APDA provides information, services, and publications for their members.

Applesoft BASIC   A variation of the BASIC programming language for the Apple II series of computers. Applesoft is an interpretive BASIC that allows floating-point numbers.

AppleTalk   An Apple Computer networking strategy built into certain products manufactured by Apple Computer, Inc., such as the Macintosh and LaserWriter. There are also AppleTalk adapter boards available from third-party vendors that allow IBM computers to be linked into an AppleTalk LAN.

AppleTalk filing protocol   A set of protocols from Apple Computer, Inc. for use on their networks. AFP is consistent with the OSI model. See also *AppleTalk*.

application   A classification of programs whose members are designed to accomplish a single task or group of related tasks. Examples of application programs include word processors and spreadsheets.

application development facility   Application generation software developed by IBM to run under the IMS database management system on mainframe computers.

application heap   In the Macintosh environment, the area of memory that contains an application program and its resources.

application layer   In the OSI communication model, this is the level at which the user or an application program interacts. It is layer 7 of the OSI model. See also *open system interconnection*.

application program   See *application*.

application program interface   A series of defined interface standards for an application. An API typically defines how an application should appear to a user, how input should be requested and obtained, and how output should be done.

application rational interface logic   (APRIL) A logic chip made by IBM that learns from its environment using neural networking techniques.

application shortcut key   In the Microsoft Windows environment, one of several special key combinations that bring an application to the foreground.

application software   See *application*.

application-specific integrated circuit   Customized chips containing a collection of predesigned circuits selected from a standard library of such circuits. Since no customized or specialized circuits are used, ASIC design is much faster than designing a chip from scratch.

application portability profile   A set of standardized tests used to determine how portable a program is among differing hardware and operating system platforms. The test was developed by the National Institute for Science and Technology for use in the federal government.

application programmer   A programmer who specializes in writing, analyzing, and maintaining application software.

APRIL   See *application rational interface logic*.

APSE   An acronym for Ada program support environment.

APT   A programming language used primarily in industrial applications for machines that automate factories. APT is an acronym for automatic programmed tools.

ARC file   In the MS-DOS environment, a file ending with the .ARC extension. This extension is short for archive. ARC files are compressed data files used for secondary, long-term storage. The file extension originated with archival programs developed by System Enhancement Associates (SEA).

architecture   The overall layout of the hardware or software components of a computer system.

archive *n*   **1.** Backup copies of information. Archives are used in case the original data is damaged or lost. **2.** Past versions of a document or file. **3.** In the MS-DOS environment, a file ending with the .ARC extension. These are compressed data files used for secondary, long-term storage.

archive *v*   To backup or make copies of data for long-term storage.

archive copy   See *archive n (1)* or *archive n (2)*.

archive file   See *archive n*.

ARCNET   An early LAN scheme developed by Datapoint Corporation that interconnects up to 255 nodes in a star topology. A token-passing scheme is used to transfer data.

argument   A variable, constant, or expression used by a command, function, or subroutine to accomplish its purpose. Arguments can either be mandatory or optional.

arithmetic conversion   In programming, the process of changing the data type of a number. For example, changing a number from floating point to integer.

arithmetic/logic unit   The portion of the processor that performs arithmetic functions on data, including comparisons and Boolean operations. On some processors, the ALU controls the settings of the bits in the CPU's flags register.

arithmetic processor   See *numeric processor extension*.

ARM   An acronym for asynchronous response mode.

ARPANET   A packet-switching wide-area network operated by the U.S. government through the Department of Defense. ARPANET is an abbreviation for Advanced Research Projects Agency network, and is used to further advanced scientific research projects.

ARQ   An abbreviation for automatic retransmission request, an error detection and correction technique used in data communications.

array   A collection of individual data items arranged in an organized fashion so the entire collection can be treated as a single piece of data. Individual elements of the array have like data types, and may be addressed individually or collectively.

array bounds   In programming, the range determined by the minimum and maximum allowable subscript for individual array elements. In some languages, the array bounds must be declared explicitly before the array is accessed. Other languages assume default array bounds unless they are explicitly declared. For example, if the following two BASIC lines are included in a program,

```
OPTION BASE 1
DIM SmallArray(50)
```

then the array bounds for SmallArray are 1 through 50.

array processor   A specialized hardware system that is optimized and specialized to perform very fast array manipulations. Sometimes implemented as a parallel or coprocessor, an array processor is used to off-load time-intensive operations from the main CPU. Sometimes referred to as a vector processor.

ascender   The portion of lowercase letters such as b, d, f, or t that extends above the main body of the letter. See also *descender*.

artificial intelligence   A branch of computer science concerned with designing computer systems capable of exhibiting limited attributes of human intelligence.

ascending   Going from lowest value to highest.

ascending sort   The arrangement of information based upon a sequence progressing from low to high (i.e., 0 to 9, A to Z, and a to z).

ASCII   See *American standard code for information interchange*.

ASCII file   A file that contains only ASCII characters. It contains no encoded numeric values or special formatting characters—only straight text or text representation of numbers.

ASCIIZ   An ASCII string terminated with a null character (ASCII value of 0). ASCIIZ strings are used extensively in certain languages and operating systems. For instance, C maintains string variables in this format.

ASIC   See *application-specific integrated circuit*.

ASM   See *Association for Systems Management*.

aspect ratio   The ratio of the horizontal to vertical dimensions of the frame used to hold an image on either the screen or a printer. Aspect ratio usually refers to the video screen itself, which has a standard aspect ratio of 4:3.

ASR   An acronym for automatic send-receive.

assembler   The software program that translates (assembles) assembly language mnemonics into machine language for direct execution by the computer.

assembly   The process of code conversion performed by an assembler. Assembly language source code is translated into machine language through this process.

assembly language   The next-to-lowest level and most direct programming language that programmers can use to generate native code, (the lowest level being machine language). Each microprocessor uses its own version of assembly language, thus the language is extremely hardware-dependent (i.e., it is not portable). Assembly languages tend to be pseudo-English in nature, and are not directly executable by a computer. The source code must first be processed by an assembler. Many people erroneously refer to programs written in assembly language as being written in assembler. The assembler is the software that converts the language to something that the CPU can execute—it is not the language itself.

assign   In programming, to declare a value for a variable.

associate   In the Microsoft Windows environment, the process of establishing a logical link between a filename extension and a certain application. Once the link is established, anytime you select the file with that extension, the associated application is automatically run.

Association for Computing Machinery   A professional organization working toward the goal of advancing the information processing industry. The ACM was founded 1947. Its offices are located at:

Association for Computing Machinery
11 West 42nd Street
New York, NY 10036
(212) 869-7440

Association for Systems Management   An international organization consisting of administrative executives and specialists in information systems from business, education, government, and the military. You may contact ASM at:

Association for Systems Management
24587 Bagley Road
Cleveland, OH 44138
(216) 243-6900

Association for Women in Computing   A professional organization for people interested in furthering the education and development of women in computer-related industries. The address is:

Association for Women in Computing
407 Hillmoor Drive
Silver Spring, MD 20901

Association of Computer Users   An organization whose members are interested in the use of small computers for business purposes. Founded in 1979, the ACU evaluates products and services from the user's point of view and publishes a monthly newsletter. The ACU can be contacted at:

Association of Computer Users
P.O. Box 9003
Boulder, CO 80301
(303) 443-3600

Association of Data Processing Service Organizations   A business organization composed primarily of time-sharing service companies. Founded in 1960, ADAPSO is oriented toward improving management techniques, defining performance standards for computer services, and affecting government regulations related to the industry. ADAPSO is located at:

Association of Data Processing Service Organizations
1300 North 17th Street
Arlington, VA 22209
(703) 522-5055

associative dimension   In AutoCAD, a dimension whose values are up-dated automatically to reflect any modifications to the dimension.

associative memory   A type of memory in which an entry is located by its contents instead of by address. Also referred to as content-addressable memory.

associative storage   A type of mass storage device in which an entry is located by its contents instead of by address.

asymmetrical modem   A full-duplex modem that transmits data at dif-fering speeds in each direction.

async   Short for *asynchronous.*

asynchronous   1. A series of events (such as data transmission) that are not synchronized in any manner. 2. In the SNA environment, events that are independent rather than concurrent.

asynchronous communication   The transmission of information between two devices (such as modems) in which intercharacter timing is not strictly synchronized. Instead, start and stop bits are transmitted to indicate the beginning and end of data packets. See also *synchronous communication.*

asynchronous event scheduler   An IPX (NetWare) process that starts execution of specific events at predetermined intervals.

asynchronous transmission   See *asynchronous communication.*

AT command set   A series of commands that control modems compatible with those manufactured by Hayes Microcomputer Products. See also *Hayes-compatible.*

atom   In the LISP programming language, a single element in a list.

atomic operation   An operation that cannot be divided into smaller operations.

ATOTAL   In the NetWare environment, a utility that provides daily or weekly audit trail information.

a-trap   In the Macintosh environment, a call to the toolbox or operating system. See also *trap*.

attached processor   Another name for a coprocessor, as long as the coprocessor is another CPU. Attached processors are viewed by the system as an extension of the primary CPU and are used in multiprocessing environments.

attenuation   A reduction in signal strength that may be caused by a variety of factors. Attenuation can be purposeful or inadvertent, desirable or disastrous — it all depends on the purpose of the signal and the needs of the system.

attribute   **1.** A specific characteristic that describes properties of an item. For example, a file may have attributes that define it as hidden or read-only. Display characters may have attributes that define color and brightness. A variable may have the attribute of being a fixed-point number or an array with certain dimensions. **2.** In the PICK operating system, an object or collection of logically related objects within a data file. An attribute is analogous to a field under other operating systems. An attribute can be divided into values and subvalues. **3.** In AutoCAD, a piece of text information in which you can store any type of information associated with a block.

attribute mark   In the PICK operating system, a reserved ASCII character used as a delimiter between attributes. An attribute mark has an ASCII value of 254.

attribute mark count   In the PICK operating system, the relative number of an attribute within a data file.

attribute tag   In AutoCAD, a one-word label for the attribute being defined.

audio   Sound within the frequency range audible to the human ear (15 to 20,000 Hz).

audit trail   A detailed record of individual transactions, typically used in database or financial systems. Audit trails assist in later verification of steps taken to manipulate data.

authentication   The process of verifying the accuracy of a result, or the validity of a user seeking access to a system.

authoring language   See *computer-assisted instruction*.

authority level   In the SQL database language, the authority level determines the type of operations a user can perform in a database. The authority level is granted by the system administrator (SYSADM).

authorization code   An ID number or password used to gain access to a computer system or a program running on a computer system.

auto answer   The ability of a modem to recognize an incoming call, answer the call, and establish a communications link.

autocoder   An assembly language designed for IBM 1400 and 7000 series computers.

auto dial   The ability of a modem to dial a telephone number automatically.

AUTOEXEC.BAT   In an MS-DOS environment, a file containing commands to be executed by the system when it is first started.

autoindex   A feature of some database systems that automatically updates the database index as changes are made to individual records in the database.

automatic call distributor   A piece of switching hardware for data communications systems that automatically distributes incoming calls to the next available modem connected to the host computer system.

automatic calling unit   In data communications, a device that automatically dials the telephone, thereby enabling a modem connection. In many of today's modems, the ACU is an integral part of the modem.

automatic error correction   A classification of error detection and correction schemes implemented in hardware. This frees the software from the necessity of including code to do what can be done by the hardware more quickly and efficiently.

automatic variable   In certain programming languages (such as Quick-BASIC), a temporary variable used in procedures. It is similar to a local variable in that its value is not saved during recursive calls.

automation   The replacement of manual operations by computerized or mechanical methods.

autoscrolling   In a GUI environment, a technique of scrolling the screen if the user drags the mouse outside the window boundaries while a mouse button is depressed. Commonly used in selecting a large amount of information with the mouse.

AUX   The auxiliary port under the MS-DOS, UNIX, or OS/2 operating systems. Usually synonymous with a communications port.

A/UX   Apple Computer, Inc.'s version of UNIX for their Macintosh line. A/UX is based on AT&T's UNIX System V with Berkeley extensions.

auxiliary carry flag   In the 80*x*86 (Intel) family of microprocessors, a bit in the flags register that indicates whether the previous decimal operation resulted in a carry out of or borrow into the four low-order bits of the byte.

auxiliary memory   High-speed memory that is not directly addressable by the CPU. As used in large-scale and supercomputers, information stored in auxiliary memory is transferred to and from main memory over a high-speed channel.

auxiliary storage   A mass storage device (such as a disk or tape drive) used to hold information while the computer is not processing it, or when the computer is turned off.

AWC   See *Association for Women in Computing*.

AX   On the 80x86 (Intel) family of microprocessors, a 16-bit general-purpose register.

axis   An imaginary line along which position or movement can be measured. In a two-dimensional system there are two axes, x and y, denoting a plane. The z axis is added when referring to three-dimensional space. All three axes are located at right angles to each other.

axis of revolution   In AutoCAD, the axis around which a path curve revolves.

B   A suffix indicating that a number is in binary form. May be upper- or lowercase. For instance, 101011B and 101011b both indicate that the number is binary.

Bachman diagram   A graphical representation of relationships in database systems. It was developed by and named after C. W. Bachman in the late 1960s. Bachman diagrams use boxes, lines, and arrows to define the relationships between database fields, records, and files. Figure B-1 shows an example of a simple Bachman diagram.

backbone   In data communications, a high-speed communications channel connecting several network bridges.

back end   A portion of a program with which users do not interface directly. Often used to refer to database engines, which work with a front-end program that accepts input and commands from users.

background   **1.** The portions of the screen that are not representing actual characters or graphics symbols contained in a character set. (Those sections comprise the foreground.) **2.** See *background operation.*

background category   A priority classification for processes in the OS/2 environment. It consists of processes not currently operating in the foreground; these are processes associated with a screen group not currently displayed. See also *foreground category.*

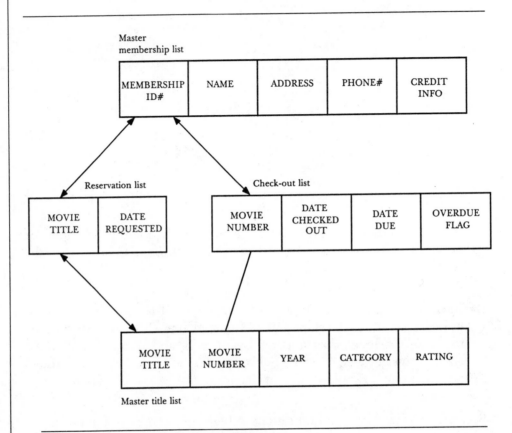

Figure B-1. A sample Bachman diagram

background operation   The execution of secondary tasks by a computer system during brief pauses in the execution of the system's primary (foreground) task or tasks.

background processing   See *background operation*.

background task   See *background operation*.

backplane   See *motherboard*.

backslash   The \ character, it is the reverse of the slash character. The backslash points left at the top and right at the bottom. Its ASCII value is 92; the EBCDIC value is 224.

backspace   The operation performed by software when the Backspace key is pressed. The results of pressing the key will vary depending on the computer system and software. On most systems, pressing Backspace results in moving the cursor one space to the left and erasing the character that was there (destructive backspace). Some systems simply move the cursor one space to the left without erasing any characters (nondestructive backspace). The ASCII value for the backspace is 8, the EBCDIC value is 22, and the abbreviation is BS.

backtrack after fail   In Prolog, a method that uses the fail predicate to backtrack in a database so all possible clauses are visited and examined for the intended purposes.

backtracking   In Prolog, a mechanism where satisfaction of a previous goal is attempted through alternate means after the evaluation of a subgoal is completed successfully.

back up   To make copies of information for long-term archival purposes.

backup   **1.** Secondary information that is used when the current information is rendered unusable by corruption or system failure. **2.** The "fall-back" hardware or software to be used if the primary systems fail.

Backus-Naur form   Developed in the late 1950s by John Backus and Peter Naur, the Backus-Naur form was actually a language used to define programming languages (a metalanguage). The Backus-Naur form is sometimes referred to as the Backus normal form, and commonly abbreviated BNF.

Backus normal form   See *Backus-Naur form*.

backward chaining   In Prolog, a control procedure that starts with a primary goal and attempts to satisfy each unresolved subgoal. This is done recursively until either a solution is found or all subgoals have been expanded into their simplest components.

BAF   See *backtrack after fail*.

BAK file   In the MS-DOS environment, a file ending with the .BAK extension. These are files created with the DOS BACKUP command or files created by software as backups to the current file.

balun   A contraction for balanced/unbalanced, a balun is a device used to connect dissimilar transmission media in network environments. Typically a balun is a type of transformer used to connect high-impedance (balanced) to low-impedance (unbalanced) lines.

band printer   A type of line printer that uses a metal loop containing the printable characters. The loop spins horizontally around the print hammers until the proper character is in front of a hammer, and then the hammer strikes the character to produce an impression on the paper.

bandwidth   The information-carrying capacity of a communications channel. Technically, the bandwidth is the frequency range. This range denotes the number of communications channels (hence, capacity) for the line.

bank   An array of identical hardware components. For example, a memory bank is a group of identical memory chips.

bank switching   A method of expanding beyond its normal constraints the memory that can be accessed by a CPU. This is accomplished by manipulating the address lines of a CPU so it acts as though it is accessing a legal area of memory when in fact it is accessing an area of memory outside its normal bounds. For example, if a computer has two complete sets of memory chips mapped to the same memory addresses, then special circuitry can be used to specify which bank (set) of memory chips is active at any given moment.

bar chart   A chart in which the data being displayed is represented as a series of bars, either horizontal or vertical (see Figure B-2).

bar code   A code made up of a series of variable-width vertical lines (bars), which can be read by an optical scanner. Bar coding is used in many inventory and retail systems for fast identification. The code is interpreted

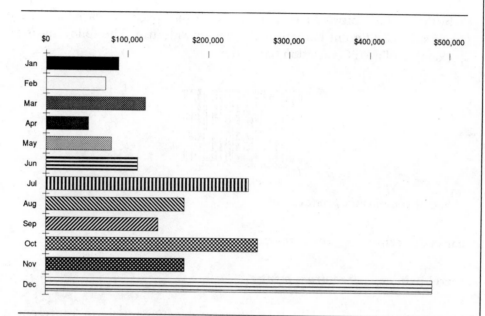

Figure B-2a.   A horizontal bar chart

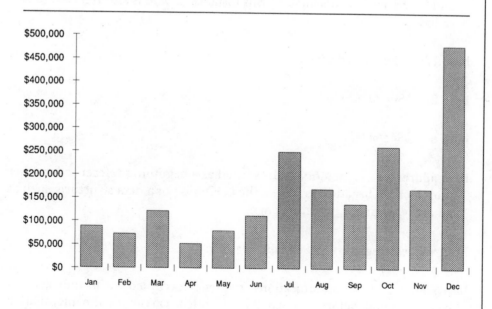

Figure B-2b.   A vertical bar chart

by the scanner software based on the width and spacing of each bar. There are several different bar code schemes in wide use. The following is an example of a UPC variation bar code:

See also *universal product code*.

bar code scanner   See *scanner*.

barrel printer   See *drum printer*.

base   **1.** A term used in logarithms and exponentials to represent a number being raised to a power. **2.** A number that defines the numbering system being used; i.e., base 2 is binary, base 8 is octal, base 10 is decimal, and base 16 is hexadecimal. In this instance, a base is also referred to as a radix.

base 16   See *hexadecimal*.

base 2   See *binary*.

base 8   See *octal*.

base address   A memory address used as a beginning reference for other operations. This address can be the beginning of a data structure, such as an array, segment, table, or page.

base address register   See *base register*.

baseband   The communications frequency occupied by an information-bearing signal before it is combined with a carrier in the modulation process. See also *carrier frequency*.

baseband transmission   A digital transmission technique utilizing low-frequency transmission over relatively short distances (up to several miles). Transmission speeds are generally limited to under 10 megabits per second. See also *broadband transmission*.

base displacement addressing   See *base relative addressing*.

base FID   In the PICK operating system, the first disk frame set aside for a file. A frame is analogous to a sector or cluster.

base group   A set of 12 communications frequencies capable of carrying the human voice over a telephone line.

base indexed addressing   In the 80*x*86 (Intel) family of microprocessors, a method of assembly language addressing in which one of the operands is composed of three parts. The first part is a register that contains the address of (a pointer to) a memory location. The second part is an index register (either SI or DI) whose contents are added to the address in the register. The third part is an offset that is added to the sum of the first two parts. This provides the final address, the contents of which are used in the operation to be performed. Examples of this addressing mode are:

```
MOV    AX,TABLE[BX][DI]
MOV    AX,[BX+8+SI]
MOV    AX,[SI+BX+8]
MOV    AX,[BX+8][SI]
MOV    AX,[BX][SI+8]
MOV    AX,8[BX][SI]
MOV    AX,8[BX+SI]
```

See also *addressing mode; indexed register indirect addressing*.

baseline document   The primary written information used to log changes to a software or hardware system.

base memory   **1.** The portion of a computer's addressable memory set aside for execution of software. **2.** In the MS-DOS environment, that portion of memory under the 640K memory boundary.

base name   In the MS-DOS and OS/2 environments, the portion of a filename to the left of the period. The base name may contain up to eight characters. For example, in the filename COMMAND.SYS, the base name is COMMAND. See also *filename extension*.

base point   In AutoCAD, a reference point, located anywhere in a drawing, that AutoCAD needs to complete a command.

base register   A register containing an address that is used as a base in indirect addressing methods. In 80*x*86 (Intel) family microprocessors, the base register is usually the BP or BX register or its extended counterpart (EBP or EBX).

base relative addressing   A method of assembly language addressing in which one of the operands is composed of two parts. The first part is a register that contains the address of (a pointer to) a memory location. The second part is a displacement that is added to the address in the register. This provides the final address, the contents of which are used in the operation to be performed. Examples of this addressing mode are:

```
MOV    AX,[BX]+8
MOV    AX,[BX+8]
MOV    AX,8[BX]
```

Sometimes referred to as base displacement addressing. See also *addressing mode*.

base table   In relational database systems, a table (file) containing data.

BASIC   An acronym for beginners' all-purpose symbolic instruction code, this programming language was developed in the mid-1960s at Dartmouth College by John Kemeny and Thomas Kurtz. It is a general-purpose language that uses English-like commands. Originally developed as an interpretive language, there are now many BASIC compilers available that aid in program development. There are hundreds of BASIC dialects available; the most popular and widespread is the version of BASIC written by Microsoft Corporation (GW-BASIC or BASICA) for MS-DOS machines. The most popular compiler version of the language is

QuickBASIC, published by Microsoft Corporation. The following is a short BASIC program to request a number from a user, find the square of the number, and then display the result:

```
100 INPUT "What is the number:"; A
110 S = A * A
120 PRINT "The square of"; A; "is"; S
```

The exact syntax used depends on the implementation of BASIC. In some of the modern BASIC compilers, the line numbers are optional.

BASICA   A variation of the BASIC programming language. BASICA stands for BASIC Advanced, and comes with the PC-DOS operating system. It runs on the IBM PC family of computers, and uses language routines stored in ROM. See also *BASIC*.

basic input/output system   On microcomputers, the set of routines contained in ROM, necessary to proper booting of the system and rudimentary communication with basic hardware components of the computer system. The routines provided by the BIOS form the building blocks that DOS and other programs use in their operations.

batch   A group of information to be processed at a single time. See also *batch processing*.

batch command   In the MS-DOS or OS/2 operating systems, a command stored within a batch file.

batch file   An MS-DOS file containing a series of commands that can be sequentially executed by the operating system's command processor. A batch file must have the filename extension .BAT. See also *command file*.

batch processing   A data processing model that involves completing the processing of an entire group (batch) of information at a single time, as opposed to on-line or individual record processing.

BAT file   See *batch file*.

battery backup   A source of emergency power. Battery backup systems can be built to provide power for either entire computer systems or for critical areas of memory. See also *uninterruptable power supply*.

baud   See *baud rate*.

Baudot code   An early data coding scheme using five bits to make up each character. Developed in the late 19th century by Emile Baudot. The formal name for Baudot code is ITA #2. The Baudot code is shown in Table B-1.
     Notice that there are two characters assigned to almost every value in Table B-1. Code values 27 and 31 are used to select from which column the characters following will come.

baud rate   **1.** The electrical switching speed of a transmission line; the number of times a line changes its electrical state each second. **2.** The transmission speed of a communications channel; at low speeds, baud rate is often used interchangeably with bits per second (bps) even though they mean different things.

BBS   See *bulletin board system*.

BCC   See *block check character*.

BCD   See *binary coded decimal*.

BCH   In data communications, an error detection and correction technique named after its developers, Bose, Chaudhuri, and Hocquengham.

BCNF   An acronym for Boyce/Codd normal form.

BDOS   An acronym for basic disk operating system.

beacon   In network (LAN) terminology, a special message, or frame, sent by a node indicating a serious network problem.

Decimal	Hex	Character	Character
0	0	Blank	Blank
1	1	E	3
2	2	LF	LF
3	3	A	—
4	4	Space	Space
5	5	S	'
6	6	I	8
7	7	U	7
8	8	CR	CR
9	9	D	WRU
10	A	R	4
11	B	J	BELL
12	C	N	,
13	D	F	
14	E	C	:
15	F	K	(
16	10	T	5
17	11	Z	+
18	12	L	)
19	13	W	2
20	14	H	
21	15	Y	6
22	16	P	0
23	17	Q	1
24	18	O	9
25	19	B	?
26	1A	G	
27	1B	FIGS	FIGS
28	1C	M	.
29	1D	X	/
30	1E	V	=
31	1F	LTRS	LTRS

Table B-1.   The Baudot Code

bead   A small subroutine, a series of which comprises a thread.

before-image log   In the SQL language, a file maintained by the system that contains an image of the original version of any records changed by a user during a transaction. The log is kept until the transaction is rolled back or committed.

beginning of file   The logical position prior to the first byte of information or first record in a file. Abbreviated as BOF or TOF (top of file).

BEL   See *bell character*.

Bell 103   The standard protocol defining how information is to be transmitted at low baud rates (110 and 300 bps) over telephone lines. This standard applies to full-duplex communications in North America.

Bell 212   The standard protocol defining how information is to be transmitted at 1200 bps over phone lines in North America.

bell character   A control character that results in the sounding of an audible alarm on a computer system. The common abbreviation is BEL, the ASCII value is 7, and the EBCDIC value is 47.

benchmark   A performance-measurement testing program.

Berkeley software distribution   Versions of the UNIX operating system developed at the University of California at Berkeley bear this title.

Berkeley Standard UNIX   The version of UNIX developed at the University of California at Berkeley. It is comprised of UNIX along with extensions designed for easier use.

BERT   An acronym for bit error rate testing; used in data communications.

beta testing   Hardware or software testing performed by a limited number of users under normal conditions. Beta testing occurs after in-house (alpha) testing.

Bezier curve   A type of curve generated by an algorithm. Named after French mathematician Pierre Bezier, it is used to display nonuniform curves based upon a fitting algorithm. An example of a Bezier curve is shown here:

BGI   An acronym for Borland graphics interface, a protocol and group of library routines from Borland International for use with languages they publish.

bias   **1.** A constant added to the true exponent of a real number to obtain the exponent field of that number's floating-point representation. **2.** In data communications, signal distortion related to bit timing.

biased exponent   The exponent as it appears in a floating-point representation of a number, interpreted as an unsigned, positive number.

bidirectional printer   A printer that can print regardless of the direction the print head is moving.

bifurcation   A choice or condition that has two (and only two) possible solutions.

big-endian   A storage technique for multibyte quantities in which the most significant byte is physically stored in memory first. This technique derives its name from a fictitious political party in the book *Gulliver's Travels*. See also *little-endian*.

billion   One thousand times one million (1,000,000,000). This is roughly equivalent to a giga; thus a gigabyte is approximately one billion bytes.

binary   A numeric system based upon powers of 2. Binary is the native numbering system used by computers. It uses only the digits 0 and 1. See also *bit; numbering system*.

binary coded decimal   A binary format for representing decimal digits. A single byte is used for each digit of the number, with the 4 low-order bits (0-3) representing a value between 0 and 9. The hexadecimal values A through F (normally represented in the 4 high-order bits) are not used.

binary/decimal conversion package   A standard Macintosh package used to convert numbers from binary to ASCII. Thus, the binary number 101 is converted to decimal 53, the ASCII code for 5. This package is provided in the system resource file, or in ROM beginning with the Mac Plus. See also *package*.

binary digit   See *bit*.

binary field   A field, typically within a database, containing binary numbers.

binary file   A file in which data is expressed only as combinations of ones and zeros. A binary file typically contains binary data or programs. Although a processor reads this type of file, it is unintelligible to humans.

binary point   Similar to a decimal point, except that a binary point is used in floating-point binary numbers. Each binary digit to the left of this point is multiplied by an increasing positive power of 2; each binary digit to the right is multiplied by an increasing negative power of 2.

binary search   A search technique to locate individual items in ordered lists quickly. It is implemented by successively dividing the possible range of records in half by determining which half the desired record would reside within. For example, if the list to be searched contains 500 sorted items, you examine the 250th record for a match. If this record is greater than desired, then you look at the 125th record. If this one is smaller, then you divide the range again and examine the 187th record. This process continues until the desired match is found or you cannot divide the remaining range any further (in which case, the desired information cannot be found). In the example, locating any given record requires (at maximum) only nine comparisons. If the list is increased to 1,000 items, then only ten comparisons are needed.

binary synchronous communication   A synchronous communications protocol developed by IBM, sometimes abbreviated as BSC. Bisync requires the precise synchronization of sender and receiver before data transmission can occur. Bisync is bit-oriented in nature and used extensively in mainframe networks for extremely fast data transmission.

binary synchronous transmission   See *binary synchronous communication*.

binary tree   A data organizational structure in which each element contains one parent (superior element) and no more than two children (inferior elements), as shown in Figure B-3. Each circle in the figure represents a data element, and each line represents a link between data elements. See also *tree*.

bindery   In the NetWare environment, the bindery is made up primarily of components called objects and properties. These contain information on network clients, and are the foundation of NetWare's client security, password system, and accounting.

binding   In language compilers, the assignment of a size and value to a variable name, or the conversion of logical references to physical addresses.

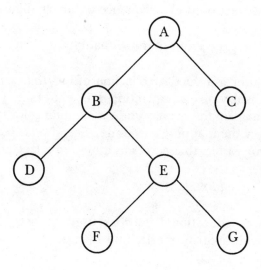

Figure B-3.   A binary tree

BIOS   See *basic input/output system.*

BIOS parameter block   In the MS-DOS environment, a portion of a disk's boot sector. The BPB indicates enough information about the disk to enable the boot program to locate the beginning of the directory and file space. See also *boot sector; master boot record.*

bisync   See *binary synchronous communication.*

bisynchronous   See *binary synchronous communication.*

bit   A contraction of binary digit, the smallest unit of storage on a computer. Each bit can have a value of 0 or 1, indicating the absence or presence of an electrical signal. See also *binary.*

bit block   See *bitmap* or *bit pattern.*

bit cell   See *domain (3).*

bit density   The number of bits that can be stored within a given area.

bit field   A data unit composed of a sequence of binary digits, or bits.

bit manipulation   The processing of individual bits.

bitmap   1. In computer graphics, a collection of bits that represent the status of individual display pixels or printing dots, either on or off. This is an actual memory image of the display and can contain color information (depending upon how the mapping was done). See also *bit pattern.* 2. In general, any collection of bits that serves as a map to a larger data area.

bit-mapped display   See *bitmap.*

BITNET   A wide-area educational network used by over 1,000 postsecondary institutions in North America and Europe.

bit-oriented protocol   A communications protocol that uses individual bits as control codes. See also *binary synchronous communication; byte-oriented protocol.*

bit pattern   A layout of bits that defines a larger object; for example, many GUIs use bit patterns to define icons. Each bit within the pattern specifies the on/off condition of an individual pixel. See also *bitmap*.

bit plane   A conceptual model of video graphics in which it takes more than a single bit to represent each pixel. For instance, if there is a full byte assigned to each pixel, bit 0 of each byte may represent the pixels in the first bit plane. Bit 1 of each byte then represents the pixels in the second bit plane, and so on.

bit rate   The transmission speed of binary coded data. See also *bits per second*.

bit slip marks   In the Apple DOS environment (used on the Apple II series of computers), a trailing section of a data field on disk. The marks are used to double-check that the disk head is still in sync and the sector has not been damaged.

bits per inch   The number of bits stored in a linear inch of a storage medium, such as a disk or magnetic tape. The acronym is bpi.

bits per second   The measurement of how many bits are transferred across a communications link per second. The acronym is bps.

bit stream   The continuous transfer of bits across a communications link.

bit string   An arbitrary-length sequence of binary digits, or bits, that make up a data unit called a string. Typically, a string may contain both alphanumeric and numeric characters, or their binary representations.

bit stuffing   In data communications, once a message or packet is constructed, the protocol used may demand the addition of a number of bits to round out a fixed length for the message or packet. The adding of these additional bits is called bit stuffing.

bit test   An algorithm to test the condition of a specific bit without changing its value.

bit transfer rate   See *bits per second*.

bit twiddler   A nickname for a person who likes to program.

BIU   An acronym for bus interface unit.

black box   A hardware device specifically designed to connect otherwise incompatible hardware or software systems.

blank character   Same as a space character; an ASCII value of 32 or an EBCDIC value of 64.

blank segment   See *main segment*.

BLERT   An acronym for block error rate testing; used in data communications.

blip   In AutoCAD, a symbol that AutoCAD places on-screen to indicate points that have been digitized. This symbol is usually a small cross (+).

block   **1.** A group of database records treated as a single unit. **2.** In word processing, a series of text characters that can be treated as a single object for actions such as moving or copying. **3.** In graphics programs, a set of grouped entities treated as a single object. **4.** In data communications or storage systems, a set of contiguous bits or bytes that make up a definable quantity of information.

block check character   In cyclic redundancy checking (see *cyclic redundancy check*), a character or code sent after the transmittal of the information block. The BCC is recalculated at the receiving end and checked against the one transmitted. If they match, it means that no error was detected. If they do not match, then a retransmission is necessary.

block device   A computer peripheral that accesses, transfers, or accepts more than one character at a time. These groups of information are called blocks. See also *character device*.

block diagram   A type of flowchart that depicts the relationship between hardware and software components in a computer system. See also *flowchart*.

block header   In the Macintosh environment, the first 8 bytes of a heap block. Also called a heap block header.

blocking factor   A numeric value representing the number of records in a block. Sometimes referred to as a grouping factor.

block length   The size of a block, measured in bytes, characters, words, or records.

block mode   A method of data transmission where information is sent as each record or group of characters is completed. See also *character mode*.

blow up   **1.** To enlarge a picture. **2.** Synonymous with *crash* or *bomb*.

BNC connector   A type of connector used to connect coaxial cable to hardware devices, as shown here:

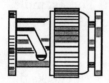

BNF   See *Backus-Naur form*.

board   Another name for an electronic circuit board.

BOF   See *beginning of file*.

boilerplate   Common predefined and standardized words, phrases, or paragraphs designed to be copied into different word processing documents as needed.

bomb   The condition of a program ending abnormally, or the operating system hanging so that all operations cease. See also *abend* or *crash*.

Boolean algebra   See *Boolean mathematics*.

Boolean expression   Using Boolean operators in a logical statement (or equation) that, when resolved, is either true or false.

Boolean mathematics   A branch of mathematics developed by George Boole, an English mathematician. Boolean math deals with logical expressions, and operators such as AND, OR, NOT, XOR, NOR, and NAND according to set rules to produce a result of either true or false.

Boolean operator   In programming, a keyword that causes two values to be combined in a logical fashion. The resulting combination can be determined through several different methods. See also *Karnaugh map* or *truth table*.

Boolean search   A search for specific data that utilizes Boolean logic to express the search condition. For example, "List all records for which conditions A and B, but not condition C, are true."

boot   The process of starting a computer system. It generally involves internal, hard-coded software that checks the computer memory, peripherals, and I/O channels to verify that they are working. Then the operating system is loaded, and control is turned over to a command processor that awaits user input. Boot is short for bootstrap, from pulling yourself up by your bootstraps.

boot disk   The disk or disk drive used to boot, or start up, a computer.

boot sector   The data sector on a disk (floppy or hard) that is used to boot the computer system. It generally contains a small amount of information defining a portion of the disk's layout, along with some programming code to load the booting routines off the disk. See also *BIOS parameter block; master boot record*.

bootstrap   See *boot*.

BOT   An acronym for beginning of tape.

boundary   A line of demarcation indicating where a particular operation is to begin or end. In computer graphics, a boundary is often used to denote the outline of an object or the line at which an operation (such as color or pattern filling) is supposed to stop.

Bourne shell   In the UNIX environment, the user interface shell used in implementations of UNIX from Bell Labs.

bozo bit   In the Macintosh environment, a file attribute bit that controls whether the file can be copied to a different disk. If set, then the file cannot be copied by normal means.

BP   On the 80*x*86 (Intel) family of microprocessors, the 16-bit base pointer register.

BPB   See *BIOS parameter block*.

bpi   See *bits per inch*.

bps   See *bits per second*.

branch   A change in the linear progression of program execution caused by a processor instruction. See also *jump*.

breadboard   A blank circuit board used for developing electronic proto-types. Breadboards are usually thin plastic boards (of varying sizes) with hundreds of evenly spaced holes for inserting electronic components such as transistors, wires, connectors, chips, and so on. The term derives from the early days of radio when hobbyists tinkered with radio kits at home, using actual breadboards to hold their projects.

break   **1.** To stop something, usually a computer program or task. **2.** To send a break signal. See also *break signal*.

break code   A numeric value passed to the computer by the keyboard when a key is released. See also *make code; scan code*.

break key   A key used to stop a computer program, task, or transmission.

breakout box   A device designed to aid in the testing and analysis of communications channels.

breakpoint   A predefined address in a program where execution is stopped and control is passed to debugging software.

break signal   In data communications, a special signal used to stop the transmission of a remote computer. The signal is defined as a space condition (signal is held at low—meaning voltage is low—which is equivalent to digital 0) lasting approximately 0.275 seconds.

BRI   An acronym for basic-rate interface, used under ISDN.

bridge   In network terminology, a device linking similar networks together and allowing communication between them.

bridgeware   Hardware or software used to convert data or programs from one format to another.

broadband   A method of transmitting information over a communications link that will handle a greater range of frequencies than is available over a regular voice-grade line. Because of the wide bandwidth, a broadband network will handle many communications channels simultaneously. This is usually accomplished by using multiplexers.

broadband transmission   A transmission technique utilizing high-frequency transmission over long distances. Transmissions can be digital or analog and generally employ coaxial cable or optical fibers. See also *baseband transmission*.

broadcast   To disseminate information simultaneously to a broad range of recipients.

broadcast messages   In a NetWare environment, communications between workstations or between a workstation and its file server. These messages appear on the bottom screen line (line 25) of the receiving workstation or file server console.

BS   See *backspace*.

BSC   See *binary synchronous communication*.

BSD   See *Berkeley software distribution*.

b-tree   A self-maintaining method of data indexing that minimizes the access time to any given piece of data and provides for fast information retrieval.

bubble memory   A type of data memory in which information is stored as a series of magnetized "bubbles" on a thin film. Bubble memory is nonvolatile in nature, and requires low power.

bubble sort   A sorting technique that functions by repetitively arranging successive pairs of elements in the proper order until all elements are in the desired sequence. Named after the characteristic of the smallest elements "bubbling" to the top of the list.

buffer   A temporary storage area for data, typically in RAM. Buffers are used extensively in I/O operations.

buffer pool   A memory area set aside for buffers.

bug   An error in either hardware or software that causes a computer operation to malfunction, or to function unexpectedly.

bulletin board system   An on-line computer system, accessible through dial-up modems, that functions as a centralized information source for files, programs, and messages. A BBS is analogous to public bulletin boards in lunchrooms or grocery stores. Users connect with the BBS and download or upload files and leave messages for each other.

burn in   A testing process that entails running hardware for a time to determine if there are any weak components or system errors.

burster   A piece of mechanical equipment designed to separate multipart forms into their individual parts.

burst error   In data communications, a series of consecutive errors.

burst mode   A condition of data transmission in which a large amount of information can be sent without interruption by other external events. The result is high-speed data transfer of what is typically critical information.

bus   **1.** The common internal data channel used by a computer system for transferring data to and from the CPU. **2.** One or more conductors used to transmit electrical signals or power.

bus extender   A device that allows additional boards to be connected to an existing computer bus.

business graphics   The presentation of business data in a graphic format for clarity. Common presentation methods include line, bar, and pie charts. See also *bar chart*.

BX   On the 80*x*86 (Intel) family of microprocessors, a 16-bit general-purpose register.

BYP   An abbreviation for bypass, an EBCDIC control code with a value of 36.

byte   A basic unit of data storage and manipulation. A byte is usually equivalent to 8 bits (binary digits) and can contain a value ranging from 0 through 255. While 8 bits is the most common size for a byte, computer manufacturers are free to define a differing number of bits as a byte. For instance, some computer systems define a byte as 6 bits.

byte addressable   A condition that exists when the smallest unit of memory that a computer can independently address is a byte.

byte-oriented protocol   A communications protocol that uses full bytes as control codes. See also *bit-oriented protocol*.

C   A high-level programming language developed by Dennis Ritchie at
Bell Laboratories in the early 1970s. C combines the benefits of a
high-level language (ease of programming and maintainability) with
portability and low-level machine access capabilities. C is typically implemented as a compiler-based language, and sometimes in an integrated
development environment, which combines the compiler capabilities with
an editor and debugger. The following example of C program code
requests a number from a user, finds the square of the number, and then
displays the result:

```
#include <stdio.h>

main()
{
  float i,s;

  puts( "Enter a number:" );
  scanf( "%f", &i );
  s = i * i;
  printf( "The square of %g is %g", i, s );
}
```

C is a language much touted for its portability; this program should work
under most C compilers currently available.

C++   A high-level programming language developed by Bjarne Strous-
trup at Bell Laboratories. C++ encompasses all the abilities of C, but also
adds object-oriented programming capabilities.

C3 – C0   The four condition-code bits of an 80x87 (Intel) family NPX status word. These bits are set or cleared by the compare, test, examine, and remainder functions of the coprocessor.

cache   A relatively small, fast memory area that holds the most active parts of a larger, slower memory. Using caching technology in computers can dramatically improve response times and overall system performance. See also *disk cache*.

cache flush   On the Intel 80486 chip, an operation that marks all cache lines as invalid. The 80486 has individual instructions for flushing internal and external caches.

cache hit   A request for access to memory that is contained within the cache.

cache line   The smallest storage unit that can be allocated in a cache.

cache line fill   An operation that loads an entire cache line from non-cache (main) memory.

cache miss   A request for access to memory that is not within the cache and thus requires reading non-cache (main) memory.

CAD   See *computer-aided design*.

CADD   An acronym for computer-aided design and drafting.

CAE   See *computer-aided engineering*.

CAF   See *cut and fail*.

CAI   See *computer-assisted instruction*.

CAL   An acronym for computer-assisted learning. See also *computer-assisted instruction*.

call   A programming term representing the temporary branching to a different routine. The point at which the call was executed is maintained, and execution of the main program continues at the next instruction when the routine has finished execution. Different computer languages implement this process with differing commands.

callback modem   A modem that has the additional capabilities of a callback unit. See also *callback unit*.

callback unit   A hardware device that, in response to a call from a remote computer, disconnects the line and calls the remote computer back. Callback units are used to ensure system security.

call by reference   See *pass by reference*.

call by value   See *pass by value*.

call gate   On certain members of the 80x86 (Intel) family, a special LDT or GDT entry used to define a subroutine entry point.

calling convention   The protocol followed by a function or process in calling other routines. See also *pass by reference; pass by value*.

calling program   A program that calls another program or subroutine; the program from which a call is invoked. See also *call*.

CAM   See *computer-aided manufacturing*.

Cambridge Polish notation   A variant of prefix notation used in implementations of the LISP programming language. See also *prefix notation*.

CAN   An abbreviation for cancel, a control character used in some systems to indicate that information received in the most recent block is in error and should be discarded. The ASCII and EBCDIC values for CAN are both 24.

cancel character   See *CAN*.

canonical   The property of acting in accordance with a well-defined set of rules or according to a predefined model.

canonical synthesis   The process of designing a database model without redundant data items.

Caps Lock key   A specialized keyboard key that, when pressed, causes all alphabetic characters to appear as uppercase. The Caps Lock key has no effect on any other key on the keyboard.

captive thread   In the OS/2 environment, a thread created, owned, and residing wholly within a dynlink subroutine. A captive thread never transfers back to the main process' code.

card   **1.** Another name for a printed circuit board, or circuit card. **2.** See *punched card*.

card cage   A cabinet or metal frame designed to hold printed circuit cards.

cardinal number   A number that expresses a quantity.

card punch   Another name for a keypunch machine or a computer peripheral that punches paper cards under computer control.

card reader   **1.** A computer input device that reads the punched holes on paper cards. **2.** A device designed to read the magnetic strip on the back of credit cards.

caret   The ^ symbol, typically produced by pressing the Shift-6 combination on a keyboard. In some software systems, the caret is used as the cursor.

carriage return   A control code that causes the cursor to return to the left side of the current line. This code is generated when the Enter or Return key is pressed. The ASCII and EBCDIC values for a carriage return are both 13, and the acronym is CR.

carrier   See *carrier frequency*.

carrier frequency   In communications, a fixed-frequency signal that acts as the "guide" for a broadcast transmission. The carrier frequency is modulated with the baseband signal to produce the final output signal. The frequency is measured in cycles per second (Hertz).

carrier sense multiple access/collision avoidance   A technique for collision detection and resolution in network systems. If a node connected to a CSMA/CA network plans to transmit a message, it must first send a jam signal, wait a short amount of time, and then start transmission. If another node's jam signal is detected while transmission is in progress, then the node must stop, wait a random amount of time, and then try access again.

carrier sense multiple access/collision detection   A technique for collision detection and resolution in network systems. When multiple network nodes are attempting to use the network at the same time, CSMA/CD dictates that each node stop the attempt, wait a random amount of time, and then try access again.

carrier system   In data communications, a method of extracting several channels from a single communication link by combining multiple signals at the transmitting end of the link and reversing the process at the receiving end to recover the individual signals. A carrier system is implemented over a wideband or high-speed communications channel.

carry flag   A bit in the processor flags register that indicates whether the previous operation resulted in a carry out of or borrow into the high-order bit of the resulting byte or word.

Cartesian coordinate system   A coordinate system that uses three axes (x, y, and z) to locate any given point in three dimensions.

cartridge font   A font or series of typefaces contained in ROM chips mounted within a plastic module called a cartridge. The cartridge is placed in a compatible printer to allow it to use the fonts. See also *soft font; internal font*.

CAS   An acronym for column address strobe.

CASE   An acronym for computer-aided software engineering.

case insensitive   A program that treats upper- and lowercase letters the same way; thus, the letter *A* is treated the same as the letter *a*. See also *case sensitive*.

case sensitive   A program that differentiates between upper- and lowercase letters; thus, the letter *A* is treated differently from the letter *a*. See also *case insensitive*.

CASE statement   In certain programming languages, a CASE statement is a variation of the IF-THEN-ELSE statement. It is used when there are many successive conditions to test for. An example is:

```
DO CASE
    CASE KEY=49
        DO ADD
        EXIT
    CASE KEY=50
        DO EDIT
        EXIT
    CASE KEY=51
        DO CHECK
        EXIT
    CASE KEY=52
        QUIT
ENDCASE
```

The exact syntax of the structure will vary depending on the programming language being used.

catalog   **1.** A directory of files on a computer system; synonymous with directory. **2.** In database systems, an internal system file that keeps track of other files in the database application; similar to a data dictionary.

cathode ray tube   The display screen of a computer monitor or television set. The cathode, or electron emitter, is used to energize phosphor bits inside the screen, resulting in a displayed image. The following is an example of a CRT:

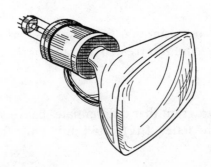

CBEMA   See *Computer and Business Equipment Manufacturers Association*.

CBT   An acronym for computer-based training. See also *computer-assisted instruction*.

CC   An acronym for cursor control, an EBCDIC control code with a value of 26.

CCEP   An acronym for commercial COMSEC endorsement program.

CCIS   An acronym for common channel interoffice signaling.

CCITT   See *Consultative Committee for International Telephony and Telegraphy*.

CCP   See *Certificate in Computer Programming*.

CCR   See *condition codes register*.

CD   See *compact disc*.

cdev   In the Macintosh environment, a control program that customizes the user interface. The word cdev is a contraction for control device. A cdev program must be placed in the system folder, after which it will appear as an icon in the control panel (beginning with Macintosh System 4.1).

CDP   See *Certificate in Data Processing*.

CD-ROM   An acronym for compact disc, read-only memory. CD-ROM is a read-only storage medium for digital data. A standard 4.75″ CD-ROM can hold over 600,000,000 bytes of information. It is closely related to similar storage methods for audio (compact disc, or CD) and video (videodisc).

CD-ROM extensions   Additions to the MS-DOS operating system in the form of device drivers, that allow normal access to information stored on a CD-ROM. The extensions cause the CD-ROM to appear as an additional disk drive.

cell   **1.** A data storage location in a spreadsheet. A cell is typically defined as the intersection of a row and column, and can contain either text or numeric data. **2.** See *character cell*.

center justification   See *justification*.

centimeter   A linear measurement equal to one-hundredth of a meter.

centralized data processing   A systems configuration in which all computing tasks are done at a central location within a company. Users access the computer through terminals connected to the system either directly or through a network. This methodology is the opposite of distributed data processing.

centralized processing   See *centralized data processing*.

central processing unit   The full name for the acronym CPU. See also *processor*.

centronics interface   See *centronics parallel interface*.

centronics parallel interface   A defacto standard for connecting printers and other peripheral devices to a computer via a parallel channel. The interface defines the type of connector used as well as the use of each pin in the connector. An example of a Centronics parallel interface connector is shown here:

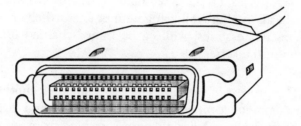

CERT   An acronym for character error rate testing, used in data communications.

Certificate in Computer Programming   The CCP examination is given annually at test centers throughout the United States. It is an in-depth examination designed to test a person's knowledge of computer programming and programming fundamentals. Upon successful completion, the CCP certificate is awarded by the Institute of Certification of Computer Professionals (ICCP).

Certificate in Data Processing   The CDP examination is given annually at test centers throughout the United States by the Institute of Certification of Computer Professionals (ICCP). It is an in-depth examination designed to test a person's knowledge of hardware, software, systems analysis, computer programming, management, and accounting.

CGA   An acronym for color graphics adapter, a display adapter for IBM-compatible microcomputers.

CGM   See *computer graphics metafile*.

chad   The tiny piece of paper punched from a punched card or a paper tape.

chained list   A series of items (usually indexed) in which each item contains the location of the following item. A forward-chained list contains the next item in the series, while a backward-chained list contains the previous item in the series.

chaining   The process of running one program after another. When one program is complete, control is passed to the second program. Some languages offer the capability to pass variables from one program to another during the chaining process.

chain printer   A type of line printer that uses a print mechanism consisting of characters connected together in a chain. The chain spins around a set of print hammers, and the hammer strikes the character to produce an impression on the paper.

chamfer   A beveled edge between two intersecting lines, as shown here:

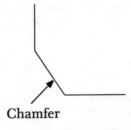

Chamfer

channel   A pathway dedicated to the transmission of data or communications between computers or computers and their peripherals.

channel bank   Data communications hardware used to perform multiplexing, usually on voice grade channels.

character   A single letter, digit, or symbol. A character is synonymous with a byte.

character cell   A rectangular area of dots used to form a character on a printer or video display. An example of a character in a character cell is shown here:

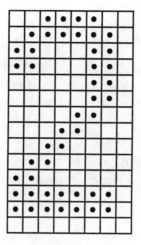

Each dot in the illustration represents a pixel within the cell.

character code   See *American standard code for information interchange; Baudot code; extended binary coded decimal interchange code.*

character device   A computer peripheral that accesses, transfers, or accepts information a single character at a time. See also *block device.*

character generator   A device, either hardware or software, that converts numeric code values (either ASCII or EBCDIC) to an actual character than can either be displayed or printed.

characteristic   **1.** An attribute of an object. **2.** The exponent field of a floating-point number.

character matrix   In display or printing systems that represent characters as a series of dots, the rectangular array of dots that makes up the box in which each character resides. See also *character cell.*

character mode   A method of data transmission where information is sent as it is typed, one character at a time. See also *block mode.*

character printer   A printer that produces a single character at a time. Contrast with *line printer.*

character recognition   The ability of either hardware or software to recognize and accept printed text as input.

character set   A collection of characters and symbols that fulfill a specific purpose. See also *American standard code for information interchange; Baudot code; extended binary coded decimal interchange code.*

characters per second   A measurement of speed indicated by the number of characters (bytes) that can be transmitted, printed, or otherwise processed in a second. The term cps is most commonly used to indicate the speed of a printer.

character string   A series of alphanumeric characters, typically referred to simply as a string. A character string's contents are treated as though they were text, even if the string contains numbers.

check bits   A series of one or more bits used for error checking. See also *parity; checksum; cyclic redundancy check.*

check box   In a GUI environment such as Microsoft Windows, Presentation Manager, or the Macintosh, a small rectangular box shown beside an option. The box acts as a toggle; when the option corresponding to the box is selected, there is an X in the box, otherwise it is blank. An example of a check box from a software program for the Macintosh is shown here:

⊠ Bold
☐ Italic
☐ Small Kaps
☐ Hidden
☐ Underline
☐ Word underline
☐ Double underline

See also *command button.*

check digit   A digit used to validate previously entered numbers. For instance, a credit card number is composed of an account number and a check digit (the last digit), which is used to make sure the rest of the digits are correct. This check digit is derived by various formulas that result in a unique digit between 0 and 9, which is then appended to and becomes part of the account number.

check exception   In the 680x0 (Motorola) family of microprocessors, an exception caused by a failed CHK instruction.

check key   One or more characters appended to a block of data, which can be used to detect errors in the block. The check key is typically derived from the information in the block. See also *cyclic redundancy check*.

checksum   A calculated value used to ensure the accuracy of information transferred across networks, telecommunication systems, or between computers and peripherals. The value is transferred with the data, and a new checksum is calculated by the receiver. The two values are compared; if they are the same, the probability of transmission error is very low. See also *cyclic redundancy check*.

child process   A subordinate program (process) that is executed within an environment created by another program. The program that creates the environment for the child process is called the parent.

chip   A small piece of semiconducting material, such as silicon, on which an integrated circuit is fabricated.

choose   To select an item from a list of choices.

Chooser   In the Macintosh environment, a desktop accessory (utility program) that allows the user to select a device driver to be used by the system.

Chooser resource   A device driver for the Macintosh environment. These resources are installed in the system folder, after which they appear as options in the Chooser. See also *driver*.

chop   The process of dropping the fractional portion of a number (or that portion to the right of the decimal point). This is done without rounding. Sometimes used interchangeably with truncate.

chord   A line segment connecting the endpoints of an arc, as shown here:

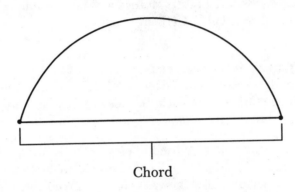

Chord

chroma   See *chrominance*.

chrominance   The part of a composite video signal used to define the color portion of a picture. From chrominance, a color receiver can determine shade, hue, and saturation. See also *luminance*.

CICS   An acronym for customer information control system, an enhancement for certain IBM operating systems running on mainframe computers.

CIM   An acronym for computer-integrated manufacturing.

cipher   An algorithm used to encode or encrypt data.

ciphertext   Data that has been encoded or encrypted.

circuit   **1.** A set of electronic components that perform a particular function. **2.** The path that electricity follows between the electrical source (such as a generator) and an electrical device. **3.** In data communications, a channel.

circuit board   See *printed circuit board*.

circuit breaker   An electrical device that breaks, or opens, a circuit to prevent an overload condition, which may cause physical harm to the media making up the physical circuit. Circuit breakers can be reset once tripped, usually by flipping a switch. See also *fuse*.

circuit card   See *printed circuit board*.

circuit diagram   A schematic or blueprint of an electronic circuit.

circular buffer   A memory storage area in which data is stored in a FIFO fashion. Besides the buffer area, pointers to the head and tail of the buffer are maintained, indicating where information should be added and retrieved from the buffer. When the pointers reach the end of the buffer area, they "wrap around" to the beginning, thus the circular nomenclature. Keyboard drivers generally use circular buffers.

circularity   See *circular reference*.

circular queue   See *circular buffer*.

circular reference   A series of references where the last reference in the series points to an earlier reference in the series. An example is shown here:

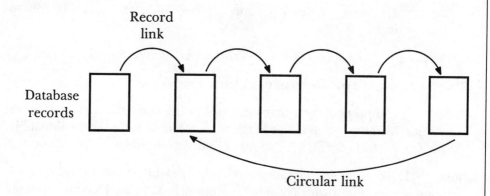

CISC   An acronym for complex instruction set chip or complex instruction set computer. See also *complex instruction set chip*.

cladding   The layer of glass that surrounds optic fibers in some fiber-optic cables.

class   In object-oriented programming, an object that specifies a structure for other types of objects based on that object. A class contains both data and algorithms that operate on the data.

class type   A common assembler directive indicating how individual segments are to be grouped when linked.

clause   In some programming languages (i.e., SQL and Prolog), a syntactical unit of a programming statement.

clear   To erase or set back to a default position. For example, clear memory, which means to wipe out the contents of a memory area.

click   To press and release a button on a mouse.

client   In a network environment, synonymous with user.

clipboard   A memory area used to hold temporary information that can be inserted in the same data area or another document or program's data area.

clipping plane   In graphics programs, a plane perpendicular to the line of sight that can be applied anywhere between the viewer's position and the target so it blocks whatever is behind or in front of it.

clobber   To destroy a file or portion of a file. The term can also apply to memory areas.

clock speed   The speed at which a computer's governing clock operates.

CLOS   An acronym for common LISP object system.

clone   A computer system that functions in the same manner as another system. The most common use of the term refers to computers compatible with the IBM PC or IBM AT family of microcomputers.

close   1. To suspend operations relating to a file, port, peripheral, or memory area, and flush all buffers relating to it. 2. In a GUI environment, to remove a window from the screen.

closed architecture   A system in which the internal workings are proprietary or withheld from public knowledge. See also *open architecture*.

closed loop   See *infinite loop*.

closed shop   A computer center in which only the data processing staff has access to the computer. Users must use the staff as intermediaries for their computing needs. Contrast this with an open shop in which users can access the computer directly.

cluster   **1.** A group of disk sectors treated as a single entity by a disk controller or an operating system. **2.** A group of terminals connected to a single controller or computer system.

cluster controller   A peripheral control unit that manages several devices, typically terminals or disk drives.

CM   An acronym for configuration management.

CMD file   See *command file*.

CMOS   An acronym for complementary metal oxide semiconductor, a type of integrated circuit used in electronic components.

CMOS RAM   A low-power memory area of the IBM AT and PS/2 series of computers. This memory area is used to maintain system configuration information. The memory contents are maintained by a battery.

CMS   See *conversational monitor system*.

coaxial cable   Often referred to simply as coax, this cable is used widely in audio, video, and communications connections due to its wide bandwidth. This bandwidth offers a greater transmission capacity than other types of wiring. Coaxial literally means that the conductors within the cable share the same axis. A cross-section of coaxial cable is shown here:

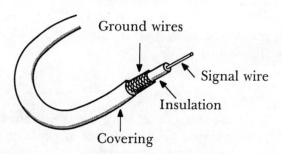

COBOL   A contraction for common business-oriented language, this high-level programming language is used extensively in mainframes and minicomputers for business applications. COBOL is a compiler-based language that has been around since the early 1960s, and claims the largest amount of program code in existence.

CODASYL   An abbreviation for conference on data systems languages, a standardization organization formed in the 1970s.

0

code *n*   **1.** A set of symbols or abbreviations used to represent other information such as data. **2.** A program, such as source code or object code.

code *v*   To program an algorithm in a programming language.

codec   A contraction for coder-decoder; an analog/digital converter. Typically, a codec is used in devices such as a telephone to translate sound waves (analog) to a digital form, which can be transmitted quickly and processed easily.

code page   In the MS-DOS or OS/2 operating systems, a table used by the operating system to designate character sets used for display purposes. Code pages are designed to adapt the operating system to international use. They allow remapping of the keyboard to differing display character sets.

code segment   A memory address space that contains executable instructions for the CPU.

coding   See *code v*.

coherency   The quality of logical consistency.

cold boot   The process of starting a computer from a cold, or powered-off condition. See also *boot*.

cold start   See *cold boot*.

collator   A device (or software) that merges records into a single group. The records can be physical (such as punched cards or copier/printer output) or logical (such as database records).

collision   In network or data communications terminology, this is what happens when two computers attached to a network attempt to send information or access a resource at the same time.

color code   A numeric value used to indicate the color used for various objects in a graphics system. In the MS-DOS environment, the various color codes are shown in the following table.

Value	Color	Value	Color
0	black	8	gray
1	blue	9	light blue
2	green	10	light green
3	cyan	11	light cyan
4	red	12	light red
5	magenta	13	light magenta
6	brown	14	yellow
7	white	15	high-intensity white

column ' In SQL database terminology, the same data field across a group of related records. A column is referred to as a field in other database systems.

column name In SQL database terminology, the name assigned to a column of data. All data within the column can then be collectively referred to by this name.

COM An acronym for computer output on microfilm.

COMCHECK In the NetWare environment, a utility program used to check nodes on the network to make sure they can communicate with the network.

COM file 1. A type of executable program file in the MS-DOS or OS/2 operating systems. COM files derive their name from the filename extension .COM, which is short for command. They have all their code and data contained within a single 64Kb segment, and are a direct image of the program as it appears when loaded into memory. 2. In the VAX/VMS operating system, a file containing a series of commands to be executed by the operating system.

comma-delimited A data file in which the individual fields are separated by commas. See also *tab-delimited*.

command A directive to a computer or computer program that causes an action to occur. The form that commands take is dictated by the software or computer meant to interpret and act upon the command.

command button   In a GUI environment such as Microsoft Windows, Presentation Manager, or the Macintosh, a small rectangular box containing commands such as Yes, No, OK, Open, Cancel, or Close. By clicking on a command button, the desired response is indicated to the system. An example of a command button from the Microsoft Windows environment is shown here:

See also *check box*.

COMMAND.COM   A command processor for the MS-DOS, PC DOS, or OS/2 operating systems.

command-driven   One of two general user interface schemes for programs. A command-driven program relies upon commands entered at a command line. The other type of scheme, menu-driven, presents all commands in a series of menus from which the user can select the desired function.

command file   A file containing the commands to be executed sequentially by a program or processor. In the OS/2 environment, command files end with the filename extension .CMD. See also *batch file*.

command interpreter   See *command processor*.

command language   A limited programming language used strictly for executing a series of commands. Examples of command languages include a query language (such as SQL) or a job or batch language (such as JCL or DOS batch files).

command line   The screen line on which the user may input commands to be processed by a program.

command line option   See *switch*.

command processor   A system program that accepts commands, interprets them, and acts upon them within the environment defined by the operating system.

command prompt   See *DOS prompt*.

command shell   See *command processor*.

comment   Information included as a part of a program for the sake of documentation or clarification. Comments are indicated in varying ways, depending on the language being used. In C, the following are comment lines:

```
/* These are comment lines in C. The compiler */
/* ignores everything between the opening     */
/* slash-asterisk combination and the closing */
/* asterisk-slash.                            */
```

In BASIC, the REM statement is used to indicate a comment, as in the following code lines:

```
10 REM  This program is designed to do
20 REM  lots of great things.
```

Comments are not translated into executable code by the compiler or assembler.

common memory   In the DESQview environment running under MS-DOS, a special memory area used for general-purpose functions. These include managing windows and maintaining the top-level menu.

communications   A broad, ambiguous term referring to the ability (or lack thereof) of hardware, software, and users to exchange information.

communication services   In the NetWare environment, a collection of services that enable applications to use the NetWare IPX and SPX protocols.

communications line   An individual circuit, or channel, that carries data within a computer or across a network. The term communications line can refer to either the logical connection or the physical communications media.

communications port   See *serial port*.

communications protocol   A scheme used for transmitting data between computers or computers and their peripherals. The scheme is defined by the hardware and software used for the actual transmission.

communications speed   See *data rate*.

compact disc   A storage medium for digital data, typically audio, that is read by a laser beam. On a standard 4.75" CD, up to 72 minutes of music can be recorded. See also *CD-ROM; videodisc*.

compaction   The process of defragmenting a heap to make free space available to processes needing it.

compact memory model   In the C programming language in the 80x86 (Intel) environment, a type of program in which programming code resides in less than 64K, but data requires more than 64K of memory.

compandor   In telecommunications systems, hardware used to improve transmission performance by compressing the outgoing signal and expanding the incoming signal.

compare   To contrast or relate two pieces of data with each other. Comparisons form the core of many computer operations.

comparison operator   See *relational operator*.

compatibility box   In the OS/2 environment, the window that simulates the MS-DOS environment. The compatibility box allows the user to run programs written for the earlier DOS environment. Sometimes called DOS mode.

compatible   Able to work together; able to function the same as a different system or a system from another vendor.

compile   The process of translating source code into lower-level code.

compiler   A program that translates source code into lower-level code, preparing it for linking to object-code libraries to form directly executable programs.

compiler directive   See *preprocessor directive*.

compile time   The length of time it takes to compile a program.

completion code   See *return code*.

complex domain   In Turbo Prolog, a domain that is built from basic domains, usually involving functors.

complex instruction set chip   A type of processor architecture that maximizes the number of instructions performed by the processor. In CISC systems, the processing burden is placed on hardware instead of software. See also *reduced instruction set chip*.

COM port   See *serial port*.

composite video   The video-only portion of an NTSC color television signal. It is a method of transmitting a video signal in which the chroma and luma signals are modulated onto a single carrier wave. Composite video signals are easily connected directly to a standard television set. See also *chrominance; luminance*.

compound statement   In certain programming languages, several programming statements occupying one line of code. The term may also apply to a single statement that requires more than a single line of code.

CompuServe   An on-line database service offering subscriber services including electronic mail, databases, and conference facilities. CompuServe can be contacted at:

CompuServe Incorporated
5000 Arlington Centre Boulevard
P.O. Box 20212
Columbus, OH 20212
(800) 848-8990

computer   An electronic device capable of doing a variety of tasks at high speed, including arithmetic and logic operations, without the intervention of humans. Computers are controlled by a series of instructions that together make up a program.

computer-aided design   The use of computer systems in the design of mechanical, architectural, or industrial products. CAD systems often consist of a powerful computer, highly specialized software and input devices (such as digitizing tablets), and plotters for producing schematics. The most popular and widely used CAD program is AutoCAD, produced by Autodesk, Inc.

computer-aided engineering   The use of software that aids in the development and analysis of engineering designs. See also *computer-aided design*, which is closely related to CAE.

computer-aided manufacturing   The use of computers in manufacturing systems and management.

computer-aided software engineering   The use of computers and computer tools (such as software) to aid in the development process for software systems. CASE goes far beyond languages and compilers, adding the capabilities of data dictionaries, authoring systems, and analysis tools. The goal of CASE systems is to speed up the software development process by doing many of the mundane, repetitive tasks that take up much of a programmer's time.

Computer and Business Equipment Manufacturers Association   An organization for computer vendors, business equipment manufacturers, and suppliers. Founded in 1916, CBEMA is involved in the development of standards for the data processing and business equipment industries. As such, it is associated closely with the computing branches of ANSI. CBEMA can be contacted at:

Computer and Business Equipment Manufacturers Association
311 First Street, N.W.
Washington, DC 20001
(202) 737-8888

computer-assisted instruction   The use of software that mixes graphics, sound, and text to aid in the teaching of subject material to students. CAI is usually interactive in nature, and allows users to progress at their own pace. Lessons can be set up within a CAI system using an authoring language, which lets instructors define the sequence of steps and material that the student should follow.

computer conferencing   In data communications, a system in which many users can simultaneously share information, in the form of messages, with each other.

computer graphics metafile   A device-independent file format for storage of object-oriented graphics images. CGM files are used for exchanging graphics files between software programs and users.

computer instruction code   See *machine language*.

computer language   See *programming language*.

computer program   See *program n.*

computer virus   See *virus*.

CON   The system name for the console under the MS-DOS, UNIX, or OS/2 operating systems.

concatenate   To combine two or more similar elements (such as character strings) to form a new, larger element.

concatenated index   In the SQL language, an index created on several columns jointly.

concatenation   See *concatenate*.

concentrator   A hardware device used to connect a group of peripherals to a computer system in such a way that there is only one data line between the concentrator and the computer system.

concurrency   The degree to which a system can be shared among users, typically on a local area network (LAN).

concurrency management   The capability of software written for use on a local area network (LAN) to ensure that data files are not corrupted by simultaneous modification or multiple input.

concurrent access   The simultaneous use of a computer system, software program, database, or other resource by more than one user. See also *concurrency*.

Concurrent CP/M   See *CP/M*.

Concurrent PC-DOS   An operating system from Digital Research that runs on IBM compatible PCs and features multitasking.

conditional branch   A change in the linear progression of program execution based upon the outcome of a comparison instruction. See also *conditional jump*.

conditional jump   A forced change in the linear progression of program execution based upon the outcome of a comparison.

conditional statement   A programming statement that is executed based upon the outcome of a comparison instruction.

conditional structure   In programming, a logical structure in which the commands or statements that are executed depend upon the values derived from a set of comparisons in a control expression. Examples of conditional structures include IF-THEN-ELSE structures, DO loops, CASE statements, and FOR-NEXT loops.

condition code   A code returned by a program, maintained by a CPU or numeric coprocessor, or returned by an interrupt handler that indicates the results of the most immediate operation or function.

condition codes register   In the 680x0 (Motorola) family of microprocessors, a register containing a series of bit settings that indicate the result of operations in the CPU. This register makes up the lower half of the status register.

conductor   A material used to carry electrical current.

CONFIG.SYS   In the MS-DOS and OS/2 environments, a file that specifies the drivers and system parameters used by the operating system. It is read when the operating system is loaded, and the instructions in it are acted upon by the OS loader.

configuration   The mix, connection, and layout of a computer system or network.

configuration file   A file created and maintained by a software program, and used to specify system parameters that are used to define the environment created by the software.

configure   To modify hardware or software to meet a specific environment or need.

conforming segment   On certain members of the 80x86 (Intel) family, a code segment that executes with the RPL of the segment selector or the CPL of the calling program, whichever is less privileged.

conjunction   See *AND*.

connectivity   The degree to which two differing systems (hardware or software) are able to work together successfully.

connector   A cable or wire linking two devices.

connect time   The length of time a user is logged on to a computer system, either local or remote.

console   A term referring to a display terminal and keyboard.

constant   A value that, during program execution, does not change.

Consultative Committee for International Telephony and Telegraphy
One of the four standing committees of the United Nations' International Telecommunication Union (ITU) involved in developing international data communications standards. The standards issued by CCITT are called recommendations. The X series of recommendations deal with digital networking, and the V series deal with data transmission over the telephone network. The abbreviation CCITT is normally used when referring to the organization.

content-addressable memory   See *associative memory*.

contention   A conflict arising in a network environment when more than one computer attempts to use a single resource at the same time.

contention network   A network protocol in which nodes on the network compete for the resources available on the network.

context-free grammar   A model of constructing sentences where the meaning of the sentence can be derived without reference to the context in which the words in the sentence are used.

context-sensitive help   Optional, user-requested help or instructions given within a program based upon the current operation or status of the software.

context switch   See *task switch*.

contiguous   Elements that are in close proximity to each other; usually immediately adjacent to each other.

continuation   In AutoCAD, the process of drawing a line or arc that starts at the end of the most recently drawn line or arc and continues from that point.

continuous forms   Computer forms connected end-to-end so they can be fed into a printer in a continuous manner.

control center   In dBASE IV, the full-screen display that enables the user to access most dBASE IV menus and tasks.

control character   A special character that triggers some action in a computer device such as a printer or display screen. See also *control code; device-control character*.

control code   Same as control character; typically ASCII codes with values in the range of 0 to 31. Control codes in the EBCDIC character set are spread throughout the 256 possible characters. See also *device control character*.

control console   See *console*.

control expression   In programming, an expression that evaluates to a true or false condition and thereby controls the order in which programming instructions are executed. See also *conditional structure*.

control key   (Ctrl) A specialized keyboard key that, when pressed at the same time as other keys, alters their meaning, function, or interpretation.

control key sequence   A specific combination of two or more keyboard keys, one of which must be the control key.

controller   A device that manages the flow of information between a computer and a peripheral device.

controller card   See *adapter*.

control menu   In the Microsoft Windows environment, a menu that allows the user to perform window-related options. This menu is activated by selecting the small box located in the upper-left corner of a window.

control panel   In the Macintosh, Microsoft Windows, and Presentation Manager environments, a program that allows the user to modify certain aspects of the user interface. With the control panel you can change screen colors, printer connections, communication protocols, fonts, and the system date and time. With the Macintosh, the control panel is selected by clicking on the apple in the upper-left portion of the screen. In the Windows and Presentation Manager environments, the control panel is displayed when you execute the CONTROL.EXE program.

control structure   In programming, a language construct that alters the flow of program execution.

control word   A 16-bit register used in certain members of the 80x86 (Intel) family to govern how the chip works.

conventional memory   In the MS-DOS environment, the first 640K of memory that can be accessed by the operating system without special programs or drivers.

conversational monitor system   An operating system for IBM mainframe computers. CMS is typically used with VM/SP. See also *VM/SP*.

conversion   The process of translating information from one format to another.

converter   Hardware or software that changes data or electrical signals from one format to another.

cooked mode   An input mode where input is accepted on a line-by-line basis, and some limited processing is done before the user presses the Enter key. For example, backspacing, insertion, deletion, and use of cursor-control keys are intercepted and acted upon by the operating system. See also *raw mode*.

coons surface patch   In AutoCAD, an interpolated bicubic surface between four curves.

coordinate   A unique point in space that can be expressed by values representing the distance from an origin point along the x, y, and z axes.

coprocessor   An extension to the base architecture and instruction set of a processor achieved by adding another processor chip to the bus. Examples of common coprocessors are specialized chips that handle numeric or graphic operations. See also *numeric processor extension*.

copy protection   Hardware or software used to prevent the unauthorized copying of software programs. Hardware protection methods are usually called locks.

core   An obsolete term for computer memory.

core dump   See *memory dump*.

coresident   Programs that reside in memory with other programs are said to be coresident.

corrupt   To mix up or partially erase information in memory or a file so it is no longer usable by the computer.

corruption   The altering of data or programs due to hardware malfunction, software failure, or deliberate sabotage.

counter   A program variable used for keeping track of how many times a certain activity has occurred.

courseware   **1.** Lessons developed for use within a CAI or CBT environment. **2.** Another name for educational or training software.

CPF   An acronym for control program facility, the operating system for an IBM System/38 minicomputer.

cpio   In the UNIX environment, a program used to copy files.

CPL   See *current privilege level*.

CP/M   A single-user operating system used extensively on microcomputer systems in the late 1970s and early 1980s. CP/M stands for Control Program for Microprocessors and was created by Gary Kildall of Digital Research. Over the years there have been many versions of CP/M, each with different capabilities. These versions include CP/M-80, CP/M-86, Concurrent CP/M, Concurrent CP/M-86, CP/M Plus, and MP/M.

CPS   See *characters per second* or *cycles per second*.

CPU   An acronym for central processing unit. See also *processor*.

CR   See *carriage return*.

crash   The sudden and unexpected termination of a program due to a hardware or software error. See also *abend; bomb*.

CRC   See *cyclic redundancy check*.

creator signature   In the Macintosh environment, a four-character string stored with a data file and used to identify the application program that created the file. If the user tries to open the data file with the finder, the creator signature is used to find and start the program that created the data file. See also *signature*.

critical error   In the MS-DOS environment, an error of such proportion that the operating system cannot allow the current program to continue. The most common types of critical errors include disk errors.

critical error handler   In the MS-DOS environment, the portion of the operating system that is invoked if a critical error occurs. It issues the familiar "Abort, Retry, Ignore" message on the screen. A programmer can create a custom critical error handler to replace the one provided with DOS.

cr/lf   An abbreviation for carriage return/line feed; a combination of those two control characters. The ASCII values for this combination are 13 and 10.

cron   In the UNIX environment, a daemon that periodically checks to see if it is time to execute any previously scheduled tasks. See also *daemon*.

crontab   In the UNIX environment, a file that contains scheduling information about tasks to be executed. This file is checked by the cron daemon.

cross assembler   A translating assembler that allows the generation of object code for a computer system to differ from the one on which the cross assembler is running.

cross compiler   A translating compiler that allows the generation of object code for a computer system to differ from the one on which the cross compiler is running.

crossfoot   A numerical error-checking method used in tabular data, such as spreadsheets, that compares the sum of the columns with the sum of the rows.

cross hairs   Two thin, perpendicular lines used in certain software as a cursor. The intersection of the lines marks the point at which a desired operation will occur.

crosshatching   A pattern of crossed or intersecting lines used primarily in monochrome or printed graphics to differentiate one graphic area from another.

crosstalk   In data communications or transmission, the interference from an adjacent communications or broadcast channel.

CRT   1. See *cathode ray tube*. 2. A computer terminal.

cryptography   A discipline specializing in the encoding and decoding of information.

CS   In the 80*x*86 (Intel) processor family, the code segment register.

C shell   In the UNIX environment, the user interface shell used in implementations of UNIX from the University of California at Berkeley.

CSMA/CA   See *carrier sense multiple access/collision avoidance*.

CSMA/CD   See *carrier sense multiple access/collision detection*.

Ctrl   An abbreviation for control. Ctrl is the abbreviation that is usually printed on a control key. See also *control key*.

Ctrl-Break   A common key combination on IBM-compatible computers. Under the MS-DOS or OS/2 operating systems, it cancels the currently executing command.

Ctrl-C   A common key combination that cancels the currently executing command. On some computer systems, Ctrl-C has the same effect as Ctrl-Break.

CTS   An acronym for clear to send, CTS is the equivalent of handshaking in communications systems.

CU1   See *customer use character*.

CU2   See *customer use character*.

CU3   See *customer use character*.

CUA   An acronym for common user access.

current directory   In an operating system that uses a hierarchical file structure, the current directory is the disk directory in which the user is currently operating. Sometimes referred to as the working directory.

current drive   In a computer system using more than one disk drive (logical or physical), the disk drive in which the user is currently operating.

current privilege level   On processors, the privilege level of the program that is currently running. The common acronym is CPL.

current record   The database record currently selected for some action (such as editing, printing, display, or deletion).

cursor   1. A mechanism used to mark, on-screen, where current input or output is to happen. It may appear as a blinking or solid box, underline, or caret. 2. In certain languages, a logical position within memory or a file that indicates where the next operation will occur.

cursor-control keys   See *cursor keys*.

cursor keys   On a keyboard, the keys that control the movement of the cursor on the screen. The following table lists some common cursor keys and what they usually do.

Key	Common Cursor Movement
⬅	One position left
➡	One position right
⬆	One line up, same horizontal location
⬇	One line down, same horizontal location
HOME	Beginning of the current line or input field
END	End of the current line or input field
PGUP	Up one full screen
PGDN	Down one full screen

customer use character   An EBCDIC control code, the use of which is left up to the programmer or user. EBCDIC allows for three specifically-defined customer use characters. They are differentiated by the numbers 1 through 3 appended to the abbreviation CU. CU1, CU2, and CU3 have values of 27, 43, and 59, respectively.

cut and fail   In Prolog, a method that uses the cut predicate to stop backtracking through a database when a certain condition is met.

cut-sheet feeder   See *sheet feeder*.

CX   In the 80x86 (Intel) processor family, a 16-bit general-purpose data register, usually used for counting.

cybernetics   A branch of science that examines the workings of humans and machinery to discover similarities and differences.

cycle   A single occurrence of a repetitive event.

cycles per second   The number of electrical cycles that occur in a second. The number is referred to as Hertz. Thus, 1,000 Hz is 1,000 CPS.

cyclic redundancy check   A numeric checksum value derived from a specific algorithm performed on the individual bits in a block of data. The CRC can later be recalculated after the block has been transmitted or copied, and the new CRC can be compared to the original CRC to verify that the copy or transmission was correct.

cyclic shift   See *end-around shift*.

cylinder   A logical division of a fixed disk comprised of the tracks that reside at the same location on each side of each platter of the disk unit, as illustrated here:

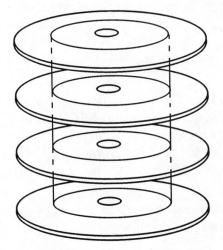

For example, if a hard disk is comprised of four platters (eight sides), then track 5 on each side (eight sides = eight tracks) makes up cylinder 5.

DAC   An acronym for digital-to-analog converter.

daemon   In the UNIX or OS/2 environments, a special type of program that, once activated, starts itself and carries out a specific task without any need for user input. Daemons are typically used to handle jobs that have been queued, such as printing, mail, and communication.

daisy chain   An arrangement of devices in which each unit in a series is connected to the previous unit, one after the other.

daisy wheel   A print head used in many typewriters and printers that consists of individual typeface characters attached to the end of "spokes" radiating from a central hub, as shown here:

To print a letter, the wheel is rotated so the desired letter is positioned in front of a print hammer, which strikes the letter against a ribbon and onto the paper. A daisy wheel produces fully formed characters.

DASD   See *direct access storage device*.

DAT   See *digital audio tape*.

data   Multiple pieces of information; plural from of datum. Used interchangeably with information.

data acquisition   The process of gathering information for a computer. The process can be either automatic or manual.

data bank   A collection of related information stored in single or multiple files on a computer system.

database   **1.** A collection of interrelated files, arranged in a highly organized fashion, that is created and managed by a database management system (DBMS). **2.** A collection of information that is electronically stored. **3.** In Prolog, a collection of clauses that contain data (facts). This data is alterable by rules and predicates that act on the database.

database integrity   The level of accuracy of information within a database. See also *data integrity*.

database machine   A computer dedicated to or optimized for database management. A database machine is designed to work closely with another computer that handles other computational needs. Used almost exclusively in mainframe environments where cocomputers are linked via high-speed communication channels.

database management system   One or more software programs that govern the organization, storage, retrieval, security, and integrity of information in a database. The DBMS typically accepts requests for data from an application program and instructs the operating system to transfer the appropriate data. Three common database management models are hierarchical, network, and relational. The term database management system can be used interchangeably with database manager.

database manager   **1.** The person responsible for overseeing a database or set of databases in an organization. **2.** See *database management system*.

database predicate   In Prolog, a predicate declared for the purpose of storing facts in the database.

database server   A node in a local area network (LAN) that handles database management. A database server is more highly specialized than a file server, which simply acts as a remote disk drive.

data bit   In data communications, one of the bits defined as specifying the character being transmitted.

data bus   A channel, internal to the computer, across which data is transferred to and from the CPU.

data collection   The process of collecting data for input to a computer system. Data collection can either be manual (data entry) or automatic (real-time acquisition).

data communications equipment   Generally, the computer or peripheral initiating a communications link. Abbreviated DCE. See also *data termination equipment* (DTE).

data communications   See *communications*.

data compression   A method of compressing information so it may be stored in less space or transmitted in less time. Compressed data may be later expanded to the original format.

data control statements   In SQL terminology, statements that create other users or determine authority levels and privileges on tables and views in the database.

data declaration   In programming, the explicit defining of data formats and constants used within the program.

data definition language   See *data description language*.

data definition statements   In SQL terminology, statements that define or change the database structure.

data description language   A specialized language used to define data and its relationships to other data. Sometimes referred to as a data definition language. The common abbreviation is DDL.

data dictionary   A listing, in the form of a file, of all the data formats, files, and relationships in a database.

data division   The portion of a COBOL program that contains data structures, files, record layouts, variables, and I/O formats. See also *identification division; environment division; procedure division*.

data-driven language   A programming language defined in terms of objects and the relationships between the objects. See also *object-oriented programming*.

data element   See *data item*.

data encryption standard   An encryption standard established by the National Bureau of Standards. The DES technique allows information to be transformed into an apparently random stream of bits for security reasons. It uses a binary number or string of binary values as an "encryption key." Each key results in a different encoding pattern.

data file   See *file*.

data flow diagram   A diagram showing the flow of data within a program. A DFD is typically constructed using symbols instead of words.

data fork   In the Macintosh environment, the portion of a file containing information that is not in a format that the system can recognize as a resource. A data fork is treated simply as a stream of bytes. See also *resource fork; resource (3)*.

data frame   See *frame*.

data independence   A condition where the structure of a program's database is independent of the processing that will occur upon the data within the database. Thus, the layout of the database can be changed without affecting the operation of the processing portion of the program.

data insertion   In a database system, the physical or logical addition of a record between two existing records.

data integrity   The validity of information; the process of securing data so it does not become corrupted.

data interchange format   A file format first developed for use with Visi-Calc, DIF files are used for exchanging data between programs. The DIF format defines a standard way of representing row- and column-oriented data.

data item   A distinct piece of information in memory or in a database file.

data line   See *communications line*.

data line monitor   A test instrument used to analyze the signals, timing, and condition of a communications line.

data link   A physical link (i.e., a wire or telephone circuit) connecting one or more devices or controllers.

data link escape   A control character used in data communications to temporarily modify the meaning of the immediately following characters. The implementation of this control code depends on the system using it. The ASCII and EBCDIC values for this character are both 16, and the acronym is DLE.

data link layer   In a network using the open systems architecture model, the layer that provides the functions and procedures used to establish, maintain, and release data link connections between network elements. This is layer 2 of the OSI model. See also *open system interconnection*.

data link level   See *data link layer*.

data manipulation   The act of processing data.

data manipulation language   A programming language used to store, retrieve, and update information in a database. The common acronym is DML.

data manipulation statements   In SQL terminology, statements that act upon the data in a database.

data model   A description of a database's organization.

data processing   The recognition, acquisition, storage, manipulation, and retrieval of information.

Data Processing Management Association   An organization of data processing managers and directors, programmers, systems analysts, and computer professionals. DPMA was founded in 1951 and can be contacted at:

Data Processing Management Association
505 Busse Highway
Park Ridge, IL 60068
(312) 825-8124

data rate   A measurement of the speed at which information is transmitted across a network. See also *bits per second; characters per second*.

data redundancy   The presence of additional, presumably identical, copies of information. Maintained for backup purposes in case the original data set is corrupted or otherwise rendered unusable.

data register addressing   In the 680*x*0 (Motorola) family of microprocessors, a method of addressing in which the contents of a data register are used as an operand. See also *addressing mode; register addressing; address register addressing*.

data register direct   See *data register addressing*.

data segment   A memory address space that contains data used by the CPU.

data set ready   In data communications, a hardware handshaking line from data communications equipment (DCE) to data termination equipment (DTE). The DSR line is defined as line 6 in RS-232 connections.

data stream   The continuous transfer of data across a communications link.

data structure   An arrangement of information in memory in such a way that it can be easily accessed and processed by a programming language. There are three general types of data structures: arrays, records, and linked lists.

data terminal ready   In data communications, a hardware handshaking line from data termination equipment (DTE) to data communications equipment (DCE). The DSR line is defined as line 20 in RS-232 connections.

data termination equipment   Generally, the computer or peripheral considered the receiver in a data communications link. Abbreviated DTE; see also *data communications equipment* (DCE).

data transfer   The movement of data within or between computers or computers and their peripherals.

data transfer rate   See *data rate*.

data type   In database systems or programming languages, a specification of the characteristics or bounds of a classification of data. Typical data types include character, numeric, logical, currency, and date. The data type also dictates the type of operations that may be done using the data.

datum   One piece of information; singular form of data.

daughter board   A small printed circuit board that adds capability to another printed circuit board. Such a board is typically piggybacked, or physically added to, the other board.

DB   See *database*.

dB   An abbreviation for decibel.

dBASE   1. A relational database management system from Ashton-Tate. 2. A programming language that originated with the dBASE product, but is now used by many different database products.

DBF file   A type of data file that has a filename extension of .DBF. It typically contains a database file stored in the dBASE format.

DBMS   See *database management system*.

DC1   See *device-control character*.

DC2   See *device-control character*.

DC3   See *device-control character*.

DC4   See *device-control character*.

DCA   See *document content architecture* or *distributed communications architecture*.

DCE   See *data communications equipment*.

D-code   Intermediate pseudocode produced by dBASE language compilers during the first stages of program compilation.

DDBMS   See *distributed database management system*.

DDCMP   An acronym for digital data communications message protocol, a communications protocol used in Digital Equipment Corporation (DEC) computers.

DDE   See *dynamic data exchange*.

DDL   See *data description language* or *document description language*.

DDP   See *distributed data processing*.

deadlock   See *deadly embrace*.

deadly embrace   A condition encountered when two computer systems or two processes on a single computer are using shared resources in a nonsynchronized manner, and each is waiting on the other to release control of resources the other needs to complete a task. Typically encountered in multiuser application software that is not programmed correctly.

deallocate   To free a computer resource (or portion thereof) so it is available to other processes, users, or files. Such resources may include CPUs, CPU time, disk drives, printers, memory, or disk sectors.

debug   The process of removing errors from either hardware or software design or logic.

debugger   A tool that aids in debugging a software program. It can either be a combination hardware/software tool, or a software-only tool. A debugger typically provides means of stopping the program at arbitrary points during execution, or displaying and/or capturing data values at pre-defined breakpoints or watchpoints. Advanced debugging tools can display source code, object code, and data values.

debugging   See *debug*.

debugging terminal   A second computer or terminal connected to the computer running software or hardware being debugged. The debugging terminal is used to display input, output, or status information about the system being debugged.

decibel   A unit of measurement used to indicate the sound power of an acoustic source.

decimal   A numeric system based upon powers of 10. Decimal is the native numbering system used by humans. It uses digits ranging from 0 to 9. See also *numbering system*.

decision box   A diamond-shaped flow chart symbol. It denotes a comparison and/or decision point within the logic flow of a program.

deck   **1.** A part of a magnetic tape unit that holds and moves the reels of tape. **2.** A set of punched cards (Hollerith or other type of computer cards).

declaration   A statement type used in some programming languages to define data or procedures. A declaration is used only by the compiler; it does not create executable code.

declarative language   A nonprocedural programming language that focuses upon *what* is wanted rather than *how* to get it. Many database languages are declarative in nature; they allow you to state what you want, and then the database software takes care of fulfilling your request. See also *nonprocedural language*.

DECnet   A communications architecture, protocol, and series of products from Digital Equipment Corporation (DEC).

decollator   A machine that separates multipart paper forms into individual parts. If the parts of the form contain carbon paper, it is removed.

decrement   Reduce by 1; subtract 1 from an existing value.

decrypt   To convert information from a secure, encoded (encrypted) condition to its original condition.

dedicated channel   A communications line or circuit used exclusively for one purpose. See also *leased line*.

dedicated line   A fixed communications line that is maintained continuously and used only for data communications between data communications equipment (DCE) and data termination equipment (DTE). See also *dedicated channel*.

dedicated server   See *server*.

dedicated service   A service or computer resource dedicated to a single user or organization.

defacto standard   A standard established through overwhelming common use, not through the actions of a standards organization (such as ANSI).

default   A response automatically provided unless overridden by explicit user input.

defragger   See *defragmenter*.

defragmenter   A program that analyzes where information is stored on the disk, and then moves files that may have become fragmented (non-contiguous) over time. Since the result of this process is contiguously stored files, disk access times are faster because the read/write head does not have to move as much to access all of a file.

degausser   A bulk demagnetizer used to remove large amounts of data from magnetic media or to remove magnetic interference from a television monitor or CRT.

degradation   A slowdown in the response time of a computer system as it spends more time doing other tasks or as more users are added to the system.

DEL   See *delete (2)*.

delay distortion   On a communications link, distortion that occurs due to the different propagation speeds of signals at different frequencies across the same transmission medium.

delayed branch   A method of instruction implementation in which a branch does not occur immediately, but is delayed so the instruction following the jump is first executed. This type of branch is common in RISC systems.

delete   **1.** To remove an item from a file, from memory, or from a disk. **2.** A control character that causes a character (either preceding or following) to be removed or ignored. How this character is implemented depends on the system. The ASCII value for this character is 127, the EBCDIC value is 7, and the abbreviation is DEL.

delimited identifiers   In SQL terminology, names that must be enclosed within quote marks because they consist of reserved keywords, contain spaces, or have other special characters.

delimiter   A character, flag, or other control mechanism that delineates one data item from another.

delimiters   Characters used specifically to set off or divide elements in character strings. Common delimiters include commas and the Tab character. In network terminology, delimiters mark the beginning and end of a transmission frame.

delta   A mathematic term representing the change between two conditions, typically "before" and "after" conditions.

demand paging   To retrieve a page of memory from disk at the moment it is needed. See also *paging*.

demodulator   The portion of a modem that converts an analog signal to digital form.

denormal   A special form of floating-point number that has a biased exponent of zero. In general, any floating-point number that is too small to be expressed in a normalized form.

dequeue   To remove items from a queue.

dereference   To convert a pointer to the value it references.

dereferencing   The process of converting a pointer (or a series of pointers) to an absolute address.

derived data   Information that is deduced from other data based on an algorithm.

DES   See *data encryption standard*.

descender   The portion of lowercase letters such as g, j, p, q, and y that extends below the letter's baseline. An example using the letter *j* is shown here:

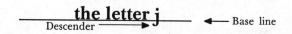

Descender ————▶   ◀——— Base line

descending   Going from highest value to lowest.

descending sort   The arrangement of information based upon a sequence progressing from high to low (i.e., z to a, Z to A, and 9 to 0).

descriptor   An identification word used to designate a document in an information retrieval system.

descriptor privilege level   In certain members of the 80*x*86 (Intel) family, the privilege level applied to a segment. The DPL is a field in the segment descriptor.

descriptor table   **1.** A data table that describes an object or collection of objects. **2.** In certain members of the 80*x*86 (Intel) family, a collection of segment descriptors. See also *global descriptor table; local descriptor table*.

desk accessory   In the Macintosh environment, a program that is available at any time regardless of what else is currently running. Desk accessories are accessed by selecting them from a special pull-down menu.

desktop   In a GUI environment, the screen that displays the available options. The desktop typically contains icons that represent programs, files, or resources available to the user. Besides being executed, these icons can be moved around the desktop in much the same way as objects are moved around a physical desktop.

desktop bus   See *Apple desktop bus*.

desktop publishing   A method of producing high-quality printed output using specialized software on a personal computer. Desktop publishing software can be used to produce near-typeset quality text and graphics.

destination operand   In computer languages, the operand that receives the results of the operation of the computer instruction.

destructive backspace   See *backspace*.

deterministic predicate   In Prolog, a predicate in which the internal unification process is controlled in such a way that only a single solution is derived.

developer   A person who designs, writes, and tests software; another name for a programmer. See also *programmer*.

development environment   The conditions under which a programmer creates software. The environment is defined by the hardware, operating system, language, test data, and tools that the programmer has available.

development system   Computers, software, and tools used by programmers to create programs.

device   A generic term for an input/output peripheral unit such as a terminal, display, or printer.

device-control character   A control code that alters the manner in which the receiving peripheral functions. The exact meaning of the character, and the result, depends on the system. Both ASCII and EBCDIC allow for four specifically defined device-control characters. They are differentiated by the numbers 1 through 4 appended to the abbreviation DC. In ASCII, DC1, DC2, DC3, and DC4 have values of 17, 18, 19, and 20, respectively. In EBCDIC, the DC1 through DC4 have respective values of 17, 18, 19, and 60. See also *control character*.

device controller port   A memory location, accessed through special CPU commands, used to control the operation of a peripheral device attached to the computer.

device dependent   A program is said to be device dependent when it will only work with one specific piece or type of hardware.

device driver   See *driver*.

device file   In the UNIX environment, a file used to represent a peripheral device attached to the system. A device file is also known as a special file.

device independence   A programming goal in which the programmer or user does not have to be concerned with how to communicate with a peripheral—all communication is done in a standard fashion for either block or character devices.

device independent   A program is said to be device independent when it will work with a wide variety of hardware devices.

device name   A device name is a near-English name assigned to a hardware device. When the computer system encounters a device name, it translates it into a physical address.

DF   See *direction flag*.

DFD   See *data flow diagram*.

dhrystone   A benchmark program that tests a computer system through a series of general-purpose instructions. Test results are expressed in Dhrystones per second.

DI   In the 80x86 (Intel) family, the 16-bit destination index register.

DIA   An acronym for document interchange architecture, used in SNA networks.

diagnostic output   Computer output used only for program testing and debugging. Diagnostic output is created by the programmer inserting temporary instructions into the program to cause runtime information about the program to be displayed or printed.

diagnostic program   A program that detects, isolates, and explains a hardware or software malfunction.

diagnostics   A class of software used to test hardware.

DIALOG   A dial-up database service offering on-line access to a large number of databases. The fees charged vary according to the database used.

dialog box   GUI terminology that refers to an on-screen box used to communicate information with and offer limited options to a user.

dialog record   In the Macintosh environment, a data structure containing information about a dialog box.

dialup   A communications channel established over telephone lines. This type of connection does not use dedicated lines or leased lines, but is established through a telephone call.

dibit   Literally translated, dibit means two bit. Thus, a dibit is any two consecutive bits.

DIBOL   A version of the COBOL programming language for PDP and VAX computers. It is marketed by Digital Equipment Corporation (DIBOL is a contraction of Digital COBOL).

dictionary   In the PICK operating system, a file used to hold information defining the structure of the file at the next level in the hierarchy.

DIF   See *data interchange format*.

digit   A single character in a numbering system.

digital   A derivation of the word digit, digital describes any system (such as a computer) that works with numbers.

digital audio tape   A recording technique that records sound as a digital signal on magnetic tape, in much the same way that digital computer data can be stored on magnetic tape. DAT technology results in extremely high-quality audio, similar to compact discs.

digitize   **1.** In CAD systems, the process of using a pointing device to randomly but accurately indicate points in a drawing. **2.** The process of converting analog information to its digital counterpart.

digitizing tablet   An input device typically used in CAD systems. The tablet is similar to a drawing tablet, and can either use a puck or a pen for indicating discrete points that the tablet's interface software can sense and act upon.

dimension   In certain programming languages, a dimension statement is used to define the number of elements in an array.

dimensioning   In CAD systems, the application and editing of dimensions to objects in a drawing.

DIN connector   A type of plug-and-socket connector commonly used in computer systems and other electronic devices. DIN stands for *Deutsche Industrie Norm,* a German committee that sets dimensional standards. Examples of DIN connectors are shown here:

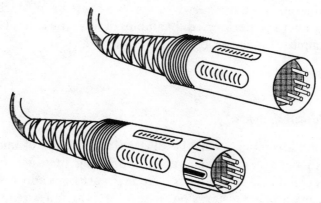

DIP   An acronym for dual in-line package.

DIP switch   A series of tiny on/off toggle switches built into a housing and commonly connected to a circuit board. The switches typically control the conditions under which the circuit board operates. DIP is an acronym for dual in-line package. A type of DIP switch is shown here:

DIR   DIR is an operating-system command used to list the file directory of a disk or subdirectory of a disk. It is used in CP/M, MS-DOS, and OS/2.

direct-access modem   A modem that does not use an acoustic coupler. Typically a direct-access modem uses telephone-type connectors such as RJ-11 or RJ-14 connectors to hook into the telephone system.

direct access storage device   A term (coined by IBM) used to refer to external data storage units, such as disk drives.

direct addressing   A method of assembly language addressing in which one of the operands is a memory location, the contents of which are used in the operation to be performed. Examples of this type of addressing (for the 80x86 family of microprocessors) are:

```
MOV   AX,TABLE
MOV   AX,[40]
```

See also *addressing mode*.

direct indexed addressing   In the 80x86 (Intel) family of microprocessors, a method of assembly language addressing in which one of the operands is composed of two parts. The first part is an address, either as a displacement or in a register. The second part is an index register (either SI or DI) or an offset. This offset, or the content of the index register, is added to the initial displacement address. This provides the final address, the contents of which are used in the operation to be performed. Examples of this addressing mode are:

```
MOV   AX,TABLE[DI]
MOV   AX,[BX][SI]
```

See also *addressing mode*.

direction flag   In the 80x86 (Intel) family, the bit in the flags register that indicates whether string operations should increment (DF clear) or decrement (DF set) the index registers.

direction keys   See *cursor keys*.

directive   See *preprocessor directive*.

direct memory access   A method of data transfer involving direct access of a RAM buffer area through specialized circuitry without going through the CPU. DMA frees the processor for other operations, which results in a more efficient use of computer resources.

directory   A list of files available on a computer system; synonymous with catalog.

directory handle table   In the NetWare environment, the file server maintains a table comprised of 255 pointers to either a volume or a directory path. One directory handle table is maintained for each workstation on the network.

directory hashing   A method of analyzing and mapping the files in a directory. The resulting hash table is kept in memory. This allows extremely fast access to any file in a directory. This technique is typically used in file servers attached to a LAN.

directory path   See *path (1)*.

directory services   In the NetWare environment, a group of services that allow an application to maintain and manipulate directories.

disassembly   The process of composing assembly language instructions from machine code; the opposite of assembly.

disjunction   See *OR*.

disk   A nonvolatile mass storage device that allows direct access to data stored on it.

disk access time   See *access time*.

disk cache   A memory buffer area that contains a large block of information read from or to be written to the disk. Since reading from and writing to memory is faster than to disk, this speeds up program throughput. When writing to disk, the information in the cache is written as the disk is able to process it when the cache is full, or when it is flushed by special program commands. See also *cache*.

disk cartridge   A removable hard disk consisting of a plastic or metal casing in which one or more disk platters are mounted. To access the information on the disk, the cartridge is placed in a disk drive and locked into place; then the disk and drive function the same as a traditional fixed disk.

disk drive   A computer peripheral that allows access to information on either floppy or hard disks.

disk duplexing   A method of implementing fault-tolerant redundancy by adding secondary disk drives, controllers, and cabling. See also *fault-tolerant system*.

diskette   See *floppy disk*.

disk file   A collection of information stored in an organized manner on a disk.

disk initialization package   A standard Macintosh package used to detect when an unreadable disk has been inserted into a disk drive. This package then gives the user the option to eject or initialize the disk. This package is provided in the system resource file. See also *package*.

diskless workstation   A computer terminal that is used only to access information on a network. The workstation has no local disk drives; it uses only those drives that are remote resources on the network.

disk mirroring   A method of implementing fault-tolerant redundancy by adding a backup file server to a networked system. See also *fault-tolerant system*.

disk operating system   A generic term for the system software used by a computer to control resources and communicate with application software. In the PC environment, DOS typically refers to either PC-DOS or MS-DOS.

disk optimization   See *defragmenter*.

disk pack   A type of disk cartridge that contains more than one hard-disk platter.

disk server   See *file server*.

disk transfer area   A memory area set aside for transferring information to or from the disk drive.

dispatcher   See *scheduler*.

displacement   An offset from a specified starting location. For example, a displacement can be used to modify a memory address so the address points to a desired location. Typically, this is done to find the beginning address of an entry in a table or array.

display adaptor   The printed circuit card that controls the format, resolution, and type of information sent to a video display.

display attribute   See *attribute (1)*.

display element   See *graphics primitive*.

display frame   See *frame*.

display list   In computer graphics, a collection of vectors that make up a graphics image.

display list processor   A graphics peripheral board used to speed up the processing of vector graphics information. A display list processor is most often used with graphics software that requires intensive computational work to display an image—for example, CAD systems.

display PostScript   A version of the PostScript language that displays fonts and graphics on-screen instead of on an output device such as a printer.

display segment   In computer graphics, a collection of graphics primitives that can be manipulated as a single element.

distributed communications architecture   A set of rules and protocols for Unisys communications networks.

distributed database   A database that is not stored in one central location. Instead, it is physically located on a number of different computers connected by a network. The database management software keeps track of the database and makes it appear as one large database file to users.

distributed database management system   The software designed to manage a distributed database.

distributed data processing   A systems configuration in which computing tasks are done at many different sites throughout a company. Users are able to perform computing tasks on a computer system dedicated to their use or the use of their department. This methodology is the opposite of centralized data processing. See also *distributed processing*.

distributed processing   A networking configuration in which data may reside on a disk drive connected to any workstation in a network. See also *distributed data processing*.

dithering   In computer graphics, the creation of additional colors or shades of gray from an existing palette based upon an algorithm. An example is shown here:

Dithering is typically used for special effects, creating halftones, and to make "hard edges" softer.

DL/1   An acronym for data language 1, this is an IBM database manipulation language used in the IMS database management system.

DLE   See *data link escape*.

DMA   See *direct memory access*.

DML   See *data manipulation language*.

document   Another name for a text file.

documentation   The printed, on-line, or in-code comments, instructions, tutorials, and support information supplied with software.

document content architecture   A set of IBM file definitions for files that contain alphanumeric data, such as word processing documents. The common acronym is DCA.

document description language   A printer control language used in Hewlett-Packard LaserJet printers. The common acronym is DDL.

DO loop   In programming, a structure that repeats a series of instructions a specific number of times. The programmer specifies a test that, if determined to be true, causes the loop to be exited. The basic structure is:

```
NO = 1
YES = 0
PROCEED = YES
DO WHILE PROCEED=YES
   GET INPUT FROM FILE
```

```
    PROCESS INPUT
    IF END OF FILE THEN PROCEED = NO
ENDWHILE
```

This type of control structure originated with FORTRAN. The exact syntax of the structure will vary depending upon the programming language being used. The example shown causes the loop to be executed while the test value (PROCEED = YES) is true. A variation on this loop uses a DO UNTIL syntax to cause repetition of the loop until a certain test is true.

domain   1. A range and type of values defined for an individual data type. 2. In communications, all the resources under control of a computer. 3. A single bit in bubble memory or on a disk. Sometimes called a bit cell or magnetic cell.

dongle   The common slang name for the I/O device used to protect software. A dongle attaches to the parallel or serial port of a computer, and acts as a key. Special instructions written into the software can test to see if the dongle is attached to the system. If so, then processing can proceed as intended. If not, then the software will not run properly. Dongles are typically used in expensive vertical-market software where piracy may be a legitimate concern to the vendor. They tend to be expensive and a nuisance to the users.

DOS   See *disk operating system*.

DOS extender   An operating system extension used under the MS-DOS operating system to access information beyond the 640K memory barrier.

DOS mode   See *compatibility box*.

DOS prompt   In the MS-DOS environment, the display, or prompt, that informs the user that the operating system is awaiting input. The default DOS prompt is the name of the current disk drive, followed by a "greater-than" sign (as in C>).

DOS protected-mode interface   A memory-extending technique used under the MS-DOS operating system. The DPMI specification was developed by Microsoft Corporation with input from other software vendors.

DOSSHELL.BAT   A batch file that initiates a command shell for the MS-DOS operating system. This shell became available with the release of MS-DOS version 4.0.

DOS/VSE   An operating system for some of IBM's mainframe computers. DOS/VSE is an acronym for disk operating system/virtual storage extended. It allows multiple users, and provides multitasking and virtual memory.

dot addressable   A condition or attribute of a system that allows the user to program each pixel on a video screen or each dot on a printer directly.

dot matrix   A printing or display technique that uses a pattern of dots to form each character or image. The following is an example of dot-matrix printing:

```
This is an example of dot matrix printer output.
```

dot pitch   In a display or printer system that uses dots, the distance from the center of one dot to the center of an adjacent dot. For example, if a laser printer has a resolution of 300 dpi, then the dot pitch is 1/300th of an inch.

dot prompt   In dBASE products from Ashton-Tate, the display that informs the user that the program is awaiting input. This prompt is nothing more than a period at the beginning of a line followed by a blinking cursor.

dots per inch   A linear measure of the number of dots a device can print in an inch. For example, laser printers are commonly rated at 300 dpi, meaning they can print up to 300 dots for each horizontal or vertical inch on the paper.

double buffering   The use of two buffers to speed up I/O operations. Each buffer is typically assigned a special purpose. For instance, one buffer could handle information coming to the computer (input), while the other is dedicated to information being output.

double bus fault   In the 680x0 (Motorola) family of microprocessors, a condition in which an exception occurs while a previous exception is being handled. A double bus fault causes the system to crash and restart.

double click   To press and release a mouse button twice in rapid succession.

double-density disk   A floppy disk with twice the storage capacity of the previously used disk type. In IBM-compatible microcomputers, a double-density 5.25″ disk is one with a capacity of 360K, while the double-density 3.5″ disk has a capacity of 720K.

double format   A floating-point format that consists of a sign, an 11-bit biased exponent, an implicit integer bit, and a 52-bit significand.

double precision   In number storage, the use of two computer words (usually two 16-bit words) to represent a number.

double quotes   Another name for the quote mark (″), often used inaccurately to distinguish the character from a single quote mark, or prime (′).

double-sided disk   A floppy disk that uses both sides for storage of information.

doublet   A byte consisting of two bits.

doubleword   Two words of memory space; a 32-bit quantity of memory. Also called a long word.

Dow Jones News/Retrieval Service   A dial-up database service for the business community. The service offers many business publications and services in a database format that can be accessed by subscribers.

down link   A communications channel from a satellite to an earth station.

download   1. To move a file from a remote computer to your computer over a communications channel; the opposite of upload. 2. To move a configuration or control file from the main computer to a peripheral. For example, a font may be downloaded to a printer before printing a document.

downstream   In network terminology, an area further along the network in the direction of data flow.

downtime   The length of time during which a computer or peripheral is inoperable due to hardware or software failure; the opposite of uptime.

downward compatible   A quality of software that enables it to run without modification on smaller or earlier models of a computer system; the opposite of upward compatible.

DPB   See *drive parameter block*.

dpi   See *dots per inch*.

DPL   See *descriptor privilege level*.

DPMA   See *Data Processing Management Association*.

DPMI   See *DOS protected-mode interface*.

d-pointer   In the PICK operating system, a dictionary record that defines a file.

drag   In graphics systems, the process of using a pointing device (such as a puck, mouse, or stylus) to move an object while holding down the control button on the device. The object is visible while it is moved across the screen.

DRAM   See *dynamic RAM*.

drive   See *disk drive; tape drive*.

drive number   A numeric value commonly used by operating systems to represent a logical disk drive.

drive parameter block   In the MS-DOS environment, a data structure used by DOS. The DPB indicates detailed layout information about disks and drives attached to the system, including the drive number, sizes of units, where the data begins, and where the root directory begins.

driver   A specialized computer program that is used by the operating system or other software to interface and correctly operate peripheral devices such as printers, mice, disk drives, or video displays.

drum printer   A type of line printer that uses a metal drum containing the printable characters. The drum contains a full character set for each possible printing position. The drum spins on a spindle until the proper character is in front of a print hammer, and then the hammer strikes the character to produce an impression on the paper.

drystone   See dhrystone.

DS   1. In the 80x86 (Intel) family, the 16-bit data segment register. 2. An acronym for digit select, an EBCDIC control code with a value of 32.

DSA   An acronym for distributed systems architecture, a communications protocol for Honeywell Bull networks.

DSDD   An acronym for double-sided, double-density. See also *double-sided disk; double-density disk*.

DSP   An acronym for digital signal processing.

DSR   See *data set ready*.

DSS   An acronym for decision support system.

DTA   See *disk transfer area*.

DTE   See *data termination equipment*.

DTR   See *data terminal ready*.

DTS   An acronym for digital termination service.

dual cable   In network terminology, a broadband cabling system that uses one cable for transmission and one for reception.

dumb terminal   A terminal designed to be hooked up to a remote computer; it has no local processing capability.

duplex channel   A communications channel that allows simultaneous two-way transmission of information.

DVST   An acronym for direct-view storage tube, an early type of display screen for computers.

DX   In the 80*x*86 (Intel) family, a 16-bit general-purpose register.

dyadic operation   A classification of operation requiring two operands. See also *monadic operation*.

dynamic allocation   The procurement of variable space while a program is running instead of when a program is compiled or assembled.

dynamic array   In certain programming languages, an array that is not explicitly declared. It is assigned a range and a memory location when it is first referred to in the program.

dynamic data exchange   A protocol used in the Microsoft Windows environment that allows application programs to request and exchange data automatically.

dynamic link   In the OS/2 environment, a method of postponing the resolution of external references until a program is loaded or run. Subroutines using the dynlink capabilities of OS/2 can be created, maintained, and updated separately from the processes that access them.

dynamic RAM   A type of random access memory that only holds its contents for a short period of time. Because of its short persistence, dynamic RAM must be refreshed many times every second. Compare with static RAM, which maintains its contents as long as power is supplied. See also *refresh*.

dynlink   Short for *dynamic link*.

dynlink library   In the OS/2 environment, a file containing the binary code for a collection of dynamically linked subroutines.

EAM   An acronym for electrical accounting machine.

EAX   On the 80*x*86 (Intel) family of microprocessors beginning with the 80386, a 32-bit general-purpose register. EAX is an extension of the AX register.

EBCDIC   See *extended binary coded decimal interchange code*.

EBP   On the 80*x*86 (Intel) family of microprocessors beginning with the 80386, the 32-bit base pointer register. EBP is an extension of the BP register.

EBR   An acronym for electron beam recording.

EBX   On the 80*x*86 (Intel) family of microprocessors beginning with the 80386, a 32-bit general-purpose register. EBX is an extension of the BX register.

ECB   See *event control block*.

ECC   An acronym for error correction code.

echo   To repeat a stream of characters. For instance, characters entered at a keyboard are echoed to the screen.

echo check   In data communications, a method of verifying the correctness of transmitted characters by the remote terminal retransmitting the received characters back to the sender. The sender then checks to make sure there is a match between the original transmission and the echoed information. This is sometimes called a loop check.

ECMA   See *European Computer Manufacturer's Association*.

ECX   In the 80x86 (Intel) processor family beginning with the 80386, a 32-bit general-purpose data register, usually used for counting. ECX is an extension of the CX register.

EDI   In the 80x86 (Intel) processor family beginning with the 80386, a 32-bit general-purpose data register. EDI is an extension of the DI register.

edit mode   An input mode that allows the editing of previously entered information.

editor   A software program used to create, edit, save, and manage text files. See also *line editor; text editor*.

edit sensing   A method used in some application software to determine whether a record, previously read from a file, should be rewritten. If alterations to the record are sensed by the software, then it can be written to the disk.

EDLIN   In the MS-DOS environment, a simple line editor provided with the operating system.

EDP   An acronym for electronic data processing.

EDX   In the 80x86 (Intel) processor family beginning with the 80386, a 32-bit general-purpose data register. EDX is an extension of the DX register.

EEMS   An acronym for enhanced expanded memory specification. EEMS is a second-generation version of the earlier EMS standard. It was developed jointly by AST, Quadram, and Ashton-Tate. EEMS is not widely in use, as most software conforms to the more-recent LIM 4.0 standard. See also *expanded memory; LIM*.

EEPROM   See *electrically erasable programmable read-only memory*.

effective address   A memory address calculated from component parts such as a base, index, and displacement.

effective transfer rate   The average amount of data transmitted across a channel in a given period of time.

EFT   An acronym for electronic funds transfer.

EGA   An acronym for enhanced graphics adapter.

EIA   See *Electronic Industries Association*.

EIP   In the 80*x*86 (Intel) processor family beginning with the 80386, a 32-bit register used to indicate the address in memory of the next instruction to be executed. EIP is an extension of the IP register. See also *instruction pointer*.

EIS   An acronym for executive information system.

EISA   See *extended industry standard architecture*.

electrically erasable programmable read-only memory   A semipermanent nonvolatile memory chip. Information stored in the EEPROM can be electronically erased by special electrical circuits, therefore a computer equipped with EEPROM chips can update them dynamically.

electronic bubble memory   See *bubble memory*.

Electronic Industries Association   An industry organization whose members include manufacturers of electronic parts and systems. Founded in 1924, the organization establishes electronic interface standards. The EIA can be located at:

Electronic Industries Association
2001 I Street, N.W.
Washington, DC 20006
(202) 457-4900

electronic mail   The composition, transmission, and storage of messages and files by and between users of a network system.

electronic messaging   See *electronic mail*.

element   An individual member of a set, collection, array, or matrix.

EM   See *end-of-medium character*.

E-mail   See *electronic mail*.

embedded system   A specialized computer used to control the device in which it is contained. For example, automotive control computers use embedded systems.

EMM   See *expanded memory manager*.

empty set   See *null set*.

EMS   An acronym for expanded memory specification; see also *expanded memory*.

emulate   To behave or function the same as another system (hardware or software).

enabled event   In the QuickBASIC programming environment, an occurrence that is actively tested for with an ON event statement.

encapsulated PostScript   A directly printable PostScript file; the output of a PostScript-compatible printer driver captured in a file instead of being sent to a printer. The typical filename extension for encapsulated Post-Script files is .EPS.

encapsulation   A programming technique in which the implementation of a program, function, or process is hidden from external programs, functions, or processes. In this way it is possible to understand *what* the encapsulated routine does, but not *how* it does it. This is a principle fully implemented in object-oriented programming.

encrypt   To convert information from an understandable condition to a secure, encoded condition.

end-around shift   A bit-wise machine language operation implemented by shifting bits to the next higher bit position. The most significant bit is then transferred to the least significant bit position. Sometimes called a cyclic shift.

endless loop   A condition that occurs when a program enters a logical loop with no chance of exiting the loop. This is often caused by inadequate escape mechanisms, faulty logic, or program errors.

end of file   The last byte of information or last record in a file. Abbreviated as EOF; in many operating systems, the end-of-file character is defined as a Ctrl-Z, or an ASCII value of 26.

end-of-medium character   A control character used in some computer systems to indicate the physical end of a recording medium. The ASCII and EBCDIC values for this character are both 25, and the abbreviation is EM.

end-of-tape marker   A physical change in a recording tape that indicates to the tape drive that the end of the tape has been reached. This change is usually a reflective surface or a transparent section of the tape.

end-of-text character   In data communications, a control character used to signal the end of the transmission of a block of text. The ASCII and EBCDIC values for this character are both 3, and the abbreviation is ETX.

end-of-transmission-block character   A control character used in data communications to indicate the successful end of a transmission block. The ASCII value for the end-of-transmission-block character is 23, the EBCDIC value is 38, and the acronym is ETB.

end-to-end encryption   A data security technique where information is encoded at the transmitting node of a network and decoded at the receiving node.

end user   The person for whom a computer program or report is ultimately designed—the person who uses a program.

enhanced small device interface   A standard method of interfacing disk and tape drives to computers.

ENQ   See *enquiry character*.

ENQ/ACK   In data communications, a handshaking protocol using the ENQ, ACK, and NAK characters. See also *acknowledge character; enquiry character; negative acknowledge character.*

enquiry character   A control character used in data communications to initiate communication or a request for information from a remote terminal. The ASCII value for this character is 5, the EBCDIC value is 45, and the abbreviation is ENQ. On older TTY systems, this may be known as WRU, or "Who are you?"

Enter key   The keyboard key usually used to signify when user input is completed. On some systems, the Enter key is referred to as the Return key.

entry point   **1.** In programming, the starting point of a program or subroutine. **2.** The first record logically accessed in a file.

environment   The conditions and circumstances under which a program or computer system is operating.

environmental variables   **1.** System variables maintained by the operating system that define special settings or values that affect the way other applications function. **2.** Within a program, variables created automatically based on information derived from the environment in which the program is functioning.

environment division   The portion of a COBOL program that provides information about the environment in which the program is to be run. See also *data division; identification division; procedure division.*

environment strings   In the MS-DOS and OS/2 environments, a series of character strings that define the operating conditions of a process. Environment strings are definable by the user or by another process (such as the parent process).

EOB   An acronym for end of block.

EOF   See *end of file*.

EOT   1. See *end-of-transmission-block character*. 2. See *end-of-tape marker*.

EOV   An acronym for end of volume.

EPA   An acronym for entry point address.

EPROM   See *erasable/programmable read-only memory*.

EPS file   See *encapsulated PostScript*.

eqn   In the UNIX environment, a troff preprocessor used to format mathematical expressions. The corresponding preprocessor for nroff is called neqn.

equalization   In data communications, a technique of line compensation accomplished by adding loss or delay to the line signals in inverse proportion to the channel characteristics.

equation   An arithmetic expression consisting of two parts, one on each side of the equal sign. For example, $total = r*s$ is an equation. An equation should be resolvable to a single value. In the example, when r is multiplied by s, the single resulting value is assigned to the variable *total*.

erasable/programmable read-only memory   A semipermanent nonvolatile memory chip. Information stored in the EPROM can be erased by exposure to ultraviolet light, and reprogrammed by use of a special EPROM burner.

ERD   An acronym for entity-relationship diagram.

ERRMSG   In the PICK operating system, the name of a file that contains the text of operating system error messages.

error-checking routine   A portion of a program that checks for valid data input, or handles errors that occur in normal processing operations.

error-correcting code   An algorithm that allows for the reconstruction of information that was damaged during transmission or transfer.

error handling   The process of identifying, processing, and compensating for errors during program execution.

error rate   In data communications, the ratio of information packets transmitted in error to the total number of information packets transmitted.

error trapping   A program's ability to recognize an error and perform a predetermined action in response to that error.

ES   In the 80x86 (Intel) family, the 16-bit extra segment register.

ESC   See *escape character*.

escape character   A control character used to signify that the characters following have special meaning. It is generated by pressing the Esc key on a keyboard. The ASCII value of the escape character is 27, the EBCDIC value is 39, and the abbreviation is ESC. See also *data link escape; escape key; escape sequence*.

escape code   See *escape sequence*.

escape key   A keyboard key typically used to signal to software that the user wishes to abort the current operation or return to the previous menu. On many keyboards it is abbreviated as Esc.

escape sequence   A series of characters, preceded by an escape character (ESC), that instructs a program or hardware device to perform a specific task as defined by the characters making up the sequence.

ESDI   See *enhanced small device interface*.

ESI   In the 80x86 (Intel) processor family beginning with the 80386, a 32-bit general-purpose data register. ESI is an extension of the SI register.

ESP   In the 80*x*86 (Intel) processor family beginning with the 80386, a 32-bit general-purpose data register. ESP is an extension of the SP register.

ETB   See *end-of-transmission-block character.*

EtherNet   A specification for baseband local area networks (LANs) developed by Xerox, Intel, and Digital Equipment Corporation (DEC). The specification calls for the use of coaxial cable configured in a bus topology, CSMA/CD network access, and data transfer rates up to 10Mbps.

ETX   See *end-of-text character.*

EU   An acronym for execution unit.

European Computer Manufacturer's Association   A European organization for computer vendors, business equipment manufacturers, and suppliers. ECMA is based in Geneva, Switzerland, and is the European counterpart of CBEMA in the United States.

even parity   See *parity.*

event   **1.** An occurrence that causes an exception or interrupt. **2.** Any discrete action or occurrence that might be of interest or significance to either hardware or software.

event control block   In a NetWare environment, a data structure containing information used to send or receive IPX or SPX packets.

event mask   See *interrupt mask.*

exception   A condition caused by an abnormal event during program execution. A forced call to a program segment. The call is generated when the CPU fails to interpret an instruction or when the CPU receives an explicit software instruction to generate the exception. Examples of events that can cause exceptions on the 80*x*86 (Intel) family include stack overflow, division by zero, undefined opcodes, and memory-protection violations. In the 680*x*0 (Motorola) family of microprocessors, exceptions can be caused by an address error, nonmaskable interrupt, and an A-trap.

exception handler   The routine executed by a CPU on detection of an exception or trap.

exception pointers   On certain members of the 80x86 and 80x87 (Intel) families, the indicators used by exception handlers to identify the cause of an exception.

exception vector   In the 680x0 (Motorola) family of microprocessors, a pointer in low-memory that indicates the address of a routine to be executed when an exception occurs.

excess representation   See *bias*.

exchange sort   A classification of sorting implemented by exchanging adjacent elements in an array. An example of an exchange sort is the bubble sort.

exclusion   See *XOR*.

exclusive-or   See *XOR*.

executable file   A program file that can be executed directly. Sometimes called a load module.

execute   To run the instructions in a program.

execute permission   A level of file access that doesn't permit any interaction with a program except to allow it to be run. See also *permission*.

execution   The orderly processing of programming instructions.

EXE file   A type of executable program file in the MS-DOS, OS/2, and VAX/VMS operating systems.

exitlist   In the OS/2 environment, a series of subroutines that are executed when a process has terminated, but before the process is removed from memory.

expand   To return compressed data to its original condition.

expanded memory   In the MS-DOS environment, memory that resides beyond the DOS 640K memory barrier, but beneath the 1M boundary. Expanded memory is accessible through an expanded memory manager. See also *extended memory; LIM*.

expanded memory manager   Systems software that handles expanded memory in an IBM-compatible microcomputer.

expansion slot   A connector slot in the back of a computer that is designed to allow compatible circuit boards to be added to the computer system.

expert system   A program that implements artificial intelligence techniques to emulate, in a limited fashion, the expertise of a human specialist. An expert system typically has the ability to manipulate data and infer conclusions from a set of given facts.

exponent   A number that indicates the power to which another number is raised.

exponential notation   See *scientific notation*.

export   To move data or information to another program, file, or peripheral.

expression   In programming, a syntactic structure that returns or can be reduced to a single value.

extended binary coded decimal interchange code   Typically referred to by the acronym EBCDIC, this is the character coding system used primarily on IBM mini and mainframe systems. It is used to convert numeric values to characters and digits that can be understood by humans, and vice-versa. The EBCDIC code uses 8 bits to define each of up to 256 characters, although many of the codes are undefined (they have no character assigned to them). Table E-1 details the EBCDIC character set as introduced in 1964 with the IBM System/360 mainframe.

Decimal	Octal	Hex	Character	Comment
0	0	0	NUL	Null
1	1	1	SOH	Start of heading
2	2	2	STX	Start of text
3	3	3	ETX	End of text
4	4	4	PF	Punch off
5	5	5	HT	Horizontal tab
6	6	6	LC	Lower case
7	7	7	DEL	Delete
8	10	8		
9	11	9		
10	12	A	SMM	Start of manual message
11	13	B	VT	Vertical tab
12	14	C	FF	Form feed
13	15	D	CR	Carriage return
14	16	E	SO	Shift out
15	17	F	SI	Shift in
16	20	10	DLE	Data link escape
17	21	11	DC1	Device control character 1
18	22	12	DC2	Device control character 2
19	23	13	DC3	Device control character 3
20	24	14	RES	Restore
21	25	15	NL	New line
22	26	16	BS	Backspace
23	27	17	IL	Idle
24	30	18	CAN	Cancel
25	31	19	EM	End of medium
26	32	1A	CC	Cursor control
27	33	1B	CU1	Customer use 1
28	34	1C	IFS	Interchange file separator

Table E-1.   IBM System/360 EBCDIC Character Set

Decimal	Octal	Hex	Character	Comment
29	35	1D	IGS	Interchange group separator
30	36	1E	IRS	Interchange record separator
31	37	1F	IUS	Interchange unit separator
32	40	20	DS	Digit select
33	41	21	SOS	Start of significance
34	42	22	FS	Field separator
35	43	23		
36	44	24	BYP	Bypass
37	45	25	LF	Line feed
38	46	26	ETB	End of transmission block
39	47	27	ESC	Escape
40	50	28		
41	51	29		
42	52	2A	SM	Set mode
43	53	2B	CU2	Customer use 2
44	54	2C		
45	55	2D	ENQ	Enquiry
46	56	2E	ACK	Positive acknowledge
47	57	2F	BEL	Bell
48	60	30		
49	61	31		
50	62	32	SYN	Synchronous idle
51	63	33		
52	64	34	PN	Punch on
53	65	35	RS	Reader stop
54	66	36	UC	Upper case
55	67	37	EOT	End of transmission
56	70	38		
57	71	39		
58	72	3A		

Table E-1. IBM System/360 EBCDIC Character Set (continued)

Decimal	Octal	Hex	Character	Comment
59	73	3B	CU3	Customer use 3
60	74	3C	DC4	Device control character 4
61	75	3D	NAK	Negative acknowledge
62	76	3E		
63	77	3F	SUB	Substitute
64	100	40	SP	Space
65	101	41		
66	102	42		
67	103	43		
68	104	44		
69	105	45		
70	106	46		
71	107	47		
72	110	48		
73	111	49		
74	112	4A	¢	Cent sign
75	113	4B	,	
76	114	4C	<	
77	115	4D	(	
78	116	4E	+	
79	117	4F	¦	
80	120	50	&	
81	121	51		
82	122	52		
83	123	53		
84	124	54		
85	125	55		
86	126	56		
87	127	57		
88	130	58		
89	131	59		
90	132	5A		

Table E-1. IBM System/360 EBCDIC Character Set (continued)

Decimal	Octal	Hex	Character	Comment
91	133	5B	$	
92	134	5C	.	
93	135	5D	)	
94	136	5E	;	
95	137	5F	¬	
96	140	60		
97	141	61	/	
98	142	62		
99	143	63		
100	144	64		
101	145	65		
102	146	66		
103	147	67		
104	150	68		
105	151	69		
106	152	6A	:	
107	153	6B	,	
108	154	6C	%	
109	155	6D	_	
110	156	6E	>	
111	157	6F	?	
112	160	70		
113	161	71		
114	162	72		
115	163	73		
116	164	74		
117	165	75		
118	166	76		
119	167	77		
120	170	78		
121	171	79		
122	172	7A	:	
123	173	7B	#	

Table E-1.   IBM System/360 EBCDIC Character Set (continued)

Decimal	Octal	Hex	Character	Comment
124	174	7C	@	
125	175	7D	'	
126	176	7E	=	
127	177	7F	"	
128	200	80		
129	201	81	a	
130	202	82	b	
131	203	83	c	
132	204	84	d	
133	205	85	e	
134	206	86	f	
135	207	87	g	
136	210	88	h	
137	211	89	i	
138	212	8A		
139	213	8B		
140	214	8C		
141	215	8D		
142	216	8E		
143	217	8F		
144	220	90		
145	221	91	j	
146	222	92	k	
147	223	93	l	
148	224	94	m	
149	225	95	n	
150	226	96	o	
151	227	97	p	
152	230	98	q	
153	231	99	r	
154	232	9A		
155	233	9B		
156	234	9C		
157	235	9D		

Table E-1.   IBM System/360 EBCDIC Character Set (continued)

Decimal	Octal	Hex	Character	Comment
158	236	9E		
159	237	9F		
160	240	A0		
161	241	A1		
162	242	A2	s	
163	243	A3	t	
164	244	A4	u	
165	245	A5	v	
166	246	A6	w	
167	247	A7	x	
168	250	A8	y	
169	251	A9	z	
170	252	AA		
171	253	AB		
172	254	AC		
173	255	AD		
174	256	AE		
175	257	AF		
176	260	B0		
177	261	B1		
178	262	B2		
179	263	B3		
180	264	B4		
181	265	B5		
182	266	B6		
183	267	B7		
184	270	B8		
185	271	B9		
186	272	BA		
187	273	BB		
188	274	BC		
189	275	BD		
190	276	BE		
191	277	BF		

Table E-1.   IBM System/360 EBCDIC Character Set (continued)

Decimal	Octal	Hex	Character	Comment
192	200	C0		
193	201	C1	A	
194	202	C2	B	
195	203	C3	C	
196	204	C4	D	
197	205	C5	E	
198	206	C6	F	
199	207	C7	G	
200	210	C8	H	
201	211	C9	I	
202	212	CA		
203	213	CB		
204	214	CC		
205	215	CD		
206	216	CE		
207	217	CF		
208	220	D0		
209	221	D1	J	
210	222	D2	K	
211	223	D3	L	
212	224	D4	M	
213	225	D5	N	
214	226	D6	O	
215	227	D7	P	
216	230	D8	Q	
217	231	D9	R	
218	232	DA		
219	233	DB		
220	234	DC		
221	235	DD		
222	236	DE		
223	237	DF		
224	240	E0		
225	241	E1		

Table E-1. IBM System/360 EBCDIC Character Set (continued)

Decimal	Octal	Hex	Character	Comment
226	242	E2	S	
227	243	E3	T	
228	244	E4	U	
229	245	E5	V	
230	246	E6	W	
231	247	E7	X	
232	250	E8	Y	
233	251	E9	Z	
234	252	EA		
235	253	EB		
236	254	EC		
237	255	ED		
238	256	EE		
239	257	EF		
240	260	F0	0	
241	261	F1	1	
242	262	F2	2	
243	263	F3	3	
244	264	F4	4	
245	265	F5	5	
246	266	F6	6	
247	267	F7	7	
248	270	F8	8	
249	271	F9	9	
250	272	FA		
251	273	FB		
252	274	FC		
253	275	FD		
254	276	FE		
255	277	FF		

Table E-1.   IBM System/360 EBCDIC Character Set (continued)

In subsequent generations of IBM mainframe systems, additional code values have been defined. Because of this, it is impossible to find one standard version of EBCDIC. See also *American standard code for information interchange*.

extended character set For character sets that define only the first 128 of 256 possible values, those characters that comprise the upper values between 128 and 256. For example, Table E-2 shows the extended character set for the original IBM PC. See also *American standard code for information interchange*.

extended industry standard architecture A 32-bit extension to the standard IBM AT bus for microcomputers. EISA was developed in the late 1980s by a group of computer and peripheral manufacturers as a counter

Decimal	Hex	Character	Decimal	Hex	Character
128	80	Ç	148	94	ö
129	81	ü	149	95	ò
130	82	é	150	96	û
131	83	â	151	97	ù
132	84	ä	152	98	ÿ
133	85	à	153	99	Ö
134	86	å	154	9A	Ü
135	87	ç	155	9B	¢
136	88	ê	156	9C	£
137	89	ë	157	9D	¥
138	8A	è	158	9E	Pt
139	8B	ï	159	9F	ƒ
140	8C	î	160	A0	á
141	8D	ì	161	A1	í
142	8E	Ä	162	A2	ó
143	8F	Å	163	A3	ú
144	90	É	164	A4	ñ
145	91	æ	165	A5	Ñ
146	92	Æ	166	A6	ª
147	93	ô	167	A7	º

Table E-2. The IBM PC Extended Character Set (ASCII Values 128 Through 255)

Decimal	Hex	Character	Decimal	Hex	Character
168	A8	¿	202	CA	⊥⊥
169	A9	⌐	203	CB	⊤⊤
170	AA	¬	204	CC	⊩
171	AB	½	205	CD	=
172	AC	¼	206	CE	╬
173	AD	¡	207	CF	⊥⊥
174	AE	«	208	D0	⊥⊥
175	AF	»	209	D1	⊤⊤
176	B0	░	210	D2	⊤⊤
177	B1	▒	211	D3	⊔
178	B2	▓	212	D4	⊔
179	B3	│	213	D5	⊏
180	B4	┤	214	D6	┌┌
181	B5	╡	215	D7	╫
182	B6	╢	216	D8	╪
183	B7	╖	217	D9	┘
184	B8	╕	218	DA	┌
185	B9	╣	219	DB	█
186	BA	║	220	DC	▄
187	BB	╗	221	DD	▌
188	BC	╝	222	DE	▐
189	BD	╜	223	DF	▀
190	BE	╛	224	E0	α
191	BF	┐	225	E1	β
192	C0	└	226	E2	Γ
193	C1	┴	227	E3	π
194	C2	┬	228	E4	Σ
195	C3	├	229	E5	σ
196	C4	─	230	E6	μ
197	C5	┼	231	E7	τ
198	C6	╞	232	E8	φ
199	C7	╟	233	E9	Θ
200	C8	╚	234	EA	Ω
201	C9	╔	235	EB	δ

Table E-2. The IBM PC Extended Character Set (ASCII Values 128 Through 255) (continued)

Decimal	Hex	Character	Decimal	Hex	Character
236	EC	∞	246	F6	÷
237	ED	∅	247	F7	≈
238	EE	∈	248	F8	°
239	EF	∩	249	F9	•
240	F0	≡	250	FA	·
241	F1	±	251	FB	√
242	F2	≥	252	FC	^{n}
243	F3	≤	253	FD	^{2}
244	F4	⌠	254	FE	■
245	F5	⌡	255	FF	(blank)

Table E-2.   The IBM PC Extended Character Set (ASCII Values 128 Through 255) (continued)

to the IBM micro channel architecture. Unlike MCA, EISA is downward-compatible with existing peripheral adapters developed for the 16-bit IBM AT bus. See also *micro channel architecture*.

extended memory   In the MS-DOS environment, normal RAM that resides beyond the 1M address mark. This memory is accessible when in protected mode. See also *expanded memory*.

extensible language   A programming language that can be expanded by the user.

extension   See *filename extension*.

external command   In the MS-DOS, OS/2, or UNIX operating systems, an operating system command stored in a file. It is not intrinsically a part of the operating system. There is no difference between an external command and a program file. See also *internal command*.

external event   An occurrence outside the computer system. External events often cause interrupts or exceptions that can then be acted upon by the computer system.

external goal   In Prolog, a goal that is not determined by the program itself. Usually this is a goal entered by the user while the program is running.

external interrupt   An interrupt caused by a source external to the computer.

external modem   A modem that is not on a printed circuit card inserted in the computer. An external modem is usually connected to a computer with a serial communications cable and has its own housing, control switches, and power supply. See also *internal modem*.

external reference   In programming, a reference to a label outside the current program file or current code segment. See also *external symbol*.

external sort   A sorting operation that cannot occur entirely in main memory.

external storage   See *auxiliary storage* or *secondary storage*.

external symbol   A label that is not contained in the same source code file in which it is referenced. Externals are resolved during linking of object files.

extract   In database terminology, to select individual records based upon a set criteria and copy them to a smaller database file.

F

factorial   A number derived by applying the following equation:

$$n! = n * (n - 1) * (n - 2) * (n - 3) \ldots * 3 * 2 * 1$$

Thus, the factorial of 4 is 24 and is derived by $4 * 3 * 2 * 1$. The factorial represents the number of possible sequences that can exist with a fixed set of items. The factorial of a number is represented by appending an exclamation point to the end of the number; for example, 4! is read "4 factorial."

failsoft   In fault-tolerant systems, a failure of the primary equipment that causes the use of backup equipment without apparent downtime or data loss.

far pointer   In a segmented memory model (such as that used on the Intel family of microprocessors), an address that includes both a segment and offset designation. Usually written in the format *SSSS:OOOO*, where *SSSS* is the segment address and *OOOO* is the offset address.

far procedure   In a segmented memory model (such as that used on the Intel family of microprocessors), a procedure that does not reside within the same memory segment as the calling routine.

fast Fourier transforms   In digital signal processing, a class of algorithms used to break down complex signals into their elementary components.

FAT   See *file allocation table*.

151

fatal error   A software error that causes the program to quit running and either exit to the operating system or hang.

fault-tolerant system   A system in which hardware, software, and data are duplicated to provide redundancy in case of failure. Fault-tolerant systems often include control systems that monitor operations, detect errors, and switch to the redundant system if the error cannot be corrected.

FCB   See *file control block*.

FDDI   See *fiber distributed data interface*.

FDM   See *frequency division multiplexing*.

FDX   See *full duplex*.

FEA   See *finite element analysis*.

feasibility study   An analysis done in the early stages of developing a computer system (hardware or software) to determine if development is desirable. Feasibility studies generally focus on cost, time, effort, efficiency, effectiveness, benefits, and reliability.

FEC   An acronym for forward error correcting, used in data communications.

feedback *n*   **1.** Information about the current operating condition of hardware or software. **2.** A condition that exists when system output is used as input into the same system.

feedback *v*   To provide feedback.

feedback loop   A configuration of hardware and/or software so that a portion of the system output is used as input for the routines generating the output. See also *feedback n (2)*.

fetch   To retrieve or get something, usually a record, discrete piece of data, or processor instruction.

FF   See *form feed*.

fiber distributed data interface   A specification for an optical fiber local area network (LAN) that operates at high-speed (100Mbps). The acronym is FDDI.

fiber optic cable   See *optical fiber*.

Fibonacci numbers   A series of integers in which each number is the sum of the two preceding numbers. For example, the series 1 2 3 5 8 13 21 is a Fibonacci series.

FID   See *frame ID*.

field   **1.** In database systems, a discrete location in a database record that contains a single piece of information. **2.** In SQL systems, a field is another name for a column. **3.** In the PICK operating system, a field is referred to as an attribute.

field separator   See *delimiter; file separator*.

FIFO   See *first in, first out*.

file   A related body of information stored as a single logical unit on a mass storage medium. Files may contain virtually any type of information, including data, text, or programs.

file allocation table   In MS-DOS or OS/2 environments, a linked-list method used by the operating system to track the disk space currently in use.

file attribute   See *attribute (1)*.

file control block   A data structure used in CP/M and early versions of the MS-DOS operating system for maintaining information about a file. The FCB is used to perform functions on the file.

file extension   See *filename extension*.

file format   The layout or structure of a file.

file handle   In the MS-DOS, OS/2, and UNIX environments, an integer value used by the operating system to refer to an open file. Similar to file reference number in the Macintosh environment. See also *handle*.

file layout   The organization and structure of a file.

file locking   A method of data security typically used in multiuser or networked environments. An in-use file is locked by a user's software to prevent other users from accessing and changing data before the locking user is through. When the original user has finished updating the file, it is unlocked so it can be used by the next user.

filename   A unique label assigned to a file for reference purposes. See also *base name; filename extension*.

filename expansion   The process of substituting characters for wildcard characters in a filename specification to determine if a match can be made.

filename extension   In the MS-DOS operating environment, the three characters to the right of the period in a filename. For example, in the filename COMMAND.COM, the extension is COM. See also *base name*.

file pointer   A numeric value maintained by the operating system that indicates the position in a currently open file where the next read or write operation will occur; sometimes called a mark. See also *record pointer*.

file protect ring   A plastic ring attached to the hub of a magnetic tape reel to either allow or prevent it from being erased. The actual function of the ring depends on the tape drive being used. If the ring permits writing to the tape, it is often called a safety ring or a write ring.

file reference number   In the Macintosh environment, an integer value used by the operating system to refer to a file. Similar to a file handle in the MS-DOS environment. See also *handle*.

file separator   A control character used on some computer systems to indicate logical boundaries between data structures such as fields or files. The ASCII value for this character is 28, the EBCDIC value is 34, and the acronym is FS. See also *interchange file separator*.

file server   A computer dedicated to maintaining the files for a local area network (LAN). Sometimes called a disk server or network server.

file services   In the NetWare environment, a collection of services that enable applications to work with files.

fillet   In CAD programs, the representation of a filled-in or rounded intersection of two entities. An example is shown here:

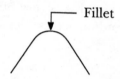

Fillet

fill justification   See *justification*.

filter   A device (either software or hardware) that limits or changes the information retrieved from the source of that information.

Finder   In the Macintosh environment, the program with which the user can manipulate files and start up applications. The Finder is normally the first program the user sees when the Macintosh is turned on.

finder flag   In the Macintosh environment, one of several file attributes used by the Finder to control how it treats the file. The finder flags are a series of on/off bits associated with each file on the disk.

finite element analysis   A mathematical discipline used to analyze stress on physical structures.

firmware   The software stored in nonvolatile memory such as a ROM, PROM, or EPROM. See also *hardware; software*.

first in, first out   A queueing method in which the first element added to the queue is the first element removed. Abbreviated as FIFO.

fixed disk   A nonremovable disk system; a term often used interchangeably with the term hard disk.

fixed-length fields   Fields within the records of a database that contain a predefined data length regardless of the actual length of the data stored in the field. Unused space in the field is "filled out" either with spaces or null characters.

fixed-length record   A database record that has a uniform length. Every record in the file is the same length as every other record. This type of record is typically used in random-access files. See also *variable-length record*.

fixed pitch   See *monospace*.

fixed point   A number storage technique where the decimal or binary point is always in a set location; there is always a specific number of digits to the left of the decimal point.

FKey   In the Macintosh environment, a utility program that, once installed in the system folder, is activated by pressing a specific character sequence regardless of what the computer is currently doing.

flag   An indicator that shows the result of some operation or the existence of a condition, which can later be used to control how a program operates. Synonymous with delimiter or semaphore.

flags register   A special-purpose register used to store bit patterns that indicate the status of the most recent CPU operations.

flat file   A database file that is not linked or related to other data files. Flat files typically contain data that is not encoded; it is stored in ASCII format.

flat model   A memory organization model in which all memory is viewed in a contiguous, linear fashion.

flexible disk   See *floppy disk*.

floating point   A number storage technique where the decimal point is not in a "fixed" location; the number of digits to the left of the decimal point can vary.

floating-point arithmetic package   A standard Macintosh package that performs floating-point mathematical functions using SANE. This package is provided in the system resource file, or in ROM beginning with the Mac Plus. See also *package*.

floating-point operand   A method of representing numbers as a base, a sign, a significand, and a signed exponent. The value of the number is the product of its significand and the base raised to the power of the exponent.

floating-point processor   See *numeric processor extension*.

floating-point unit   The portion of a CPU specialized and optimized for performing advanced mathematical functions. For those processors that do not contain an FPU, a numeric processor extension (NPX) is often used.

floppy disk   A nonvolatile storage medium for information. It is composed of a flat, circular mylar disk coated with a magnetic oxide material. This disk is enclosed in a square protective sheath. The entire disk is flexible, thus the term floppy. The front and back of a 5.25" floppy disk are shown here:

Data is magnetically stored and accessed on floppy disks through read/write heads that operate much like the recording and playback mechanisms in tape recorders. Floppy disks come in several varieties and capacities. Typical floppy disk sizes and capacities for IBM-compatible systems are shown in the table following this entry. Specifications for other types of systems depend upon the size of the disk, the operating system being used, and the capabilities of the disk drive.

Size	Sides	Density	Capacity
5.25"	1	Single	160K
5.25"	2	Single	320K
5.25"	1	Double	180K
5.25"	2	Double	360K
5.25"	2	High	1.2M
3.5"	2	Double	720K
3.5"	2	High	1.4M

FLOPS   A contraction for floating-point operations per second. A measure of the speed at which a system can process floating-point numbers.

flowchart   A pictorial representation of logic flow within a program. Flowcharts typically use standard symbols that represent specific operations, as shown in Figure F-1. Several different companies make flowchart templates to assist in drawing the symbols.

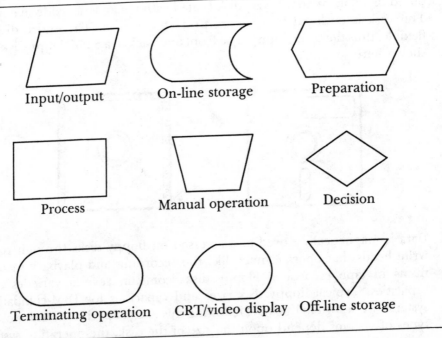

Figure F-1.   Common flowchart symbols

flow control   See *handshaking*.

flush   See *cache flush*.

flush left   See *justification*.

flush right   See *justification*.

focus   In a GUI environment, the active window receiving user input.

folder   In the Macintosh environment, a file system structure analogous to a subdirectory in the MS-DOS, OS/2, or UNIX environments. A folder holds other files or folders.

folder number   In the Macintosh environment, an integer value used by the Finder to identify a folder.

font   A set of display or printable characters of a specific typeface. A font may also contain different treatments of the same typeface such as bold or italic.

font cartridge   See *cartridge font*.

foreground   **1.** The portion of the screen representing an actual character or graphic symbol in a character set. All other sections of the screen are referred to as background. **2.** See *foreground operation*.

foreground category   A priority classification for processes in the OS/2 environment. It consists of processes associated with the currently active screen group. See also *background category*.

foreground operation   A program executing as the primary task of the computer.

foreground processing   See *foreground operation*.

foreground task   See *foreground operation*.

fork   See *data fork* or *resource fork*.

format *n*   The layout, structure, or design of an item.

format *v*   1. To prepare a disk to store information. This is accomplished through special programs that divide the disk into the necessary storage units such as tracks and sectors. 2. To arrange text or data into a form that is visually acceptable.

format file   In dBASE systems, a file containing a screen or report layout.

form feed   A code that, when received by a printer, causes the current piece of paper to be ejected. The standard form-feed character has ASCII and EBCDIC values of 12; the acronym is FF.

formula   A mathematical expression of an algorithm.

FOR-NEXT loop   In programming, a structure that repeats a series of instructions a specific number of times. The basic structure is:

```
FOR J = 1 TO 100
    READ RECORD
    PROCESS RECORD
NEXT
```

The exact syntax of the structure will vary depending upon the programming language being used. The example shown causes the loop to be executed 100 times.

FORTH   A high-level programming language developed by Charles Moore in 1970. FORTH is used in many scientific applications, as it allows direct control of hardware devices.

FORTRAN   A high-level language developed by IBM in 1954. FORTRAN is a contraction for formula translator, and was the first compiler language developed for computers. It is used extensively in scientific and engineering applications.

forward chaining   **1.** A method of linking data records in which each record contains a pointer to the next record in the series. **2.** In Prolog, a control procedure that starts with an initial set of facts, and applies rules to infer new facts until one of the rules satisfies a goal or until no further inferences can be made.

fourth-generation language   A computer language that uses an English-language-like command structure.

FPS   See *frames per second.*

FPU   See *floating-point unit.*

fractals   In computer graphics, a mathematic modeling method of describing real-world surfaces. Fractals can be used for stunning graphic effects, and can approximate the randomness of nature.

fragmentation   The noncontiguous storage of information on a disk or in memory. See also *compaction* or *defragmenter.*

frame   **1.** In animation or live-action video, a frame is a single picture. A series of frames that differ slightly from each other, shown in rapid succession, create the illusion of movement or animation. There are usually a set number of frames per second in any given medium. For example, television uses a frame rate of 30 frames per second. **2.** In data communications, the unit of transmission in a network or data communications system. A frame typically includes delimiters, control characters, information, and error-checking characters. **3.** In the PICK operating system, the smallest element of data storage. A frame consists of 512 bytes of information.

frame buffer   In computer graphics, a memory buffer intended to store one individual frame or graphics image.

frame grabber   A device used to capture a still video image for storage or processing in a computer.

frame ID   In the PICK operating system, the logical address of a disk frame.

frame pointer   In the 680x0 (Motorola) family of microprocessors, an address register used to point to a process' variables and parameters.

frame rate   In animation or live-action video, the measure of how many frames are displayed each second. This rate is typically expressed in frames per second.

frames per second   In animation or live-action video, a measurement of the number of individual pictures that are displayed for each second of action.

framing   In data communications, the process of dividing a message into a series of frames. See also *frame (2)*.

framing error   In data communications, an error that occurs when the sender and receiver are not in sync; the incoming bits are translated in error.

free-form   Information entered into a system without rigid formatting.

free variable   A variable that is not currently bound to any value.

freeware   Contraction for free software.

frequency division multiplexing   In data communications, a technique to speed up data transmission by dividing the available frequency band into two or more channels and transmitting on each of the resulting channels.

frequency shift keying   In data communications, a digital-to-analog modulation technique to speed up data transmission by shifting between two close frequencies and transmitting data on both frequencies. On one frequency, zeros are transmitted, and on the other frequency ones are transmitted.

front end   An interface program (or computer system) designed to accept input and commands from a user, perform minimal processing on the input, and then pass the information to a back-end program (or computer system) for full processing.

front panel   The control panel of a computer. This term is used generally with older computer systems where an interactive terminal was not used to control the computer. In these systems, control was achieved through a series of switches and lights that were physically attached to the front of the computer (the front panel).

FS   **1.** In certain members of the 80x86 (Intel) processor family, a 16-bit general-purpose segment register. **2.** See *file separator*.

FSK   See *frequency shift keying*.

FTAM   An acronym for file transfer access and management.

full duplex   A data communications protocol that allows for data transmission in both directions at the same time.

full justification   See *justification*.

fullword   Another name for word.

function   A self-contained program or portion of a program designed to do a specific task and optionally return a value. A function is sometimes referred to as a procedure or subroutine.

functional specifications   A set of plans or detailed outline for what a program should accomplish. Functional specifications should be completed before the development of the software begins.

function key   A specialized keyboard key that, when pressed either alone or at the same time as other keys, performs a specific, predefined task. Function keys are usually numbered, and begin with the letter *F*. For example, on keyboards associated with IBM computers, there may be 12 function keys. They are identified F1, F2, F3, . . . F10, F11, F12.

functor   In Prolog, a name for a compound object.

fuse   An electrical device that breaks, or opens, a circuit when it becomes overloaded. This prevents damage to the media making up the physical circuit. Fuses must be replaced once they have been tripped. See also *circuit breaker*.

G   An abbreviation for *giga*.

game paddle   An input device used to move the cursor on the screen through the use of a dial. Game paddles are commonly used in video games. There are many different types of game paddles in use; one common type is shown here:

garbage collection   **1.** A system routine, typically part of the operating system, that searches RAM for memory that is no longer needed or in use and returns it to the pool of memory available to other routines. **2.** A system routine for analyzing, updating, and compressing file indexes.

gate descriptor   In certain members of the 80x86 (Intel) family, a segment descriptor that can be the destination of a CALL or JUMP. They can be used to invoke a procedure or task in another privilege level. There are four types of gate descriptors: call gates, trap gates, interrupt gates, and task gates.

gateway   A connection between differing communications networks.

GDDM   An acronym for graphical data display manager.

GDI   See *graphics device interface*.

GDT   See *global descriptor table*.

gender   The type of connecter being used. Male connectors have pins, and female connectors have receptacles for those pins.

gender changer   A coupling unit that allows two like connectors (two male or two female connectors) to be joined.

gender mender   See *gender changer*.

general-purpose interface bus   The IEEE 488 standard interface used for connecting peripherals to a computer. The GPIB is a 24-pin parallel connector. Hewlett-Packard's version of the GPIB is called the HPIB (Hewlett-Packard interface bus).

general-purpose register   Any register within the CPU that may be used for more than one purpose.

general recursive rule   In Prolog, a method in which a rule is built through recursive means.

geosynchronous   An orbital condition in which a satellite is positioned at the proper distance from the earth and at the proper relational speed to appear stationary to an observer on earth. Geosynchronous satellites are critical to effective telecommunications over vast distances.

GFE   See *group format error*.

giga   A prefix denoting one billion; thus a gigabyte is approximately one billion bytes. The abbreviation for giga is G.

GIS   An acronym for generalized information system.

GKS   An acronym for graphical kernel system.

glitch   See *bug*.

global   Universal in nature.

global data segment   In the OS/2 environment, a data segment that is used by a dynlink subroutine, but which is accessible to all processes using that subroutine.

global descriptor table   On certain members of the 80x86 (Intel) family, an array of segment descriptors for all programs in a system.

global frame pointer   In the 680x0 (Motorola) family of microprocessors, address register A5. This register is used to locate a program's global variables.

global memory   In the Microsoft Windows environment, any memory not under direct control of your program. This memory can be located anywhere and is under the control of Microsoft Windows' memory manager.

global variable   A program variable that is accessible by all the modules in a system.

glue routine   In the Macintosh environment, a procedure or function used to interface a high-level language with routines in the ROM.

goal   In Prolog, a collection of subgoals that the program attempts to satisfy. A goal may be internal or external to the program.

GOSIP   An acronym for government open systems interconnections profile.

GPIB   See *general-purpose interface bus*.

GPSS   An acronym for general-purpose system simulator.

gradual underflow   In certain members of the 80x87 (Intel) family, a method of handling a floating-point underflow error condition that reduces the loss of accuracy in the result. Rather than returning a value of zero in the case of an underflow condition, a denormal number that most closely represents the correct result is returned (if such a number exists).

graphical user interface   A user interface system for either an operating system or a program that relies upon pictures and objects for the communication of information. Contrast with traditional text-based interfaces, which are command or menu driven. The common acronym is GUI.

graphics   A video presentation method consisting mostly of pictures and figures instead of letters and numbers.

graphics card   A display adapter that allows the display of graphics as well as text. In the IBM PC environment, the CGA, EGA, and VGA are all examples of graphics cards.

graphics device interface   In the Microsoft Windows environment, a collection of Windows routines that allows you to display information without concern for the specific hardware used. The common acronym is GDI.

graphics primitive   In computer graphics, an elemental graphics element such as a dot, line, arc, or circle. The term may also apply to the routines that create the primitives. Also referred to as display elements.

graphics tablet   See *digitizing tablet*.

gray-scale   In computer graphics, the use of various shades of black and white to represent colors.

gray-scale scanner   See *scanner*.

grep   In the UNIX environment, a utility program used to search for specific text in a file or group of files.

grid   A rectangular array of reference points that define the intersection of a parallel series of lines running perpendicular to another series of parallel lines. A grid is typically used for reference purposes in graphics software.

ground   An electrical connection to earth, used for safety or as a reference for other signal voltages.

group   In the PICK operating system, a frame or series of linked frames in a file.

group format error   In the PICK operating system, an error that indicates that the system data structure has become corrupted. There can be many causes of a GFE.

grouping factor   See *blocking factor*.

group separator   A control character used on some computer systems to indicate logical boundaries between data groups. The ASCII value for this character is 29, and the acronym is GS. See also *interchange group separator*.

groupware   Software that is oriented toward use by a small group of individuals.

GRR   See *general recursive rule*.

GS   1. In certain members of the 80x86 (Intel) processor family, a 16-bit general-purpose segment register. 2. See *group separator*.

GUI   See *graphical user interface*.

GW-BASIC   A variation of the BASIC programming language. Developed by Microsoft Corporation, the GW stands for gee-whiz, as this was an early interpretive BASIC that had "bells and whistles" not available on other implementations of BASIC at the time. GW-BASIC is distributed with the MS-DOS operating system, so it is available on many millions of computer systems. See also *BASIC*.

H   A suffix indicating that a number is in hexadecimal form. May be upper- or lowercase. For instance, ABC987H and ABC987h both indicate that the number is hexadecimal.

hacker   A person who is very technically skilled in some aspect of computer technology. When first used, the term was nonderogatory, but more recently it has been used to refer to people who use their prodigious technical skills in an unethical or illegal manner (such as breaking into networks or writing computer viruses).

half duplex   A data communications protocol that allows for data transmission in only one direction at a time.

half-height drive   A disk drive (floppy or hard disk) that occupies only half the vertical space of earlier disk drives, due to advances in technology and manufacturing.

handle   **1.** An alias for a connection defined between two different objects. For example, a file handle may be a number used to designate a file to the operating system. All access to the file can then occur by referencing the handle number. **2.** In the Macintosh environment, the address of a master pointer to a relocatable block in the heap.

handler   A program or subroutine dedicated to a particular task. For example, an interrupt handler is used to control the results of a system interrupt or exception.

handshaking   In data communications, the process of adhering to communications protocols so that exchange of information may occur. Handshaking can be handled either by the hardware or software, depending upon the type of data link established.

hang   A condition that occurs when a program is caught in an endless loop, doesn't respond to user input, or branches to an address in a data area, which causes the system to be unresponsive.

hard coded   A term referring to the condition of a program when parameters that could have been variable in nature are instead programmed as constants—and thus cannot be changed by the user.

hard copy   Output on paper from a printer or plotter.

hard disk   See *fixed disk*.

hard error   An error that cannot be corrected without user intervention.

hard limit   An operating limitation due to hardware restrictions.

hard-sectored   A disk is said to be hard-sectored when the beginning mark of sectors is controlled by hardware. For example, many hard-sectored floppy disks have a series of holes surrounding the hub. These holes are read by special circuits in the disk drive so the system recognizes where sectors begin. If there is only one hole around the hub, then the disk is soft-sectored (the hole is used for timing). See also *soft-sectored*.

hardware   The physical equipment that makes up a computer system. You can touch hardware. See also *firmware; software*.

hardware interrupt   See *interrupt*.

hardwire   To connect directly and (more or less) permanently.

hashing   A method of indexing information by using an algorithm that generates a hash value, which indicates the ordered position of the item.

hash table   An index created by a hashing algorithm.

hatching   In CAD programs, the process of filling a specified area with a design for purposes of identification.

Hayes command set   The collection of ASCII commands used to control modems compatible with those manufactured by Hayes Microcomputer Products. The Hayes command set includes the following commands:

Command	Action
A	Answer the line
C0	Turn carrier off
C1	Turn carrier on
D	Dial the following number (there are additional command characters valid within a phone number)
R	Switch to answer mode when finished dialing
E0	Do not echo characters to the screen
E1	Echo characters to the screen
H0	Hang up the line (go to on-hook state)
H1	Pick up the line (go to off-hook state)
O	Go on-line (enter data mode)
Z	Reset modem

This is not a complete list of the Hayes command set. There are many other commands that have been added in different versions of Hayes modems, and many other modem manufacturers who make Hayes-compatible modems have added their own commands. Each command begins with the letters AT (meaning attention), and may be combined with other commands on the same line. For instance, the following command sequence tells the modem to dial a number and then switch to answer mode:

```
AT DT 9W1,801-555-7639 R
```

Hayes-compatible   A modem that is compatible with the modem command language developed by Hayes Microcomputer Products.

HDA   An acronym for head/disk assembly.

HDLC   An acronym for high-level data link control.

HDX   See *half duplex*.

head   See *read/write head*.

head crash   A destructive condition occurring when a hard disk read/write head touches the surface of a spinning hard disk. The magnetic coating of the disk is scratched, and the resulting dust contaminates the rest of the disk surfaces. This is probably the worst damage that can happen to a hard disk. Complete loss of the information on the disk is virtually assured.

header   In data communications or networking terminology, the first part of a packet; it precedes the user text. The header typically contains control codes and information about the source, destination, and security level of the packet.

heading   1. A portion of a hard-copy report that indicates global information about the report. This may include items such as the title, date, program name, and column headings. 2. See *header*.

heap   An area of memory set aside for the temporary storage of values. Where a stack has a LIFO orientation, a heap allows random access to information contained in it. See also *stack*.

heap block header   See *block header*.

heap zone   See *heap*.

help screen   A listing or explanation of commands available within a software package. Help screens are typically displayed by pressing a special key or combination of keys.

Hertz   A unit of measurement equivalent to cycles per second. Hertz is abbreviated Hz.

heuristic   A method of solving problems by applying knowledge gained through experience. Heuristic systems "learn" from their attempts at earlier problem solving, and thus get better as they progress.

Hewlett-Packard graphics language   A device-control language developed by Hewlett-Packard for use in controlling their line of printers and plotters. HPGL commands are sent to the device and translated by firmware in the printer or plotter.

hex   An abbreviation for *hexadecimal*.

hexadecimal   A numeric system based upon powers of 16. It uses the digits 0 through 9 and the letters A through F. Hexadecimal is often used by computer programmers because it is easier to work with than binary (the native numbering system of computers) or octal systems. See also *numbering system*.

HFS   See *hierarchical filing system*.

HGA   An acronym for Hercules graphics adapter.

HGC   An acronym for Hercules graphics card; the same as HGA.

hidden file   An attribute commonly applied to a disk file to prevent its display or change. Hidden files occupy disk space but do not appear in directory listings.

hierarchical   An organizational structure that is layered. Examples of hierarchical structures are directory systems (UNIX, MS-DOS, OS/2, and Macintosh), family trees, and company organization charts.

hierarchical database structure   A database model in which records are linked together as in an organization chart, and an individual data field can be "owned" by only one owner (database file). Hierarchical structures were widely used in the first computer database management systems.

hierarchical directory structure   See *hierarchical*.

hierarchical filing system   The formal name of the filing structure used in recent versions of the Macintosh operating system. The common acronym is HFS. See also *hierarchical*.

high-level language   A programming language that has a certain degree of machine independence. Examples of high-level languages are C, COBOL, BASIC, FORTRAN, and Pascal. See also *low-level language*.

highlight   To make something stand out; usually in reference to a selection or object on the screen that is shown in a color or color combination that draws attention to it.

high memory area   In the MS-DOS environment, the first 64K of extended memory.

high-order bit   See *most significant bit*.

high-order byte   See *most significant byte*.

high-order digit   See *most significant digit*.

high-performance file system   An enhanced file system used under OS/2 beginning with OS/2 1.2. HPFS allows longer filenames and faster access to disk files.

high RAM   In the MS-DOS environment, another name for the memory between 640K and 1024K (1M).

hi-res   A contraction for high resolution.

histogram   A graphic representation of the frequency of occurrence of a set of discrete events.

history   **1.** A UNIX facility that maintains a list of previous commands entered into the system and provides a shorthand notation for recalling the commands. **2.** In certain programs, a log of an arbitrary number of the most recently executed commands.

hit   **1.** A positive result to a comparison. **2.** See *cache hit*.

HLLAPI   An acronym for high-level language application program interface, a PC-to-mainframe programming interface.

HMA   See *high memory area*.

hold file   A temporary file used to store information until it can be processed or otherwise disposed of. For example, a hold file may be created to house a print job until it can be printed.

Hollerith card   A punched card named after its inventor, Herman Hollerith. Hollerith cards were first used in the 1890 U.S. Census. See also *punched card*.

home *n*   **1.** The position at the upper-left corner of the video screen. **2.** See *home key*.

home *v*   To move the cursor to the home position.

home directory   In the UNIX environment, a user's current directory immediately upon logging on to a system. Also called the login directory.

Home key   A keyboard key that has differing meanings based on the computer system to which the keyboard is attached. On some computer systems, pressing the Home key results in clearing the screen and moving the cursor to the upper-left corner of the display. On others, it simply results in moving the cursor to the leftmost position of the current input field. See also *cursor keys*.

home position   See *home n*.

horizontal redundancy checking   An error-correction method performed on the individual bits in a block of data. The HRC can later be recalculated after the block has been transmitted or copied, and the new HRC can be compared to the original HRC to verify that the copy or transmission was correct.

horizontal tab   A control code that causes the cursor on the display or a printer to move to the next predefined tab stop location on the current line. The ASCII value of a horizontal tab is 9, the EBCDIC value is 5, and the acronym is HT.

host   1. In a time-sharing environment, the computer that performs the majority of the processing. **2.** In data communications, the computer being connected to—the computer providing the reason for establishing the data link in the first place.

hot fix   In the NetWare environment, a data integrity feature that marks bad areas on the disk so they will not be written to. See also *fault-tolerant system*.

hot key   A keyboard key or key combination that causes a specified action to occur regardless of what else the computer is currently doing. The term is most widely used in relation to terminate and stay resident (TSR) programs in the MS-DOS environment.

housekeeping   Software or operating system functions invoked to "clean up" the environment. Housekeeping includes clearing unused variables, closing files, and reclaiming available memory previously assigned to a no longer needed purpose.

HPFS   See *high-performance file system*.

HPGL   See *Hewlett-Packard graphics language*.

HPIB   An acronym for Hewlett-Packard interface bus, Hewlett-Packard's version of the GPIB. See also *general-purpose interface bus*.

HP-UX   Hewlett-Packard's implementation of UNIX.

HRC   See *horizontal redundancy checking*.

HT   See *horizontal tab*.

huge memory model   In the C programming language in the 80x86 (Intel) environment, a type of program in which program code can occupy more than 64K of memory and a single data element (such as an array) may require more than 64K of memory.

HyperCard   An implementation of a hypertext system for the Macintosh family of computers.

hyperlink   In a hypertext system, a link established between a word or phrase and a related issue or further explanation of that word or phrase.

hypermedia   A term describing hypertext-based systems that combine text, graphics, video, and sound with traditional data. Sometimes referred to as multimedia.

HyperScript   In the Macintosh environment, the command language provided with Wingz software developed by Informix, Inc.

HyperTalk   The programming language used in the HyperCard database program from Apple.

hypertext   A technique for linking information together in a free-form fashion based upon links between words in text. For example, if a hypertext system contains an article about dogs, and it mentions that dogs are mammals, the reader may be able to use the word mammals to find another article in the system on mammals.

Hz   An abbreviation for *Hertz*.

i486   See *80486*.

iAPX 86   See *8086*.

iAPX 88   See *8088*.

IC   See *integrated circuit*.

ICAS   An acronym for Intel communications application specification.

ICCP   See *Institute of Certification of Computer Professionals*.

icon   A symbolic representation of an object in a computer system. For example, systems using a graphical user interface (such as Microsoft Windows, Presentation Manager, X Window, or the Macintosh) use graphic icons to represent objects such as files, programs, documents, and disk drives. When these icons are selected using a pointing device (such as a puck, mouse, or stylus), they can be moved or accessed. Icons are a visual way of telling the user what is happening or what choices are available. A few icons common in GUI systems are shown next.

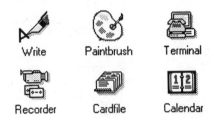

Write   Paintbrush   Terminal

Recorder   Cardfile   Calendar

IDE   An acronym for integrated development environment or integrated drive electronics.

identification division   The portion of a COBOL program that provides mandatory documentation for a program. See also *data division; environment division; procedure division*.

identifier   A label, name, or handle used to represent or refer to an object, function, or variable.

idle character   See *synchronous idle*.

idles   In network terminology, the signals sent along a network when neither frames nor tokens are being transmitted.

IDMS   An acronym for integrated database management system.

IDT   See *interrupt descriptor table*.

IEC   An acronym for International Electrotechnical Commission, an organization concerned with establishing international electrical standards.

IEEE   See *Institute of Electrical and Electronic Engineers*.

IEEE 488   See *general-purpose interface bus*.

IEEE 696   See *S-100*.

IEEE 754   A defined set of standard formats and operations that apply to floating-point numbers. The standard covers 32-, 64-, and 80-bit operand sizes. This standard was formalized by the Institute of Electrical and Electronic Engineers.

IEEE 796   See *Multibus*.

IEEE 802.3   An industry standard for a CSMA/CD bus LAN. This standard was formalized by the Institute of Electrical and Electronic Engineers.

IEEE 802.5   An industry standard for a token-ring LAN. This standard was formalized by the Institute of Electrical and Electronic Engineers.

IEEE 842.4   An industry standard for a token-passing bus LAN. This standard was formalized by the Institute of Electrical and Electronic Engineers.

IFS   See *installable file system* or *interchange file separator*.

IF-THEN-ELSE   In programming, a structure that executes a series of instructions based on the result of a comparison. The programmer specifies an IF condition that, if determined to be true, causes the THEN condition to be executed. The ELSE condition is optional. An example is:

```
IF TODAY = MONDAY THEN
    PRINT "Oh, No!  Not another Monday!"
ELSE
    PRINT "Friday is on the way!"
END IF
```

The exact syntax of the structure will vary depending upon the programming language being used.

IGES   See *initial graphics exchange specification*.

ignore character   See *CAN*.

IL   An abbreviation for idle, an EBCDIC control code with a value of 23.

imaging   The recording of graphic images on a recording media such as videotape.

immediate addressing   A method of assembly language addressing in which one of the operands is a constant within the instruction itself. An example of this type of addressing (for the 80x86 family of microprocessors) is:

```
MOV   AX,657
```

See also *addressing mode*.

immediate operand   Data encoded as a portion of an instruction.

immediate window   In the QuickBASIC environment, the window at the bottom of the screen that provides for immediate interpretation and execution of programming statements.

impact printer   A printer that relies upon physical impact between objects to produce a character on paper. Dot matrix, daisywheel, and line printers are all examples of impact printers; a laser printer is not an impact printer.

implicit integer bit   A part of the significand in a floating-point numeric representation that is not explicitly given because the entire significand is considered to be right of the binary point. The implicit integer bit is always one, except when the biased exponent is zero.

implied addressing   The same as *register indirect addressing*.

implied register addressing   See *register indirect addressing*.

include file   In programming, a file to be inserted at the place in the source file where an include directive occurs. See also *preprocessor directive*.

inclusive-or   See *OR*.

increment   To increase a value by another value. For example, if a number is incremented by 1, this means that 1 is added to the value of the number.

incremental backup   A backup of only information that has changed since the last backup.

incremental compiler   A type of language compiler that processes the lines of a program as they are typed into the computer, or converts each line of a program into intermediate pseudomachine language as it is entered. Incremental compilers are usually a feature of an integrated development environment.

incremental coordinates   See *relative coordinates*.

incremental vector   See *relative vector*.

indefinite   A special numeric value derived from a mathematical operation that otherwise results in a nonsensical answer.

indent   To offset text from the margin.

indentation level   The current width of the left margin in a text file.

index   1. A special file containing values that specify a logical order for records in another file. An index is typically composed of a series of pointers to actual records, sequentially ordered and stored in a separate file from the original database. The ordering of the pointers is determined according to a predetermined key field in the original database. 2. A number used as an offset to access a data item within a table or array.

indexed register indirect addressing   In the 680x0 (Motorola) family of microprocessors, a method of addressing in which the operand's address is obtained by adding the contents of an address register to an index and an offset. Similar to base indexed addressing. See also *addressing mode*.

indexed sequential access method   A file access method that stores information sequentially, yet maintains a separate index file that indicates a sorted order for the records. This allows the file to be accessed as either a sequential file or quickly through the index. The common acronym is ISAM.

index hole   A physical hole in a floppy disk that indicates the starting location of the first sector, as shown here:

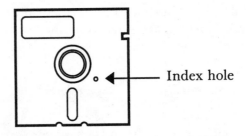

Index hole

indexing   1. The process of ordering records based upon a key data field. 2. Use of an index to access data in a table or array. See *index (2)*.

index key   In database terminology, the column or field used to produce an index of the database.

index register   A CPU register assumed to contain an address for use in indirect addressing modes.

index track   In fixed disk systems, a track used to guide the read/write head assembly in locating information on other tracks stored on other platters of the disk unit. Sometimes referred to as a servo track.

indirect addressing   See *register indirect addressing*.

indirection operator   In certain programming languages, an operator that indicates a label does not represent a specific value, but represents a pointer to a value. In C, the indirection operator is an asterisk (*).

induction variable   A variable used in a programming loop as a counter. For example, in the construct FOR I = 1 TO 100, I is the induction variable.

inference engine   The part of an expert system that generates inferences from a set of facts.

inference program   In expert systems, a program that derives conclusions by making inferences based upon available data.

infinite loop   An unending repetition of a series of programming instructions. Sometimes called a closed loop.

infinity   A floating-point number that has greater magnitude than any integer or any real number. In mathematics, infinity is often treated as another number, subject to special rules of arithmetic.

infix notation   The common method of indicating mathematic relationships between values. With infix notation, the mathematic operators are in line with the values they affect. For example, A + B − C uses infix notation. This causes the values A and B to be added; the value C is then subtracted from this sum. See also *postfix notation; prefix notation*.

information   The meaning applied to symbols, values, or other data stored in a computer system. Used interchangeably with data.

information processing   See *data processing*.

inheritance   In object-oriented programming, the ability of a class of derived objects to inherit the properties of another class.

inherited error   An error condition passed to a controlling process by a subroutine that the controlling process had invoked. The controlling process may handle the error or pass it to a higher-level procedure for further treatment.

INIT   In the Macintosh environment, a program that automatically runs when the system is started. This program must be placed in the system folder. It is analogous to AUTOEXEC.BAT in the MS-DOS environment.

init bit   In the Macintosh environment, one of several finder flags. The init bit indicates whether the Finder resources belonging to an application file have been installed in the desktop file of the disk on which the file resides.

initial graphics exchange specification   An ANSI-approved standard file format for representation of three-dimensional wire frame models.

initialization   The process of setting up a computing environment either when the system (hardware or software) is first started or after a reset.

initialize   **1.** To prepare a program for execution by resetting variables to their beginning state and procuring the necessary resources, such as memory. **2.** To format a disk. See also *format v (1)*.

initial program loader   A portion of the operating system responsible for first booting the computer. The common acronym is IPL. See also *boot*.

ink-jet printer   A printer that produces high-quality output using liquid ink sprayed through small jets.

in-line   Any element of a program or file that is included as an integral part of another program or file. For instance, several modern language compilers allow for in-line assembly language statements. This means that the statements can be mixed in the high-level language source code, and they will be handled properly by the compiler.

input *n*   Information presented to a computer for processing.

input *v*   To deliver information to a computer for processing.

input area   See *input buffer*.

input block   See *input buffer*.

input buffer   A memory area set aside for receiving input from either another program, a user, or an external device.

input/output   A term that applies to the process of moving data to a place where the computer can use it (input) or to another place after the computer has processed it (output). The common acronym is I/O.

insert   To place data between other previously existing pieces of data.

insertion sort   A sorting algorithm that is implemented by examining every item in an unordered list and shifting each element up or down until all elements are in the proper order.

Insert key   A keyboard key typically used to signal to software that the user wishes to insert text at the current cursor position. On many keyboards it is abbreviated Ins. The result of pressing the Insert key depends on the software being used. For instance, pressing Insert may result in switching to insert mode, or it may only place a space at the cursor position.

insert mode   An input condition in which what you type is inserted at the current cursor position and the information there moves to the right and/or down to the next line.

install   The initial process of making hardware or software operational.

installable file system   In the OS/2 environment, the portion of the operating system that provides the functions necessary to manage files on a mass storage device.

installation   **1.** A physical location or facility for computers and computer-related functions. **2.** The process of installing hardware or software.

installer   **1.** A program that adds software to a computer system and prepares it for subsequent execution. **2.** A person who installs, configures, and otherwise makes operational a new computer system or peripheral.

install software   See *installer*.

instance data segment   In the OS/2 environment, a memory segment used to hold data for each instance of a dynlink routine.

instantiation   In Prolog, the act of replacing a variable in a pattern or formula with a possible constant, usually as a result of searching and pattern-matching.

Institute of Certification of Computer Professionals   A professional certification association that offers a series of examinations geared toward certifying the abilities of computer professionals. The ICCP offers the Certificate in Data Processing (CDP) and Certificate in Computer Programming (CCP).

Institute of Electrical and Electronic Engineers   A professional organization founded in 1963 for the furthering of education, research, and standards in the electronics and electrical fields, the IEEE has over 250,000 members including students and professionals from the electrical engineering, electronics, and related fields. It sponsors many educational opportunities and publications for members. The IEEE can be contacted at:

Institute of Electrical and Electronic Engineers
345 East 47th Street
New York, NY 10017
(212) 705-7900

instruction   In common use, a programming command or statement, including any operands or variables needed to accomplish the command or statement.

instruction address   The memory address from which the next instruction to be executed will be fetched. See also *instruction pointer*.

instruction cycle   The amount of time it takes to fetch and execute a CPU instruction at a machine language level.

instruction pointer   On the 80x86 (Intel) family of microprocessors, the IP register. This register indicates the address in memory of the next instruction to be executed.

instruction pre-fetch   Reading the next CPU instruction in advance of execution.

instruction register   A special-purpose CPU register that maintains the address of the next instruction to be executed.

instruction restart   The ability to attempt a second execution of an instruction when an error or exception occurs.

instruction set   **1.** In assembly language, the group of mnemonics that the assembler understands and can translate into machine language. **2.** In machine language, the group of machine language instructions that the CPU can execute.

integer   A finite whole number; a number that has no fractional value attached to it. An integer may be either positive or negative.

integer BASIC   A version of the BASIC programming language that only uses integer numbers.

integer bit   A part of the significand in normalized floating-point formats. The integer bit is the part of the significand to the left of the binary point. When the biased exponent is zero, the integer bit is also zero; otherwise it is always one.

integrated circuit   An electronic component fabricated on a semiconductor material such as silicon. Integrated circuit is synonymous with chip.

integrated services digital network   An international telecommunications standard that allows the transmission of voice, video, and data over the same communications channel.

integrated software   A general classification of software, characterized by software packages that combine several differing applications under the umbrella of a main controller program. For instance, an integrated software package may combine spreadsheet, database, and word processor programs all into one unit.

intelligent database   A database with the ability to accept queries written in a language close to that used by humans.

interactive   An attribute describing the ability of a program and a user, or multiple programs, to interface with each other during execution.

interactive processing   The on-line execution of programs under the direct control of a user. The user may provide feedback to the program or operating system as it is needed. Interactive processing is the opposite of batch processing.

interactive video   The use of videodisc or CD-ROM technology with computer technology. The video unit is under the control of the computer, and, along with special software, is used for education, training, or entertainment purposes.

interblock gap   A space between two adjacent blocks of information stored on a magnetic tape. Synonymous with interrecord gap.

interchange file separator   An EBCDIC control character used to indicate logical boundaries between files. The EBCDIC value for this character is 28, and the acronym is IFS. See also *file separator*.

interchange group separator   An EBCDIC control character used to indicate logical boundaries between data groups. The EBCDIC value for this character is 29, and the acronym is IGS. See also *group separator*.

interchange record separator   An EBCDIC control character used to indicate logical boundaries between data records. The EBCDIC value for this character is 30, and the acronym is IRS. See also *record separator*.

interchange unit separator   An EBCDIC control character used to indicate logical boundaries between data units. The EBCDIC value for this character is 31, and the acronym is IUS. See also *unit separator*.

interface   The interconnection and interrelationships between two devices, two applications, or the user and an application or device.

interleave   See *sector interleave*.

intermittent error   An error that occurs periodically instead of regularly. This intermittent nature makes these errors more difficult to locate and correct.

internal command   In the MS-DOS, OS/2, and UNIX operating systems, a command that is an intrinsic part of the operating system; a built-in command. See also *external command*.

internal font   A font or series of typefaces contained within ROM chips built into a printer. See also *cartridge font; soft font*.

internal goal   In Prolog, a goal that is determined by the program itself. Conversely, an external goal is one entered from a source outside the program.

internal interrupt   An interrupt caused by a source internal to the computer, such as a division-by-zero error.

internal memory   Another name for the memory built into a computer. Synonymous with internal storage.

internal modem   A modem that resides on a printed circuit card that can be inserted directly into the bus of a computer system. See also *external modem*.

internal sort   A sorting operation that may be completely executed in main memory.

internal storage   Another name for the memory built into a computer. Synonymous with internal memory.

International Standards Organization   A voluntary international organization that sets standards in all industries (not just computers). The membership of the ISO is made up of national standards organizations, including ANSI, which represents the United States. The technical committee of the ISO maintains liaison with the CCITT. See also *Consultative Committee for International Telephony and Telegraphy*.

International Telecommunications Union   An international organization founded in 1865 to establish and further standards in the communications industry. The ITU has over 150 member countries and is headquartered in Geneva, Switzerland.

international utilities package   A standard Macintosh package that is used for standard formatting of numbers, dates, times, and other international conventions. This package is provided in the system resource file. See also *package*.

InterNet packet exchange   In a NetWare environment, an implementation of the Xerox Network Services InterNet Transport Protocols. IPX is accessed through communications services.

interpress   A page description language used on Xerox's larger laser printers.

interpreter   A program that interprets and executes programming commands in real time. Unlike a compiler (which translates the commands and produces a directly executable file), an interpreter introduces a layer of processing that slows down operation of the computer. There may be times, however, when an interpreter actually speeds program development. Because separate compile and link steps are not needed, more programming can be accomplished in the same amount of time.

interprocess communications   In multitasking operating systems, the communication that may occur between concurrently executing processes (programs). The common abbreviation is IPC.

interrecord gap   A space between two adjacent data records on a magnetic tape. Synonymous with interblock gap.

interrupt   A transfer of program control forced by a hardware signal or execution of an explicit software instruction.

interrupt descriptor table   In certain members of the 80x86 (Intel) family, an array of gate descriptors for invoking exception and interrupt handlers.

interrupt-driven   An implementation scheme for software that relies on interrupts from external sources to signal when there is information available to process. See also *polling*.

interrupt flag   In the 80x86 (Intel) family, the bit in the flags register that indicates whether the CPU should handle maskable interrupts. If this bit is set, interrupts are handled; if clear, interrupts are ignored.

interrupt handler   A routine called by the system when an interrupt occurs. The interrupt handler allows for the orderly processing of the interrupt and then returns control to the program that was interrupted.

interrupt mask   A series of switch or flag settings used by the CPU to determine if specific types of interrupts should be trapped and processed by the system. This mask is usually implemented as a series of bytes in which each bit controls the on/off condition of each interrupt.

interrupt register   A special-purpose CPU register used to facilitate the processing of interrupts.

interrupt vector table   In the 80x86 (Intel) family, an area in low memory that indicates the address of routines to be called when various interrupts occur.

intersection   See *AND*.

intersegment jump   In the 80x86 (Intel) family of microprocessors, a jump requiring both a segment and offset address (32 bits). This type of jump can be to anywhere in memory.

invert   To change from one condition to the opposite condition.

inverted file   A file in which the fundamental organization of data has been reversed. For instance, if the information in a file is originally stored as rows and columns, the inverted file would store the rows as columns and the columns as rows.

invisible bit   In the Macintosh environment, one of several finder flags. The invisible bit indicates whether the file's icon should be displayed on the screen.

I/O   See *input/output*.

IOB   An acronym for input/output block.

IOC   An acronym for input/output controller.

IOCTL   In the MS-DOS environment, a series of operating system functions for controlling I/O devices. IOCTL is a contraction for I/O control.

I/O redirection   See *redirection*.

IP   See *instruction pointer*.

IPC   See *interprocess communications*.

IPL   See *initial program loader*.

IPX   See *InterNet packet exchange*.

IR   An acronym for information retrieval.

IRD   An acronym for information resource dictionary.

IRDS   An acronym for information resource dictionary system.

IRG   See *interrecord gap*.

IRM   An acronym for information resource management.

IRQ   An abbreviation for interrupt request.

IRS   See *interchange record separator*.

ISAM   See *indexed sequential access method*.

ISDN   See *integrated services digital network*.

ISO   See *International Standards Organization*.

isometric   A two-dimensional representation of a three-dimensional object.

isotropic mapping   A translation and mapping scheme designed so the graphic representation of an object is consistent with its intended shape. This compensates for the display ratio of a video screen. For example, through isotropic mapping a circle still looks like a circle instead of an ellipse.

ISR   An acronym for interrupt service routine. See also *interrupt handler*.

ISV   An acronym for independent software vendor.

ITA   An acronym for international telegraph alphabet.

item   In the PICK operating system, a collection of logically related attributes. In other operating systems, an item is called a record.

item-ID   In the PICK operating system, a unique key representing an item in a file.

iteration   A single, complete repetition of a sequence of instructions.

ITU   See *International Telecommunications Union*.

IUS   See *interchange unit separator*.

Iverson Language   See *APL*.

Iverson notation   A notation system for the APL programming language. The system was named after its developer, Kenneth Iverson.

J

jam signal   In local area networks (LANs), a special signal that indicates that other nodes on the network should stop broadcasting for a specified period of time. In CSMA/CD implementations, a jam signal indicates a collision has occurred. In CSMA/CA systems, the signal indicates that a sending node will attempt to transmit a message.

JCL   See *job control language*.

JES   See *job entry subsystem*.

job   A user-defined task to be completed by a computer system.

job control language   A simple system control language that governs the execution of application programs in certain environments. JCL typically is used in mid- to large-size computer systems.

job entry subsystem   An integral part of IBM's MVS operating system for mainframe computers. The JES manages the use of JCL to process jobs on the system.

job management language   Synonymous with *job control language*.

job number   In multitasking and multiuser environments, an ID number assigned by the operating system or resource manager to a process awaiting execution.

job queue   See *queue*.

join   In SQL terminology, a query that draws data from several tables at the same time.

journal   A chronological record of operations performed in a computer system.

journaling   A method of tracking database modifications during a session to ensure the integrity of the database in the case of a system failure.

JOVIAL   A high-level programming language used in the 1960s and 70s. JOVIAL stands for Jules' Own Version of the International Algebraic Language, and was developed by Jules Schwartz and patterned after the ALGOL language.

joy stick   An input device used to move the cursor on the screen. Joy sticks are commonly used in video games. There are several different types of joy sticks in use; one common type is shown here:

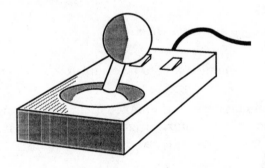

Julian date   A sequential numeric representation of the days in a year. The Julian value for January 1 is 1, while the Julian value for December 31 is 365 (or 366 in a leap year).

jump   A forced change in the linear progression of program execution; a change that was not based on the outcome of any comparisons. See also *branch*.

jumper   A short wire or connector used to establish a circuit between two electrical terminals.

jump table   A data structure comprised of addresses of other routines in memory. An algorithm is used to determine from where in the table an address should be extracted, and then program control is transferred to that address.

justification   The alignment of text on a display or a printed page. Left justification means that the left margin is even; another name for this is flush left or ragged right. Right justification means that the right margin is even; another name for this is flush right or ragged left. Center justification, fill justification, full justification, or justification (no qualifier) refers to text that has both the left and right margins even. The following are common types of justification:

```
‖ This text is left justified.      ‖
‖    This text is center justified.  ‖
‖          This text is right justified. ‖
‖ This    text    is    fill    justified. ‖
```

K   An abbreviation for kilo, meaning one thousand.

KAPSE   An acronym for kernel Ada program support environment.

Karnaugh map   A simple method of representing the outcome of Boolean operations using up to four variables. The method was developed by E. W. Veitch and M. Karnaugh in the early 1950s. The following is an example of a Karnaugh map, or K-map for short, for the AND operation using two variables:

	0	1
0	0	0
1	0	1

See also *truth table*.

Kb   An abbreviation for kilobyte, equivalent to 2^{10}, or 1,024 bytes.

KEE   An acronym for knowledge engineering environment.

Kermit   An asynchronous communication protocol developed at Columbia University. Traditional versions of Kermit use a 7-bit data format, so they tend to be slower than other types of protocols. However, this also allows them to be used on many dissimilar computer systems.

kernel   The core of an operating system. The kernel is the lowest level of the operating system; it is responsible for mediating between the hardware and the higher levels of the system.

key *n*   **1.** A button on a keyboard. **2.** A code used by an encryption algorithm to encrypt and decrypt data. **3.** A software protection device, implemented as either a key disk or a hardware protection device. See also *dongle; key disk.* **4.** *See index key.*

key *v*   To enter information into a terminal or a computer program.

keyboard   A typewriter-like computer input device that allows a user to enter commands directly to the operating system or application software. The layout and complexity of the keyboard will depend on the manufacturer, purpose, and system to which it is connected. A typical keyboard for an IBM PC is shown here:

keyboard enhancer   A software program or driver that expands the functions performed by a standard keyboard. A keyboard enhancer may implement a larger type-ahead buffer, a faster key repeat rate, or simple macros.

keyboard mapping   The process of reassigning the meaning of keys on the keyboard. Using keyboard mapping, the user can determine how the system interprets and acts upon individual keys. For example, the user can specify that when an asterisk (*) is typed, the system interprets it as either an asterisk, a different character, or a series of characters.

key disk   A method of software protection that requires the presence of a specific disk in a disk drive before the software will function properly.

keypunch   A device that punches holes in punched cards.

keystroke   The process of pressing a key on a keyboard.

keyword   In programming, any of the special terms reserved for a special purpose in the language being used. In most programming languages, keywords cannot be used as variable names. A few languages (such as PL/I) allow keywords to be used as variables if their use does not compromise syntax.

keyword analysis   A method of parsing text strings by using selected words as keys to perform predetermined functions.

kill   **1.** To terminate a program, process, or communications link before it is finished. See also **abort** *v*. **2.** To delete or erase a file.

kilo   A prefix meaning one thousand. The abbreviation is K.

kludge   A temporary, improvised patch to a software or hardware system.

K-map   See *Karnaugh map*.

knowledge base   A dynamic database, usually manipulated and maintained in an expert system. A knowledge base is composed of rules and facts that can be analyzed to develop inferences about another set of facts or conditions.

Korn shell   In the UNIX environment, the user interface shell developed by David G. Korn. This shell combines elements from both the Bourne and C shells.

label   **1.** An identifier or name used for referring to objects or functions. **2.** A data record used to identify a disk volume or magnetic tape.

lag   The delay between two successive events.

LAN   See *local area network*.

landscape   A printing orientation in which printing is done parallel to the wide side of the paper. An example of landscape orientation is shown here:

language   See *programming language*.

LAN Manager   Systems software for controlling local area networks. LAN Manager was developed jointly by Microsoft Corporation and 3Com Corporation.

LAN Server   Systems software for controlling local area networks. This is IBM's version of LAN Manager from Microsoft and 3Com.

large memory model   In some programming languages in the 80*x*86 (Intel) environment, a type of program in which programming code and data both require more than 64K of memory, but in which individual data structures are smaller than 64K.

laser prep file   In the Macintosh environment, a header file that prepares a laser printer to receive PostScript commands.

laser printer   A printer that uses the same printing technology used in copy machines. Instead of the image being taken from a lens, input is taken from a computer. Laser printers print a full page at a time.

last in, first out   A queueing method in which the most recently added queue element is the first element removed. Abbreviated as LIFO. A memory stack is a LIFO implementation.

latch   A temporary data storage register used by the CPU when processing data.

latency   In disk drives, the delay time between the request for data and the start of the data transfer. This delay is the result of waiting for the sector containing the information to pass under the read/write head.

layer   **1.** In networking terminology, a group of closely related functions and services that perform information handling at increasing levels of abstraction. Each level is called a layer. **2.** In graphics programs, a drawing overlay on which specific data can be stored. **3.** See *open system interconnection*.

LC   See *lowercase*.

LCD   An acronym for liquid crystal display.

LDT   See *local descriptor table*.

leader   The header portion of a magnetic tape that is used for threading. No information is recorded on the leader.

leading decision   In logical programming loop structures, the initial conditional statement executed to determine if the body of the loop is executed. See also *trailing decision*.

leading zeros   Zeros that appear before (to the left of) a number. Leading zeros are used to fill out a certain field width and are not significant.

leased line   A permanent, dedicated telephone line used only for communications. Data rates on leased lines are typically in the 4,800 to 19,200 bps range.

least significant bit   The rightmost bit in a series of bits.

least significant byte   The rightmost byte in a series of bytes.

least significant digit   The rightmost digit in a series of digits.

LED   An acronym for light-emitting diode.

left justification   See *justification*.

length attribute   In SQL terminology, the attribute that specifies the data length of a column. It indicates the number of characters that the column may contain.

letter quality   Print quality comparable to that produced by an electric typewriter.

lexical analysis   A method of analyzing a text string where a lexicon (dictionary), which contains symbolic definitions of words and phrases, is searched for possible matches.

lexicographic sort   A sorting technique that sorts alphabetic characters without regard to the case of the letters.

LF   See *line feed*.

library   **1.** A collection of small object-file modules intended for inclusion in other programs. The library is searched during linking. **2.** In AutoCAD, a collection of entity blocks used in other drawings.

LIFO   See *last in, first out*.

light pen   An input device that contains a light-sensitive circuit that senses light emitted by a CRT, as shown here:

The pen is used to point to areas on the CRT. The position on the screen being pointed to is sensed by the circuitry, and the positional information is fed to the software using the light pen. Light pens are typically used to select options from an on-screen display.

light-pen detection   The condition that occurs when the circuitry in a light pen senses that a pixel, pointed to by the pen, is illuminated. Also called a light-pen hit.

light-pen hit   See *light-pen detection*.

LIM An acronym for Lotus-Intel-Microsoft, the developers of an expanded memory standard for use on MS-DOS systems. The standard allows software to access memory beyond the 640K limit imposed by MS-DOS. The most current version of the standard is LIM 4.0, released in 1987. It supports memory areas of up to 32MB in size for both programs and data.

limit check A test to determine the relation of a value to a specific limit.

line **1.** In programming, one programming command or statement terminated with a carriage return/line feed combination. **2.** See *communications line*.

line analyzer A device that monitors and analyzes the condition of information transmitted over a communications line.

linear search A search for information in which the list to be searched is examined sequentially. A nonindexed search.

line driver A device to boost serial communications signals on a dedicated line. Line drivers are used to increase the distances over which a signal can be used.

line editor A rudimentary text editor that operates on a single line of text at a time.

line feed A character code that advances the cursor to the next line without changing its horizontal position. In some operating systems, the LF character signals the end of a line of text. The ASCII code for the line feed character is 10, the EBCDIC value is 37, and the acronym is LF.

line level The signal strength within a transmission line, usually measured in decibels.

line number In interpretive BASIC, a numeric value assigned by the user to each line in the program.

line printer A printer that prints an entire line at once. Contrast with *character printer*.

lines per minute   A measure of the speed at which a printer is capable of printing. The common acronym is LPM.

line styling   In computer graphics, the type of line used when a line is drawn on the screen. For instance, line styling may call for the use of a solid, bold, or dashed line.

link *n*   **1.** A logical connection between two differing objects, either hardware or software. **2.** In the UNIX operating system, an entry in a directory file that attaches a user-specified name to a file.

link *v*   **1.** To establish a logical connection between two differing objects, either hardware or software. **2.** The process performed by a linkage editor. See also *linker*.

linkage   In the PICK operating system, the first 12 bytes of a frame, which are used to define bidirectional links to other frames.

linkage editor   See *linker*.

linked list   In a database system, a collection of records may be stored in a file sequentially. These records may be in no particular order. In a linked list, there is a field in each record that points to the next logical record in the series. Thus, this chain of links maintains a desired order for the records in the file.

link encryption   A data security technique where information is encoded only as it passes between nodes.

linker   When using assembled or compiled programming languages, a linker combines object code files into an executable file. The primary purpose of a linker is to resolve external references in the object code files.

linking   The process of resolving external references and address references in object code, resulting in machine language instructions that are directly executable by the computer.

link layer   See *data link layer*.

link level See *data link layer*.

LIPS See *logical inferences per second*.

LISP A high-level programming language developed in the early 1960s by John McCarthy at MIT. LISP is a contraction for list processing, and is widely used in programming needs that do not require large amounts of numeric processing. Typical applications for LISP include expert systems and artificial intelligence software. LISP is a declarative language that makes no distinction between programs and data. There are many versions and implementations of LISP on many different computer systems. With so many different versions, LISP programs tend to be nonportable.

list A collection of data items that are to be processed in a certain order.

list box In the QuickBASIC or GUI environments, a window used to display a group of items from which the programmer makes a selection.

listing In programming, a listing is a printout of the source code of a program.

literal In computer programming, an operand that represents an actual value to be used. See also *constant*.

little-endian A storage technique for multibyte quantities in which the least significant byte is physically stored in memory first. See also *big-endian*.

load **1.** To transfer a file from a mass storage device into the memory of the computer. **2.** To mount a tape or disk pack so that it is ready to operate.

loader A routine, usually part of an operating system, that loads a program into memory prior to execution. See also *initial program loader*.

load module See *executable file*.

lobe See *node*.

local   In network terminology, any peripheral attached to the computer the user is physically using.

local area network   Two or more computers connected in a linear or circular arrangement in order to share data or other resources. A LAN does not extend across a public right-of-way, such as the phone system.

local descriptor table   In certain members of the 80x86 (Intel) family, an array of segment descriptors for a single program. If no LDT is defined, the GDT (global descriptor table) is used as a default.

local variable   In programming, a variable that is valid only within the bounds of the subroutine or function in which it is declared and used.

lock   A mechanism for restricting access to database records or other network resources to prevent corruption or enforce security.

locked instruction   In the 80x86 (Intel) family of microprocessors, an instruction using the LOCK keyword as a prefix. This instruction prevents other devices from interrupting the bus while the locked instruction is reading or writing memory. This mechanism is necessary for reliable communications among multiprocessors.

logic   A rational sequence of instructions executed by a computer to perform a task.

logical address   A memory address used to reference a location in virtual memory. In a segmented memory model, this address consists of two parts: a segment and an offset.

logical and   See *AND*.

logical comparison   The comparison of two data elements to determine their logical relation to each other.

logical coordinates   The location (either two- or three-dimensional) of a point within an area of the screen. The designation of coordinates is under the control of whichever software is being used, but is commonly designated as a series of numeric values, each representing an offset from an origin point along the x, y, and z axes. Each value is separated by a comma, as in 4.57,3.68,12.42.

logical drive   A portion of a physical disk drive set aside as a drive in its own right. This logical drive is given a drive name and responds to all operating system commands as if it was a physical drive.

logical exclusive-or   See *XOR*.

logical field   A data field that contains only values that represent yes, no, true, or false.

logical inclusive-or   See *OR*.

logical inferences per second   Used in artificial intelligence systems, a measure of the speed at which inferences can be drawn from existing data.

logical multiply   See *AND*.

logical not   See *NOT*.

logical operator   See *Boolean operator*.

logical or   See *OR*.

logical record   A data record whose relation to other records in the same file is independent of its physical location.

logic bomb   See *virus*.

logic chip   A chip that performs logic functions, such as processing and controlling. In the strict sense of the word, all CPUs are logic chips, but not all logic chips are CPUs.

logic operator   See *Boolean operator*.

log in   See *log on*.

login directory   See *home directory*.

login name   The name by which a user logs in to a computer system.

Logo   A high-level program language developed by Semour Papert at MIT in the mid-1960s. Logo is not well suited to applications that require large amounts of numeric processing. It is closely related to LISP, and is often used to teach programming practices to computer newcomers.

log off   To terminate a computing session and sign off the computer.

log on   To sign on to a computer system, thereby gaining access to system resources.

long branch   In the 680x0 (Motorola) family of microprocessors, a branch requiring an offset value that can be contained in 16 bits. Thus, a long branch can be to a point 32,768 bytes before or 32,767 bytes after the current program counter location.

long-haul   In data communications, devices capable of transmitting information over long distances.

long integer   A large-capacity integer format that consists of a two's complement value. The capacity and length of a long integer depends on the programming environment and the computer system. On some systems, a long integer is defined as 32 bits, on others it is 64.

longitudinal redundancy check   A numeric checksum value derived from a specific algorithm performed on the individual bits in a block of data; similar in nature to a cyclic redundancy check. The LRC can later be recalculated after the block has been transmitted or copied, and the new LRC can be compared to the original LRC to verify that the copy or transmission was correct. LRC algorithms are widely used in tape drives where information is stored on the tape in a series of rows. The LRC is computed for each row and compared to the LRC stored at the end of each block. If these two LRC values do not match, then an error condition exists.

long jump   **1.** In the 80*x*86 (Intel) family of microprocessors, a jump requiring an offset value that can be contained in 16 bits. Thus, a long jump can be to a point 32,768 bytes before or 32,767 bytes after the current instruction pointer location. A long jump must be within the current segment. **2.** In the 680*x*0 (Motorola) family of microprocessors, a jump using a 32-bit address as a destination.

long word   See *doubleword*.

loop   The repeated execution of a group of program instructions for a specified number of iterations.

loop check   See *echo check*.

loop unrolling   An optimization process that results in the removal of loops in a program. For instance, if a series of instructions must be executed two or three times, the physical code is repeated two or three times instead of writing a loop to repeat the same code two or three times. The resulting code is larger, but the execution of the instructions may be quicker since the testing and branching typically associated with looping is gone.

lost cluster   A cluster that is marked as "in-use" by the operating system, but is not associated with a particular file. In the MS-DOS operating system, lost clusters can be recovered with the CHKDSK program.

lowercase   An EBCDIC control code that enables lowercase characters on a peripheral. The EBCDIC value for lowercase is 6, and the acronym is LC. See also *uppercase*.

low-level format   A complete formatting of a hard disk, usually accomplished by special programs stored in the firmware of the hard disk controller.

low-level language   A programming language that is dependent on the machine on which it runs. Examples of low-level languages are machine language and assembly language. See also *high-level language*.

low-order bit   See *least significant bit*.

low-order byte   See *least significant byte*.

low-order digit   See *least significant digit*.

LP   An acronym for linear programming.

LPM   See *lines per minute*.

LRC   See *longitudinal redundancy check*.

LSB   See *least significant byte*.

LSI   An acronym for large scale integration.

LU   An acronym for logical unit; any user attached to a LAN using SNA (systems network architecture).

Lukasiewicz notation   Another name for prefix or Polish notation. See also *prefix notation*.

luma   See *luminance*.

luminance   The part of a composite video signal used to define brightness. See also *chrominance*.

luminosity   See *luminance*.

M   An abbreviation for mega, meaning one million.

MAC   See *medium access control*.

Mac   A nickname for the Macintosh computer built by Apple Computer, Inc.

MacBinary   A binary file-transfer protocol for Macintosh computers. Besides storing the file information, MacBinary also stores ancillary file information such as icon, graphics, and creation date information.

machine address   See *absolute address*.

machine code   See *machine language*.

machine-dependent   Software that will only run on one computer or one type of computer.

machine language   The series of binary digits that a microprocessor executes to perform individual tasks. People seldom (if ever) program in machine language. Instead, they program in a different language, and an assembler, compiler, or interpreter translates their instructions into machine language.

machine-readable   Printed information that can be read directly by a computer.

macro   A short series of user-defined characters that, when executed, are replaced with a much longer series of characters. Depending on the implementation, a macro can almost be viewed as a command variable: It is a user-defined command that represents a longer, more complex series of commands.

magnetic bubble memory   See *bubble memory*.

magnetic card   A recording medium made up of a thin, flexible card covered with a coating of magnetic oxide. A special device is used to write and read information from the card.

magnetic cell   An individual unit of storage in which differing patterns of magnetic orientation are used to indicate the bit of information that is stored at that location. See also *domain (3)*.

magnetic media   A storage device that functions through the application of small electronic charges applied to a magnetic recording surface. This classification of storage devices includes floppy disks, hard disks, and tape cartridges. See also *optical media*.

mail   See *electronic mail*.

mail merge   The process of combining a form letter with a series of names and addresses from a separate file into customized letters.

mainframe   A large computer system.

main memory   The large memory area directly addressable by the CPU that holds programs and immediate data.

main module   In programming, the block of code that contains the first programming statement to be executed.

main program   See *main module*.

main segment   In the Macintosh environment, the application program's code segment, which contains the main body of the program. Also called the blank segment.

main storage   The memory area directly addressable by the computer. This is typically the RAM associated with the computer's main memory.

MAKE   In programming, a utility that allows the compilation and linking of multiple source code files as they are modified. MAKE utilities come in many varieties, but all use what is called a makefile, which defines the relationship between modules and the steps to be taken by the compiler and linker.

make code   A numeric value passed to the computer by the keyboard when a key is pressed. See also *break code; scan code*.

makefile   See *MAKE*.

MAKEUSER   In the NetWare environment, a utility program that enables the addition or deletion of a large number of users that have the same network profile.

management information systems   In many companies, the department responsible for computer systems within the organization. The common acronym is MIS.

Manchester encoding   A method of encoding digital data on a magnetic surface, such as a fixed disk. Each bit period is divided into two complementary halves. A signal transition in the center of the bit period represents a 1, while a 0 is represented by the opposite transition.

mandatory argument   See *argument*.

mantissa   See *significand*.

map *n*   A series of values or descriptions that represent another series of values. See also *bitmap; Karnaugh map; memory map; resource map*.

map *v*   **1.** To assign a new interpretation to a key on the keyboard. **2.** To detail the contents of memory in a written or graphical manner.

MAPSE   An acronym for minimal Ada program support environment.

mark *n*   **1.** A manual notation on a form, intended to be read by mark-sensing equipment. See also *mark sensing*. **2.** See *file pointer*.

mark *v*   To make a physical or logical notation of a form, label, or data record.

mark parity   See *parity*.

mark sensing   The ability of a system to detect pencil lines or marks on a computer input form.

mask *n*   Another term for a filter. Masks are used to restrict the extraction of certain data or to prohibit the occurrence of certain events.

mask *v*   To filter out specific elements of a data set.

master boot record   The boot record stored at the beginning of a hard disk. It includes the partition table and indicates which partition should be booted. See also *BIOS parameter block; boot sector*.

master console   The primary terminal used to control a computer system.

master dictionary   In the PICK operating system, the primary file for each account. The MD defines all files, procs, verbs, and pointers for the account.

master disk   See *systems disk*.

master pointer   In the Macintosh environment, a data structure maintained by the system that contains the addresses of relocatable blocks on the heap.

master pointer block   In the Macintosh environment, a group of up to 64 master pointers allocated together as a single heap block.

math coprocessor   See *numeric processor extension*.

mathematical expression   An arithmetic formula or algorithm.

math processor unit   A portion of the CPU specialized and optimized for the performance of mathematic operations.

matrix   A rectangular array of rows and columns. See also *character matrix; dot matrix*.

maximize button   In a GUI environment such as Microsoft Windows or Presentation Manager, a small box containing an arrow and located at the top-right corner of a window (see Figure M-1). The arrow in the button points upwards, and if clicked will expand the window so that it fills the entire screen.

maximize icon   See *maximize button*.

MB   An abbreviation for megabyte, equivalent to 2^{20}, or 1,048,576 bytes.

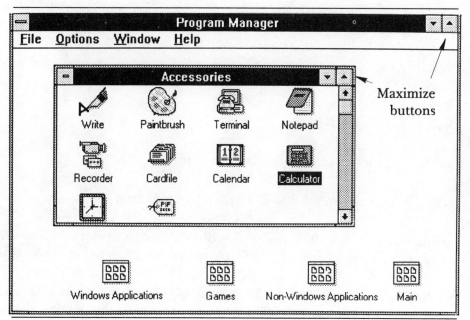

Figure M-1. The maximize buttons in Microsoft Windows

MC68000   A 32-bit microprocessor manufactured by Motorola, Inc. The MC68000 is used in some members of the Macintosh family of microcomputers, particularly the Mac 128K, 512K, 512K enhanced, Mac Plus, and Mac SE.

MC68020   A 32-bit microprocessor manufactured by Motorola, Inc. The MC68020 is used in the Macintosh II.

MC68030   A 32-bit microprocessor manufactured by Motorola, Inc. The MC68030 is used in some members of the Macintosh family of microcomputers, particularly the Macintosh SE/30, IIx, IIcx, and IIci.

MC68881   A numeric coprocessor manufactured by Motorola, Inc. This chip is used in conjunction with the MC68020 in the Macintosh II.

MC68882   A numeric coprocessor manufactured by Motorola, Inc. This chip is used in conjunction with the MC68030 in some members of the Macintosh family of microcomputers, particularly the Macintosh SE/30, IIx, IIcx, and IIci.

MCA   See *micro channel architecture*.

MCGA   An acronym for multi-color graphics array, a type of display adapter for IBM PS/2-compatible microcomputers.

MD   See *master dictionary*.

MDA   An acronym for monochrome display adapter.

MDI   An acronym for medium dependent interface.

media conversion   The conversion of information from one method of storage to another—for example, from storage on disk to storage on tape.

medium access control   In local area networks, the communications protocol used across the network without regard to the physical characteristics of the network (other than topology). The acronym is MAC.

medium memory model   In the C programming language in the 80x86 (Intel) environment, a type of program in which programming code requires more than 64K of memory, but the data requires 64K or less.

meg   An abbreviation for megabyte, equivalent to 2^{20}, or 1,048,576 bytes. Also notated as MB.

mega   A prefix meaning one million.

memo field   In database systems conforming to the standard set by dBASE, a special type of data field that can store large amounts of free-form text.

memory   The short-term electronic storage area within a computer system.

memory chip   A circuit used to hold programs and data. There are two types of memory chips: RAM holds data temporarily; ROM holds it permanently.

memory dump   The display or printout of the contents of memory or a section of memory.

memory location   A unique location in memory capable of retaining information. Each memory location in a computer is identified by a unique address.

memory management   The process of controlling the assignment, use, and access of memory areas to individual applications or processes.

memory management unit   The portion of a CPU specialized and optimized for the control of memory assigned to the CPU.

memory manager   The portion of an operating system responsible for allocating, managing, and freeing memory for use by processes running within the environment.

memory map   An organized method of depicting the use of an area of computer memory. A memory map is used to signify the uses for different parts of memory.

memory-mapped I/O   A method of input/output that is done by moving data into a specific area of memory. The most common example of memory-mapped I/O is a display device. What you see on the screen is typically an exact representation of the contents of a portion of the computer's memory (RAM).

memory-mapped video   A method of displaying video information in which what is on the screen is a direct representation of what is stored in a portion of the computer's memory (RAM).

memory model   A programming term referring to the scheme used to limit how memory is divided between code and data. Memory model use is quite common in the C programming language in the 80*x*86 (Intel) environment. For more information on memory models, refer to the actual types of memory models: *compact memory model; huge memory model; large memory model; medium memory model; small memory model; tiny memory model.*

memory overcommit   The condition of allocating more memory to a process than is physically available.

memory-resident   See *terminate and stay resident.*

memvar   Abbreviation for memory variable, often used in the dBASE language to signify a program variable.

menu   A list of options available at any given point in a program.

menu bar   A menu system implemented by a "bar" on-screen that contains the commands available at any given point in time. The bar can have either a horizontal or vertical orientation. An example of a horizontal menu bar is shown in Figure M-2.

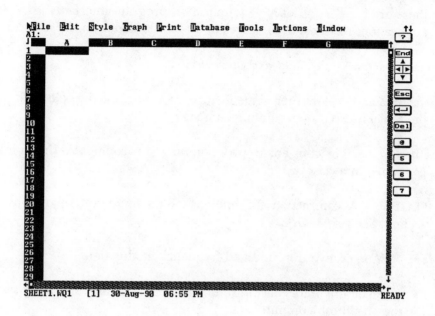

Figure M-2. A sample menu from the program Quattro Pro that has a horizontal menu bar

menu-driven   One of two general user interface schemes for programs. A menu-driven program presents all commands in a series of menus from which the user can select the desired function. The other type of scheme, command-driven, relies upon commands entered at a command line.

merge   To combine two or more sets of data into a single set. These sets of data can either be in memory (lists) or on disk (files).

merge sort   A method of sorting in which the elements to be sorted are divided into groups, the groups are individually sorted, and then the groups are merged together into the final sorted list.

message queue   A file for storing messages on a LAN until they are needed.

message services   In networks implementing the NetWare environment, these are a collection of APIs (application program interfaces) that allow applications to transmit messages to up to 100 nodes on the network.

metacharacter   See *wildcard character*.

metacommand   Another name for preprocessor directive, particularly in the QuickBASIC programming language.

method   In object-oriented programming environments, the routines contained in a class or object.

MFLOPS   A contraction for millions of floating-point operations per second. See also *FLOPS*.

MFM   An acronym for modified frequency modulation.

MFS   An acronym for Macintosh filing system, an early operating system for the Macintosh computer.

MICR   An acronym for magnetic ink character recognition or magnetic ink character reader.

micro channel architecture   The bus architecture used in certain models of the IBM PS/2 line. The MCA provides a 32-bit data bus that has more capacity than busses used in earlier computer architectures. See also *extended industry standard architecture*.

microcomputer   A computer using a microprocessor as a CPU.

microfloppy disk   A 3.5″ floppy disk.

micron   A linear measurement equal to one-millionth of a meter.

microprocessor   See *processor*.

microsecond   A unit of time equal to one-millionth of a second.

MIDI   See *musical instrument digital interface*.

milli   A prefix that means one-thousandth.

millimeter   A linear measurement equal to one-thousandth of a meter.

minicomputer   A computer system that occupies the medium range of computing power between microcomputers and mainframes.

minifloppy   A 5.25″ floppy disk.

minimize button   In a GUI environment such as Microsoft Windows or Presentation Manager, a small box containing an arrow, located at the top-right corner of a window (see Figure M-3). This arrow in the button points downward; if clicked, it will reduce the window to an icon representative of the application running in the window.

minimize icon   See *minimize button*.

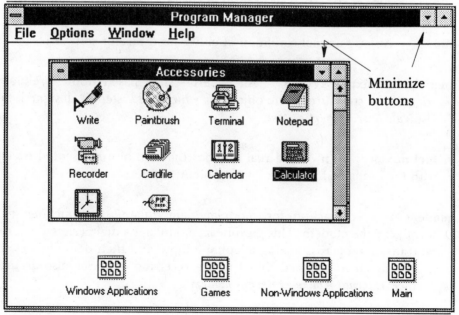

Figure M-3.   The minimize buttons in Microsoft Windows

mini-supercomputer   A smaller, less expensive version of a supercomputer.

MIPS   An acronym for million instructions per second; a measure of the processing speed of a computer system.

MIS   See *management information systems*.

miss   See *cache miss*.

mistake   An action with unintended results. A mistake is the result of human action, whereas an error is the result of computer action.

MMU   See *memory management unit*.

mnemonic   A word or code symbolic of another word, code, or function.

MNP   An acronym for Microcom networking protocol; a communications protocol from Microcom used in high-speed asynchronous modems.

mode   An operational condition of either hardware or software.

model-based expert system   An expert system based upon foreknowledge of the structure of the object for which the system is designed. See also *rule-based expert system*.

model number   In Ada, a real number that can be represented exactly with the available hardware floating-point registers.

modem   A contraction for modulate/demodulate, the functions performed by the modem. This peripheral modulates a digital signal so it can be transmitted across analog telephone lines, and then demodulates the analog signal to a digital signal at the receiving end. See also *acoustic coupler; external modem; internal modem*.

modem eliminator   See *null modem*.

modifier key   A keyboard key that doesn't generate a character by itself, but modifies the action of other keys. Modifier keys include the Shift, Caps Lock, Alt, and Ctrl keys. (In the Macintosh environment, the Option and Command keys are also modifier keys.)

Modula-2   A high-level programming language developed by Nicklaus Wirth in 1979. The language name is a contraction for modular language-2, and is based upon the Pascal programming language.

modular programming   A programming technique that relies on breaking down large tasks into smaller, more manageable tasks. Each module can be isolated from other modules as much as possible, so that the entire project can be coded and tested as a series of independent units.

modulate   The process of mixing two signals together prior to transmission over a communications link.

modulator   The portion of a modem that converts a digital signal to an analog form.

module   A subprogram; a portion of a program. See also *procedure; subroutine.*

module-level code   In the QuickBASIC programming environment, program statements located inside a module but not in a SUB or FUNCTION module.

modulo   **1.** A mathematical operation that yields the remainder of an integer division. For example, 13 modulo 5 equals 3. This is derived by dividing 13 by 5, which leaves a remainder of 3. This is the modulo value of the operation. **2.** In the PICK operating system, the number of groups in a file.

monadic operation   A classification of operation requiring only one operand. Synonymous with unary operation. See also *dyadic operation.*

monitor   **1.** Another name for a video display screen. **2.** A program used in testing and debugging to keep tabs on the operation of a system.

monochrome   **1.** Literally, single chromatic—a single color. **2.** A type of video monitor capable of displaying only a single color.

monospace   A typeface in which each character has the same width as every other character. Sometimes referred to as fixed pitch. See also *proportional space*.

Monte Carlo method   A technique of deriving a solution to a problem in a random fashion, or through the use of random numbers.

most significant bit   The leftmost bit in a series of bits.

most significant byte   The leftmost byte in a series of bytes.

most significant digit   The leftmost digit in a series of digits.

motherboard   The main printed circuit board of an electronic device such as a computer. Sometimes called a backplane or system board.

mount   To load a tape or disk pack so it is ready to function.

mouse   A hand-operated pointing device used to input positional information to a program. A mouse may be equipped with one or more (typically two or three) control buttons. Software, through a special driver, can sense the position of the mouse, its movement, and the state of the control buttons. This information is then used to control how the software functions. The following shows a typical mouse:

mouse pointer   The on-screen icon, cursor, or indicator, the movement of which is controlled by the mouse.

MPU   See *math processor unit*.

MSB   See *most significant byte*.

MS-DOS   A single-user, single-task disk operating system for IBM-compatible microcomputers. MS-DOS was created by Microsoft Corporation (the MS in MS-DOS) and released in 1981. MS-DOS has its roots in a system called 86-DOS, developed and marketed by Seattle Computer Products in 1980. 86-DOS was closely patterned after CP/M, another popular operating system of that era. MS-DOS has become the dominant operating system for microcomputers. IBM has a version of the operating system called PC-DOS. There is effectively no difference between MS-DOS and PC-DOS.

MTBF   An acronym for mean time between failures or mean time before failure.

MTTR   An acronym for mean time to repair.

Multibus   The IEEE 796 bus standard, originally developed by Intel Corporation.

Multics   An experimental operating system developed in the 1960s by MIT and Bell Laboratories. Multics was the predecessor to UNIX.

MultiFinder   A multitasking desktop manager for the Macintosh's operating system.

multimedia   See *hypermedia*.

multimode fiber   A fiber-optic cable containing several optic fibers.

multiplexer   A device used to perform multiplexing. A multiplexer allows multiple data sources to share a common communications channel.

multiplexing   In data communications and networking terminology, a technique that permits multiple data sources to share a common transmission medium.

multipoint   A method of data communications where several devices share a single communications line. See also *point to point*.

multiported memory   Memory that allows reading and writing of different bit locations simultaneously. This is accomplished by providing separate I/O channels to the memory area.

multiprocessing   Computing done by a system containing more than one processor. This can be done with either a coprocessor or parallel processors.

multisync monitor   A video display monitor that automatically adjusts to the synchronization frequency of the video source sending signals to it.

multitasking   The time-sharing of a processor among several programs. Control is passed from process to process under control of the operating system after either a set period or a certain number of instructions from each application are processed.

multithreading   The concurrent processing of different portions of the same program. Under an operating system that allows multithreading, a program can be broken down into individual tasks that can be processed at the same time. For instance, a word processing program can have one thread process spell checking, another thread process keyboard input, and a third thread process document input from other network nodes. All processes are done concurrently, resulting in a very dynamic document.

multiuser   A term describing a computer or network that can support two or more simultaneous users.

musical instrument digital interface   A standard protocol for the exchange of information between musical instruments and computers.

mux   See *multiplexer*.

MVS/ESA   An acronym for multiple virtual storage/enterprise systems architecture, an operating system for IBM System/370 series mainframes.

MVS/XA   An acronym for multiple virtual storage/extended architecture, an operating system for large IBM mainframes.

NAK See *negative acknowledge character*.

name server protocol Under TCP/IP, a protocol used to translate host and server names into the correct InterNet addresses. This protocol is typically used to facilitate file transfers.

NaN See *Not a Number*.

NAND A Boolean operation that compares corresponding bit positions of two sets of equal-length data and sets the resulting bits based on the condition of the tested bits. If both of the original bits are on, then the resulting bit is set off. If either original bit is off, then the resulting bit is set on. Sometimes referred to as a nonconjunction operation. The following is a K-map for the NAND operation using two variables:

	0	1
0	1	1
1	1	0

nano A prefix meaning one-billionth.

nanometer A linear measurement equal to one-billionth of a meter.

nanosecond   A unit of time equal to one-billionth of a second.

NAPLPS   An acronym for North American presentation-level protocol syntax; see also *PLP*.

narrowband   In data communications, voice-grade or low-speed transmission of approximately 2,400 bits per second or less.

National Television Standards Committee   A group that establishes and governs the standards for video recording, playback, and broadcast within the United States.

native code   See *machine language*.

natural language   A programming language paradigm exemplified by using English-like commands and syntax to issue commands.

NAU   An acronym for network addressable unit.

navigation line   In dBASE IV, the line at the bottom of the screen that lists currently available options.

NC   An acronym for numerical control.

NDR   An abbreviation for nondestructive read.

near-letter quality   A print quality produced by dot-matrix printers that use 24-pin print heads. The common acronym is NLQ.

near pointer   In a segmented memory organization model, a reference to a memory address within the same segment. A near pointer is nothing more than an offset address.

negation   See *NOT*.

negative acknowledge character   In data communications, the control code transmitted to signal that information has not been received or has been received with an error detected. The ASCII value for this character is 21, the EBCDIC value is 61, and the abbreviation is NAK. See also *acknowledge character*.

neqn   In the UNIX environment, an nroff preprocessor used to format mathematical expressions for character printers. The corresponding preprocessor for troff is called eqn.

nesting   Multiple levels of program execution or of menuing, with each level of program execution or each menu calling the one below it. Analogous to a hierarchical structure.

NetBIOS   The low-level interface between a network's operating system and the hardware on the network.

NetWare   A local area network operating system that operates as an extension to MS-DOS. NetWare was developed by Novell Corporation.

network   In simple terms, a communications path between computers and computer peripherals. See also *local area network*.

network administrator   An individual who manages the use and maintenance of a network.

network architecture   The overall design (both hardware and software) of a networked computer system.

network database structure   A database model in which a data field can be linked to more than one database file. In effect, the data field can be "owned" by more than one owner (database file).

network interface unit   The computer adapter card that allows a computer to attach to and communicate with a network. The common acronym is NIU.

network layer   In networking terminology, layer 3 of the OSI model. This layer is responsible for routing information through the network. See also *open system interconnection*.

network server   See *file server*.

NEU   An acronym for network expansion unit.

neural network   An artificial intelligence system designed to mimic the way the human brain works. Relationships between elements in a neural network are defined based on the way the system is used.

new-line character   A control character that moves the display or print cursor to the left margin of the next display or printing line. The EBCDIC value of the new-line character is 21, and the acronym is NL. In ASCII (and EBCDIC), the same result can be achieved by using the carriage return/line feed combination. See also *cr/lf*.

NewWave   A GUI environment from Hewlett-Packard that runs under DOS. NewWave is based upon Microsoft Windows 2.0.

nibble   One-half of an 8-bit byte, or 4 bits. A nibble can contain a value ranging from 0 to 16, so it can be expressed in one hexadecimal digit. Sometimes called a quartet; an alternate spelling is nybble.

NIU   See *network interface unit*.

NL   See *new-line character*.

NLQ   See *near-letter quality*.

node   An individual computer, server, printer, or communications device connected to a local area network (LAN). Nodes are addressable by other devices connected to the network.

node address   In a network environment, the unique number or name assigned to a node, or workstation, connected to the network.

node encryption   A data security technique where information is encoded and decoded at each node in a network.

noise   An extraneous signal or line-design problem that interferes with electrical transmissions.

nonconjunction   See *NAND*.

nondestructive backspace   See *backspace*.

nondisjunction   See *NOR*.

nonprocedural language   A programming language that does not require the programmer to define how to do many complex operations. For example, in the dBASE language, the LIST command produces a list of the records in the file, and the programmer does not have to define how to access the individual records. Those procedures are defined as a part of the language. Nonprocedural languages are typically interpretive in nature. See also *declarative language*.

nonvolatile memory   Computer memory that retains its contents without power. Examples of nonvolatile memory include ROM, PROM, and EPROM chips.

NOR   A Boolean operation that compares corresponding bit positions of two sets of equal-length data and sets the resulting bits based on the condition of the tested bits. If both of the original bits are off, then the resulting bit is set on. If either original bit is on, then the resulting bit is set off. Sometimes referred to as a nondisjunction operation. The following is a K-map for the NOR operation using two variables:

	0	1
0	1	0
1	0	0

normal   The representation of a number in a floating-point format in which the mantissa has an integer bit of one.

normalize   The process of converting a denormal floating-point representation of a number to a normal representation.

NOS   An acronym for network operating system, an operating system for Control Data's CYBER-series mainframes.

NOS/VE   An acronym for network operating system/virtual environment, an operating system for large mainframe computers from Control Data Corporation.

NOT   A Boolean operation that reverses the condition of the bits in an operand. Each bit that is set is turned off, and each bit that is off is set. This operation is monadic in nature; only one operand is required.

NOT AND operation   See *NAND*.

Not a Number   A floating-point value that does not represent a numeric or infinite quantity. They are typically generated as the result of a serious error and can contain error information that can be used to determine the source of the error.

notation   A method of expressing numbers. For example, scientific notation expresses numbers as a number between 0 and 1 followed by an exponent.

NOT OR operation   See *NOR*.

NPX   See *numeric processor extension*.

NRM   An acronym for normal response mode.

nroff   In the UNIX environment, a text formatting program used with files destined for character printers. See also *troff*.

NRU   An acronym for network repeater unit.

NRZ   An acronym for non-return to zero.

NSFNET   A wide-area network for the scientific community. NSFNET is administered by the Office of Advanced Scientific Computing at the National Science Foundation.

NTSC   See *National Television Standards Committee*.

NTU   An acronym for network translator unit.

NuBus   A computer bus developed by Texas Instruments, Inc. NuBus is used in Macintosh II computers. See also *bus (1)*.

NUL   See *null character*.

null   Empty; nothing. A null set is one containing no elements.

null character   In data communications, a control character used as a placeholder or filler. Generally, the null character has no effect on the communication in process. The ASCII and EBCDIC values of the null character are both 0, and the abbreviation is NUL.

null modem   Actually a misnomer, a null modem is a cable that switches the signals assigned to pins 2 and 3 of the RS-232 standard. This allows information sent on pin 2 at one end of the cable to be received on pin 3 at the other end. This effectively eliminates the need for a modem between two computers that are close to each other.

null set   A set that has no elements; synonymous with empty set.

null string   A character string that has a length of zero.

numbering system   The protocol used to represent numeric quantities. In computing, there are four major numbering systems used: binary, octal, decimal, and hexadecimal. Table N-1 shows the decimal values 0 through 20 in each of these numbering systems.

Binary	Octal	Decimal	Hex
00000000	00	0	00
00000001	01	1	01
00000010	02	2	02
00000011	03	3	03
00000100	04	4	04
00000101	05	5	05
00000110	06	6	06
00000111	07	7	07
00001000	10	8	08
00001001	11	9	09
00001010	12	10	0A
00001011	13	11	0B
00001100	14	12	0C
00001101	15	13	0D
00001110	16	14	0E
00001111	17	15	0F
00010000	20	16	10
00010001	21	17	11
00010010	22	18	12
00010011	23	19	13
00010100	24	20	14

Table N-1.   Binary, Octal, Decimal, and Hexadecimal Equivalents for Decimal Values 0 Through 20

numeric coprocessor   See *numeric processor extension*.

numeric overflow   See *overflow*.

numeric processor extension   A specialized chip added to a computer bus to handle advanced mathematic functions, thereby freeing up the processing power of the main CPU. The common abbreviation is NPX, although it is often referred to as a math coprocessor, numeric coprocessor, or arithmetic processor.

nybble   See *nibble*.

object   **1.** Any related group of items. **2.** The name of an individual element in an object-oriented programming language.

object code   An intermediate step between source code and executable machine language. Object code is created by a compiler and consists mostly of machine language, unresolved labels, and debugging information; it is not directly executable by the processor. It must first be linked in order to resolve external and address references. Some compilers (particularly those in integrated development environments) have a built-in linker so that directly executable code is created by the compiler.

object file   A file containing object code. See also *object code*.

object module   See *object file*.

object-oriented programming   A programming paradigm in which the focus of the programming style is on the data instead of processes. Object-oriented languages are nonprocedural in nature. The common acronym is OOP.

obliquing angle   An angle that specifies how far from perpendicular a set of letters are skewed. Italic letters are obliqued.

OCR   See *optical character recognition*.

octal   A numeric system based upon powers of 8. It uses the digits 0 through 7. The use of octal has declined in recent years; most computer professionals now use hexadecimal. See also *numbering system*.

octet   A byte consisting of 8 bits.

odd parity   See *parity*.

OEM   See *original equipment manufacturer*.

off-hook   A telephone line condition characterized by the presence of a dial tone. A telephone line is taken off-hook in preparation to originating a call. See also *on-hook*.

off-line   1. A computer system or peripheral that is not available or ready for use by other systems. 2. A function or process performed by a peripheral or system separate from the main computer system.

off-line storage   An information storage area that is not directly accessible by the computer, for instance a rack of magnetic tapes.

offset   A distance from a given base position in memory. The offset is usually given as a number of bytes.

on-hook   A telephone line condition characterized by the absence of a dial tone. A telephone line is on-hook when it is capable of receiving a call. See also *off-hook*.

on-line   A computer system or peripheral that is available and ready for use by other systems.

OOP   See *object-oriented programming*.

opaque   The opposite of transparent; a device or software program that performs limited processing on raw data, passing through the information it has not intercepted and processed.

op code   A contraction for operation code; the numeric value that instructs a processor to perform a specific task in a certain fashion. Assembly language programming instructions are translated into a series of op codes by an assembler.

open architecture   A system in which the internal workings are made public so third parties can create add-on peripherals. See also *closed architecture*.

open shop   A computer center in which users have direct access to the computer. Contrast this with a closed shop in which only data processing staff can access the computer.

Open Software Foundation   A group of seven corporations dedicated to defining and developing a new operating system based on UNIX. OSF was founded in early 1988 and initially consisted of Apollo, Bull, Digital, Hewlett-Packard, IBM, Nixdorf, and Siemens.

open system interconnection   A network communications model that divides the task of peer-to-peer communication into layers. Each OSI layer performs an individual task or set of tasks, and each layer builds on the capabilities and functions of the preceding layer until communication is complete. The layers of the OSI model are detailed in the following table. Layer 1 is the lowest level, and layer 7 is the highest. See the individual dictionary entry for each layer for more information.

Layer	Purpose
7	Application layer
6	Presentation layer
5	Session layer
4	Transport layer
3	Network layer
2	Data link layer
1	Physical layer

operand   In a programming language, the portion of an instruction that is interpreted as data necessary for the completion of the instruction.

operand-size prefix   In assembly language programming, an instruction prefix that specifies the size of an operand.

operating environment   See *shell*.

operating system   The program that controls the overall operation of the computer. Operating systems are primarily concerned with orderly system I/O, peripheral and resource management, and (in multitasking operating systems) the division of CPU time among different processes.

operation code   **1.** In the Macintosh environment, an integer value used to specify the mathematical function to be performed by a SANE call. **2.** See *op code*.

operator   **1.** A symbol that indicates an action to be performed on one or two values. The operators available to a language depend on the language, but typically consist of basic mathematic operators (addition, subtraction, multiplication, and division), logical operators (AND, OR, and NOT), and relational operators (equals, less than, and greater than). Additional operators may be added, again depending on the language. **2.** The person who operates a computer.

optical character recognition   The analysis and translation of a graphic representation of text into a coded form such as ASCII or EBCDIC. The common acronym is OCR.

optical disk   A mass storage device that uses light to store and retrieve information. Examples of optical disks include videodiscs and CD-ROMs.

optical fiber   A thin strand or wire of glass designed to channel a series of light pulses, which represent information. Due to their large transmission capacity, optical fibers are often used in transmitting information over high-speed networks or in telephone systems.

optical media   A storage device that functions through principles of light. Optical disks, which belong to this category, store information as a series of tiny, tightly packed pits or marks on a metal foil surface encased in plastic and read by a low-power laser beam. See also *magnetic media*.

optical mouse   A mouse that uses reflected light to determine position and movement. See also *mouse*.

optical reader   See *optical character recognition; scanner*.

optical scanner   See *scanner*.

optimize   To work with a program to improve performance.

option   See *switch*.

optional argument   See *argument*.

OR   A Boolean operation that compares corresponding bit positions of two sets of equal-length data and sets the resulting bits based on the condition of the tested bits. If either of the corresponding bits are on, then the resulting bit is on. The resulting bit is off only if both of the original bits are off. Sometimes referred to as a disjunction or inclusive-or operation. The following is a K-map for the OR operation using two variables.

	0	1
0	0	1
1	1	1

order   The logical arrangement of elements in an array or in a file.

ordinal   In the QuickPascal programming language, a data type comprised of members that make up an ordered set. Each member of the set is represented by an integer that indicates its assigned order. The ordinal data types are the five integer types, along with the Boolean, character, enumerated, and subrange types.

ordinal number   A number that identifies the absolute position of an element within a set. For example, if there are 20 elements in a set, the ordinal number of the sixth element is 6.

original equipment manufacturer   A company that produces computer hardware for sale either under its own name or with a private label under another company's name. The common abbreviation is OEM.

origin point The fixed location in a coordinate system where the x, y, and z axes meet and all have a value of 0 (0, 0, 0). See Figure O-1 for the origin points for two-dimensional and three-dimensional systems.

orphan In word processing and publishing, an orphan is the first line of a paragraph that appears as the last line of a printed page. Special software routines are commonly used to make sure there are no orphans when a document is printed.

ortho In AutoCAD, an input mode that permits only horizontal or vertical input.

OS/2 A microcomputer operating system from Microsoft that allows multitasking by a single user. OS/2 was introduced in 1987 and is viewed as the successor to MS-DOS. The major competitor to OS/2 is UNIX.

OS/360 An early operating system for IBM System/360 series mainframe computers.

OSF See *Open Software Foundation*.

OSI See *open system interconnection*.

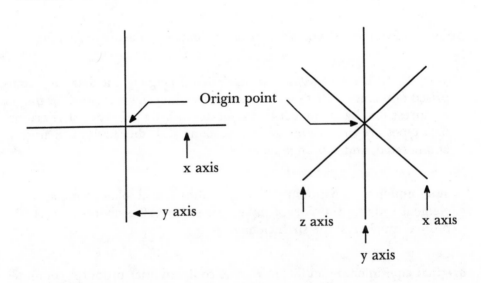

Figure O-1. Two- and three-dimensional origin points

outline font   A character type font, used in printers or screen displays, defined by mathematical values that describe the outline for each character. Outline fonts are extremely flexible, as they may be scaled to any size through special algorithms.

out-of-band   In data communications, control information that is transmitted outside the normal data stream.

output *n*   Information generated by a computer for use by the outside world.

output *v*   To generate an end product based on information stored in a computer system.

output buffer   A memory area set aside for gathering information to be sent to either another program, a user, or an external device.

output device   A computer peripheral that receives output from a computer system. Examples of output devices include video screens and printers.

output screen   A window on the display screen, or a separate monitor, that shows the output of a computer program.

overflow   An error condition in which the result of an operation is finite, but has a value too large to be represented in the destination format.

overhead   **1.** Extraneous programming code attached to a program during linking. This is typically code not used by the software, but pulled into the program from object-code libraries by the linker. **2.** Additional programming ancillary to, but necessary for completion of, the main purpose of a program. **3.** Extra work or consumption of a resource necessary to achieve a desired end. **4.** Information printed on clear acetate for projecting on a screen. Overheads are used with an overhead projector.

overlay A portion of a program called into memory only when needed. Programs that use overlays require less RAM to function, but require greater programming time and specialized programming tools that take care of the functions of loading and discarding program overlays.

overrun To exceed the capacity of a buffer; to overwrite the contents of a buffer with new information before the old information was completely processed.

overstrike In typography or printing, overstrike means to print a character, backspace, and then print a line through the character. Overstriking is a way to show corrections or editing marks on a printout. For instance, this is ~~overstriking~~.

overtype An input condition that results in typed characters replacing characters currently visible on the input line.

overwrite To record information on top of previously recorded information, thereby eliminating the original information.

owner The person, program, or network node that created a file.

pack   To convert information to a coded, compressed format.

package   **1.** A group or collection of software products that constitutes a commercial software product. **2.** In the Macintosh environment, a collection of related routines in the toolbox or operating system. A package typically resides in the system resource file, or in ROM, beginning with the Mac Plus. Further information about specific Macintosh packages can be found as follows: *binary/decimal conversion package; disk initialization package; floating-point arithmetic package; international utilities package; standard file package; transcendental functions package*.

packed BCD   A modified BCD format in which each byte is used to represent two decimal digits. See also *binary coded decimal*.

packed decimal   See *packed BCD*.

packet   In networking terminology, a self-contained block of information containing control and user information. Packets are the blocks of information transmitted across a network.

packet assembler/disassembler   In data communications, a hardware device used to pack and unpack blocks of information called packets. PADs are used in packet-switching networks.

packet switching   A data transfer scheme where information is broken into individual packets, which are transferred across a communications link and reassembled at the receiving end. In a packet-switching system (PSS), the route taken by a packet between sender and receiver is determined by each node through which the packet travels.

PAD   See *packet assembler/disassembler*.

pad character   See *padding*.

padding   The extra characters used as placeholders to fill out a field. For instance, if a data field holds ten characters, and only four are used, the additional six characters are padded with another placeholder character, usually a space or a zero. In this example, the padding can occur in either the six characters preceding or following the four used characters.

page   In the paged method of memory management, a page is a contiguous block of memory locations. It is the unit of memory used by paging hardware. See also *paging*.

page description language   A high-level language used to define how a printed page should appear. Page description languages are machine independent, which means they will work on any printer that supports the language. The actual translation of the language is done by the printer. The most common PDL is PostScript.

page directory base register   In the Intel 80386 and 80486 chips, a CPU register that holds the base address of the page directory; this is the CR3 register.

paged memory management unit   In the Macintosh environment, a chip that manages the virtual memory system in some models of the Macintosh. See also *paging*.

page fault   An exception that occurs if the desired memory page is not currently available. The operating system responds to this event by finding the page on disk and making it available in memory. The instruction that generated the page fault is then executed again.

page orientation   See *landscape* or *portrait*.

page printer   A printer that prints an entire page at a time. The most common example is a laser printer.

pagination   The process of paging information. In word processing, this means determining where page boundaries will occur.

paging   A form of memory management that simulates a large, unsegmented address space using a small, fragmented address space (pages) and some disk storage. Paging allows data structures larger than available memory by keeping them partly in memory and partly on disk.

PAL   **1.** An acronym for Paradox application language, a programming language used in the Paradox relational database management system. **2.** An acronym for programmable array logic.

palette   In computer graphics, the set of colors that can be used for display.

PAM   An acronym for phase amplitude modulation.

paper tape   A data or program storage method that consists of a series of holes punched in a long, thin paper strip. Paper tape is used in older computer systems, and has been replaced by newer and more efficient storage methods.

paradigm   This over-used buzzword is best explained by its synonyms: model, example, plan, pattern, prototype, or standard.

paragraph   A block of memory 16 bytes long, typically beginning at a memory address evenly divisible by 16.

parallel interface   A method of connecting computers or computer peripherals that allows the transfer of one or more bytes simultaneously. This is done through dedicated wires, each of which carries a single bit. Thus, if the parallel interface contains at least eight wires, it is capable of transmitting one byte at a time.

parallel port   See *parallel interface*.

parallel processing   The simultaneous processing of multiple processes within a computer. This is typically accomplished by multiple processors within the same computer.

parameter   A memory variable or other data item passed from a calling program to a subroutine, or entered by a user to modify how a program functions. Parameters can be passed either as values or as pointers to variables.

parameter RAM   In the Macintosh environment, the memory area that stores certain system information such as the current time and date, serial port configuration, default system fonts, and other system information. PRAM is 256 bytes of nonvolatile RAM; its contents are maintained by a battery inside the computer.

parent process   A superior or controlling program that executes other subordinate programs or processes called children.

parity   In data communications, a simple method of error checking that uses an extra bit to define the state of the data bits that precede it. Parity can either be EVEN, ODD, NONE, MARK, or SPACE. In all cases, the setting of the parity bit will depend on the number of ones in the data bits. In EVEN parity, the parity bit is set if the number of data bits set to 1 is odd (thus, data + parity = even). In ODD parity, the opposite is true. If the number of data bits set to 1 is even, then the parity bit is set to ODD (data + parity = odd). If parity is set to NONE, then the parity bit is either not transmitted or is ignored. In MARK parity, the parity bit is always set to 1, and in SPACE parity, it is always set to 0.

parity bit   See *parity*.

parity checking   See *parity*.

parity error   An error condition caused by the detection of an incorrect parity bit in transmitted data. See also *parity*.

parity flag   In 80x86 (Intel) systems, the bit in the flags register that indicates whether the low-order 8 bits of the result contain an even (PF set) or odd (PF clear) number of bits equal to 1.

park   To position the read/write heads of a hard drive in a safe position prior to turning off or moving the unit.

parse   To analyze a series of words to determine their collective meaning. Virtually every program that accepts user input in the form of commands must perform some sort of parsing before the commands can be acted upon.

parser   The portion of a program that does parsing. See also *parse*.

partition *n*   **1.** A section of memory assigned to a specific process or program. **2.** A portion of a hard disk used as a logical drive.

partition *v*   To divide a large object into smaller ones. For instance, you partition a hard disk by breaking it into smaller logical drives.

partition table   A data structure stored as a portion of the master boot record of a hard disk; a partition table is used to indicate the logical layout of the disk.

Pascal   A high-level structured programming language developed in the early 1970s by Niklaus Wirth. Pascal was named after the French mathematician Blaise Pascal. Pascal is a procedural language used extensively in the educational field for teaching programming principles and practices.

pass by reference   In programming, a method of providing parameters for a function by furnishing a pointer to a variable when the function is called. In this way the value of the variable can be directly changed by the function. See also *pass by value*.

pass by value   In programming, a method of providing parameters for a function by furnishing the actual value of a variable when the function is called. In this way the function has access to the necessary value, but cannot directly change the contents of the variable that first contained the value. See also *pass by reference*.

password   A series of characters used by an operating system or a program to identify an authorized user. Passwords are typically one facet of a computer security system.

patch   To make a temporary fix to a program.

patch cable   A cable used to connect two devices (one of which may be a computer). Patch cables typically are temporary in nature.

patch cord   See *patch cable*.

path   1. In operating systems based on a hierarchical file structure system, the route that must be followed to find a file in a directory or subdirectory. This route is composed of a series of directory names, with the desired filename appended to the end. The designation of the path can either start from the root directory or from the current directory. 2. In networks, the route between two nodes (devices) connected to the network.

path string   See *ASCIIZ*.

pattern matching   A process of finding results by analyzing a data set for specific patterns.

PBX   An acronym for private branch exchange.

PC   An acronym for personal computer or process controller.

PCB   See *primary control block* or *printed circuit board*.

PC-DOS   See *MS-DOS*.

PCL   See *printer control language*.

PCM   1. See *printer cartridge metrics*. 2. An acronym for pulse code modulation.

p-code   Intermediate pseudocode produced by certain Pascal compilers during program compilation. See also *UCSD p-system*.

PCS   See *print contrast signal*.

PDBR   See *page directory base register*.

PDES   See *product data exchange specification*.

PDL   See *page description language*.

peek   In certain computer languages, a command that returns the value stored in a specific memory location.

peer-to-peer   A local area network in which there is no central controller or file server. The nodes attached to the LAN each have equal access to network resources.

pel   See *pixel*.

peripheral   A hardware device that can be connected to a computer. Common peripherals include disk drives, printers, and video systems. A peripheral is sometimes referred to as an accessory.

peripheral device   See *device*.

permission   An indication of the level of access a program or user has to a file. Depending on the operating system and application software, a user or program can have read-only permission, write permission, read/write permission, or execute permission. Permission is often used interchangeably with access.

permutation   One possible combination of items out of a larger group of items.

perpendicular magnetic recording   See *vertical recording*.

persistence   1. The length of time a phosphor dot on a monitor will remain visible once it has been struck by the electron gun. 2. The ability of a storage device (such as memory, a disk drive, or a tape unit) to retain information stored on it. The persistence of RAM is short-term, as its contents disappear when power is removed. The persistence of disk and tape drives is much longer, as the information is maintained even if the power is lost.

PF   See *punch off*.

PFM   See *printer font metrics*.

PGA   An acronym for professional graphics adapter, a type of display adapter for IBM-compatible microcomputers.

phase shift keying   In data communications, a modulation technique characterized by altering the phase of the waves.

PHIGS   An acronym for programmer's hierarchical interactive graphics standard.

physical address   The memory address that appears on the hardware bus. See also *absolute address*.

physical coordinate   See *absolute coordinate*.

physical format   See *low-level format*.

physical layer   In networking terminology, layer 1 of the OSI model. This layer encompasses the lowest-level functions, those that deal with electrical, mechanical, and timing issues. See also *open system interconnection*.

physical memory   The address space on the local bus; the hardware implementation of memory.

PIB   See *primary input buffer*.

PIC   An acronym for programmable interrupt controller.

pica   1. A unit of measure used in typography. A pica is equivalent to 12 points, or one-sixth of an inch. 2. A monospace character font that has a print density of 10 characters per inch.

PICK   A multiuser, multitasking operating system that runs on a variety of hardware platforms. PICK was originally developed for the U.S. Army and is available from PICK Systems.

pick   In AutoCAD, the process of using a pointing device for selecting commands from the tablet or screen and for indicating entities or locations on-screen.

pickbox In AutoCAD, a small box that appears on-screen at the intersection of the cross hairs when prompted to select objects.

pick device See *pointing device*.

pico A prefix meaning one-trillionth.

picosecond A measure of time equivalent to one-trillionth of a second.

picture In certain programming languages, a template that specifies the type of data allowed as input to a field, or the way that data stored in a field should be displayed. The languages that use picture statements include COBOL and dBASE. As an example, the following dBASE statement results in the number of database records being displayed in a 4-digit field at the screen coordinates 1,76:

```
@ 1,76 SAY RECCOUNT() PICTURE "9999"
```

picture element See *pixel*.

pid See *process identification number*.

PIF file See *program information file*.

piggyback board See *daughter board*.

PILOT An acronym for programmed inquiry learning or teaching, this high-level programming language is used extensively in computer-assisted instruction (CAI) systems. PILOT was developed in 1968 by John Starkweather at the University of California at San Francisco.

PIM An acronym for personal information manager.

pin 1. In connectors, a male lead that is inserted into a female receptacle to make an electrical connection, as shown in the following illustration.

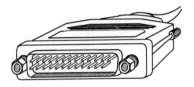

2. In printers, a series of pins are located in the print head of a dot matrix printer. Each pin is responsible for producing the dots at a specified vertical location on a printed line of text. **3.** In printers with pin-feed or tractor-feed attachments, a series of pins are located on the sprockets that guide paper past the print head.

PIN   An acronym for personal identification number.

pin feed   See *pin (3); tractor feed*.

pinouts   Graphic or text descriptions of the purpose of each pin and receptacle in a connector.

PIP   In the CP/M operating system, a program that controls the copying and transfer of files. PIP is an acronym for peripheral interchange program.

pipe   An operating system capability that causes the output of one program, command, or file to be used as the input of another program or command. In some operating systems, a pipe is used for communications between processes running at the same time. In the MS-DOS, OS/2, and UNIX operating systems, the piping character is the vertical line (|).

pipeline   See *pipe*.

piping   See *pipe*.

pitch   With monospace fonts, the pitch is a measure of the number of characters that can be printed horizontally per inch.

pixel   A contraction for picture element; a pixel is a single dot on a display screen.

PLA   An acronym for programmable logic array.

place marker   In the QuickBASIC programming environment (in the program editor), a spot in your program that can be jumped to by entering Ctrl-Q*n*, where *n* is a number in the range of 0 to 3.

planar BIOS   See *ROM BIOS*.

platform   Typically, a hardware system on which a program will run.

PLATO   An acronym for programmed logic for automatic teaching operations; an interactive, computer-based instruction system developed by Control Data Corporation. PLATO typically runs on large computer systems and combines graphics and text with touch-screen terminals to provide course instruction in many different disciplines.

platter   A recording surface (two-sided) in a hard disk.

PL/I   A high-level programming language developed by IBM in the early 1960s. PL/I is an acronym for Programming Language I, and is a general-purpose language with similarities to COBOL, FORTRAN, and Algol.

PL/M   A high-level programming language developed by Intel for use on their microprocessors. PL/M is an acronym for programming language for microprocessors, and is a dialect of PL/I.

PLP   An acronym for presentation level protocol, the videotex transmission protocol standard for North America.

PMMU   See *paged memory management unit*.

PN   See *punch on*.

POB   An acronym for primary output buffer, used in PROCs under the PICK operating system.

point *n*   **1.** An individual location that can be specified by a set of coordinates. **2.** A unit of measure used to specify the size of type. A point is equivalent to 1/72 of an inch.

point *v*   To move a cursor controlled by a pointing device (such as a puck, mouse, or stylus) so it rests on a desired object.

pointer   A reference to an address in memory.

pointing device   A hand-held device (a puck, mouse, or stylus) used as a data input alternative to the keyboard. Sometimes called a pick device.

point to point   A method of data communications where a single communications line is shared by only a single transmitter and a single receiver. See also *multipoint*.

poke   In certain computer languages, a command that stores a value in a specific memory location.

polar coordinate   A coordinate system defined in reference to a specific origin and based on distances and angles rather than on x, y, and z coordinates.

Polish notation   See *prefix notation*.

polling   A process where a series of I/O ports or devices are tested in sequence to see if any information is waiting to be processed. If so, then the information is processed before the next port or device is polled.

polygon   In computer graphics, a geometric shape with three or more sides defined by straight lines or arcs.

polyline   In AutoCAD, a series of connected lines and arcs that are treated as a single entity.

pop   To remove information from a stack or queue.

port *n*   A memory location that defines a communications channel or device interface. A port is used to interface a computer to other devices.

port *v*   To translate a computer program to another environment or hardware platform. See also *porting*.

portability   The degree to which an application can execute on a variety of machines.

porting   The process of converting software for a different computer environment than the one it was originally written for.

port I/O   A method of input/output that is done by moving data through a channel or device interface specified by one or more locations in memory. These memory locations are usually accessed through special commands to the CPU. Common examples of port I/O are disk drives and printers.

portrait   A printing orientation in which printing is done parallel to the narrow side of the paper. The following is an example of portrait orientation:

POS   An acronym for point of sale.

POSIX   An acronym for portable operating system interface for UNIX, an IEEE standard defining an interface between application programs and the UNIX operating system.

postfix notation   A method of indicating mathematic relationships between values. With postfix notation (sometimes referred to as reverse Polish notation), the mathematic operators follow the values they affect. For example, A B + C − uses postfix notation. This causes the values A and B to be added (the operator follows the values it affects); the value of C is then subtracted from this sum. (The subtraction operator follows the two values it affects, namely C and the sum of A and B.) See also *infix notation; prefix notation*.

postincrement register indirect addressing   In the 680x0 (Motorola) family of microprocessors, a method of addressing in which the operand's address is obtained from an address register. After obtaining the address, the contents of the address register are incremented by the size of the operand. See also *addressing mode*.

PostScript   The most common page description language for printers. PostScript was developed by Adobe Corporation and was originally used in the LaserWriter series of laser printers from Apple Computer, Inc. PostScript's acceptance has spread to many other types of printers because of its simple method of describing complex page layouts and its device independence. See also *page description language*.

power down   The orderly shutdown of a computer system.

power spike   See *spike*.

power up   To turn on a computer system in an orderly fashion. The power-up sequence may also include booting the operating system. See also *boot*.

pragma   A compiler directive. See also *preprocessor directive*.

PRAM   See *parameter RAM*.

precedence   The order in which mathematical operators are processed in a programming language.

precision   **1.** In mathematic functions, the number of retained decimal places to the right of the decimal point. See also *significant digits*. **2.** In database terminology, the number of digits that a numeric data field will hold.

precision control   On certain members of the 80*x*87 (Intel) family of NPXs, an option that allows for a reduced level of precision in numeric operations.

precision exception   In certain members of the 80*x*87 (Intel) family of numeric coprocessors, an FPU/NPX exception condition that results when a calculation does not return an exact answer.

precompiler   A program that translates source code into lower-level code, preparing it for further processing by a compiler. A precompiler does not create directly executable code.

predecrement register indirect addressing   In the 680*x*0 (Motorola) family of microprocessors, a method of addressing in which the address register is decremented by the size of the operand, and then the contents of the address register are used as the address for the operand. See also *addressing mode*.

predicate   In certain programming languages (such as Prolog and SQL), another name for a keyword. A predicate is followed by a series of arguments used by the predicate to complete a task.

predicate logic   The study of relationships of implications between assumptions and conclusions. Predicate logic is used in certain programming languages, such as Prolog.

pre-fetch   See *instruction pre-fetch*.

prefix   A programming instruction that has no effect in and of itself, but affects the function of any instruction immediately following it.

prefix notation   A method of indicating mathematic relationships between values. With prefix notation (sometimes referred to as Polish notation), the mathematic operators precede the values they affect. For example, + A B − C uses prefix notation. This causes the values A and B to be added (the operator precedes the values it affects); the value of C is then subtracted from this sum. See also *infix notation; postfix notation*.

preprocessor   A program that performs some preliminary processing. As an example, most C language compilers use a preprocessor to act upon certain directives that will affect how the compiler does its work.

preprocessor directive   In compiler languages, an instruction to be analyzed and acted upon by the preprocessor prior to the compiler doing its work. If the compiler does not implement a preprocessor, then there is no difference between a preprocessor directive and a compiler directive. See also *preprocessor*.

presentation graphics   Graphics used in formal presentations.

presentation layer   In networking terminology, layer 6 of the OSI model. This layer deals with data formatting and display. See also *open system interconnection*.

Presentation Manager   A graphical user interface (GUI) environment for the OS/2 operating system.

preview *n*   In the Microsoft Windows environment, the process of moving between windows by pressing Alt-Tab.

preview *v*   To examine information before it is made permanent.

PRG file   In the MS-DOS environment, a dBASE command file containing executable statements. It is a program or procedure file.

PRI   An acronym for primary-rate interface, used under ISDN.

primary control block   In the PICK operating system, the working storage area allocated to each I/O port.

primary input buffer   In the PICK operating system, a memory area used by PROCs for the temporary storage of information as it is entered at the keyboard.

primary key   See *index key*.

primitive   See *graphics primitive*.

print contrast signal   In OCR systems, a measure of the contrast between the printing and the paper. The acronym is PCS.

printed circuit board   A thin, flat plastic board that holds electronic components on one side and connectors on the other side. The circuits are usually designed to accomplish a single task.

printer   A computer peripheral that produces output on paper.

printer buffer   A memory area, peripheral, or disk area used to implement spooling. See also *spooling*.

printer cartridge metrics   A type of file in the Microsoft Windows environment that specifies font characteristics for printing. A separate PCM file is needed for each font residing on a font cartridge. PCM files end with the filename extension .PCM.

printer control language   The language used to control printers or other output devices based on the Hewlett-Packard family of laser printers.

printer driver   A device driver used to control a printer. See also *driver*.

printer font metrics   A type of file in the Microsoft Windows environment that specifies font characteristics for printing. PFM files end with the filename extension .PFM.

printing orientation   See *landscape* or *portrait*.

print server   A computer dedicated to managing one or more printers in a local area network (LAN).

print services   In the NetWare environment, a collection of services that enable applications to move print files from workstations to the printer. Print services also are used to specify control information about the print job.

print spooler   See *spooling*.

print thimble   See *thimble*.

priority   The level of importance attached to a job in the computer.

privilege level   In operating systems and some application software, a protection parameter that indicates the range of operations that can be performed by the user or application. A low privilege level results in a highly limited range of operations, while a high privilege level allows an unlimited range.

privilege mode   On members of the 80x86 (Intel) family beginning with the 80286, an execution mode capable of running code used to manipulate special system structures and tables. In the OS/2 environment, only the kernel and device drivers operate in this mode.

PRN   The system name for the printer under the MS-DOS, UNIX, and OS/2 operating systems.

PROC   1. A procedural language in the PICK operating system. 2. A common contraction for a programming procedure.

procedural language   A programming language that requires the programmer to define a series of procedures to accomplish a task.

procedure   A self-contained coding segment designed to do a specific task, sometimes referred to as a subroutine, subprogram, or function.

procedure division   The portion of a COBOL program that contains the algorithms, or processing portion, of a program. See also *data division; environment division; identification division*.

procedure file   In the dBASE language, a program file consisting of one or more procedures.

process *n*   Another name for a program, subroutine, or function; a task.

process *v*   To manipulate data or to act based on certain data.

process ID   In the UNIX environment, a unique numeric value assigned by the operating system to a currently executing process.

process identification number   In the UNIX environment, a number which the operating system kernel assigns to an active process. The common acronym is pid.

processor   The portion of a computer system that executes instructions; also called a microprocessor or CPU.

Prodigy   An on-line information service developed jointly by Sears and IBM. Prodigy is directed toward the home computer user and offers shopping, business, news, and information services.

product data exchange specification   A standard protocol used to define how information should be exchanged between CAD or CAM systems.

program *n*   A series of instructions that tell the computer what to do and when to do it. See also *software*.

program *v*   **1.** To enter programming instructions into a computer to achieve a certain goal or complete a certain task. **2.** To design, write, and test computer programs. **3.** The primary work done by a computer programmer.

program counter   In the 680x0 (Motorola) family of microprocessors, the register that indicates the address in memory of the next instruction to be executed.

program counter indirect addressing with offset   In the 680x0 (Motorola) family of microprocessors, a method of addressing in which the operand's address is obtained by adding an offset to the current program counter. See also *addressing mode*.

program counter relative addressing   In the 680x0 (Motorola) family of microprocessors, a method of addressing in which the operand's address is obtained from the current program counter. See also *addressing mode*.

program counter relative addressing with index and offset   In the 680x0 (Motorola) family of microprocessors, a method of addressing in which the operand's address is obtained by adding an offset and an index to the current program counter. See also *addressing mode*.

program file   See *file*.

program information file   A file used in the Microsoft Windows environment to hold information about applications that may be run under Windows. A PIF file has the filename extension .PIF.

program loader   See *initial program loader* or *loader*.

programmable function key   A special keyboard key that can be controlled by software.

programmable read-only memory   A permanent nonvolatile memory chip. Information can be stored in the PROM by use of a special PROM burner.

programmer   **1.** A person who creates software. **2.** A device used to write machine code to a PROM chip.

programming   The act of creating a computer program.

programming construct   A logical programming structure that affects the order in which a program executes commands. For example, many languages provide programming constructs that use the DO WHILE, FOR . . . NEXT, or CASE commands.

programming language   A set of commands, functions, and statements that form a common means of controlling a computer. A means for programmers to provide a series of instructions for a computer to follow. There are many types of languages in use in computer systems. For more information on a few of them, refer to the following entries:

Ada	*APT*
ALGOL	*assembly language*
APL	*autocoder*

BASIC	*Pascal*
BASICA	*PILOT*
C	*PL/I*
COBOL	*PL/M*
dBASE	*PostScript*
DL/1	*PROC*
FORTH	*Prolog*
FORTRAN	*QuickBASIC*
GW-BASIC	*QuickDraw*
HyperTalk	*QuickPascal*
job control language	*RPG*
JOVIAL	*SmallTalk*
LISP	*SNOBOL*
Logo	*structured query language*
machine language	*terminal control language*
Modula-2	*True BASIC*
PAL	*Turbo Pascal*

programming tools   See *software development tools*.

program overlay   See *overlay*.

program register   See *instruction register*.

program segment prefix   In the MS-DOS environment, the first part of a program (before any user data or instructions), which is used by the system to control the program. It is 256 bytes long and includes system information as well as the default FCB and DTA.

program statement   See *statement*.

program stepping   In the QuickBASIC programming environment, a program execution mode that highlights and displays each line of code as it is executing. Program stepping is used primarily to aid in testing and debugging a program.

Prolog   **1.** A high-level programming language developed in 1973. Prolog is a contraction for programming in logic, and is widely used in programming applications such as expert systems and artificial intelligence software. Prolog is similar in structure and syntax to LISP, and is based on predicate logic. Prolog is a nonprocedural language developed by Alain Colerauer and Philippe Roussel in the early 1970s. **2.** The beginning portion of a block of code that sets up the variables and environment needed for the block. **3.** See *header*.

PROM   See *programmable read-only memory*.

prompt   A character or series of characters that indicates that the system is awaiting user input.

propagation delay   The time necessary for a signal to travel from one point on a communications line to another.

properties   Characteristic qualities or attributes of an object.

property list   In a programming language such as LISP or Logo, an object that is assigned a descriptive attribute (property) and a value.

proportional space   A typeface in which each character has differing widths. See also *monospace*.

protected mode   On certain members of the 80x86 (Intel) family, an execution mode that is used for multitasking. Protected mode unleashes the full power of the CPU and allows orderly operation of multiple programs. It is called protected mode because while operating in this mode, programs are only allowed to perform operations consistent with their privilege or permission level. Thus, data areas and files used by one application can be protected from other programs.

protected virtual address mode   See *protected mode*.

protection block   See *dongle*.

protocol   A formal set of conventions defining the format and control of I/O between the devices or programs.

prototype   1. A model for a computer or software system. **2.** In the C programming language, a formal declaration of a function prior to its use.

pseudocode   1. An algorithm written in general terms, i.e., not in a specific programming language. **2.** A modified version of source code that can be interpreted and executed faster than the original source code.

pseudo-Op   A programming directive that is not meant for execution by the CPU, but is a command for the assembler, compiler, or linker to follow when producing the executable file.

PSK   See *phase shift keying*.

PSP   See *program segment prefix*.

PSS   An acronym for packet-switching system. See also *packet switching*.

PU   An acronym for physical unit; any physical node (such as a printer or terminal) attached to a LAN using SNA.

public domain   Information that is free to the public and may be used without payment of fees or acknowledgment of source.

public-key encryption   A data security technique in which only one key can encode data and one key can decode it. The decoding key is made public, and the encoding key is kept private. In this way, the file is kept safe from changes, since it cannot be decoded, recoded, and replaced with a modified version. The file is available to all those who have the public decryption key.

public variable   A variable that is available to all modules in a program; it is global in scope.

puck   A pointing device, resembling a mouse, with one or more buttons. Used in conjunction with a digitizing tablet to input information, pucks (and digitizing tablets) are used extensively in CAD systems. An example of a common puck is shown next.

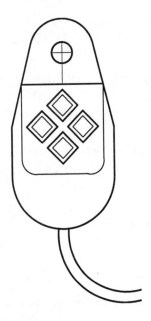

pull-down menu   A menu system that is implemented by a series of on-screen, pop-up windows, which present the choices available at any given point in time. A pull-down menu is usually used as an extension to a menu bar. When the user selects a choice from the bar, a greater selection of secondary choices is presented in menu form below the original choice. Pull-down menus are used extensively in GUI systems.

punched card   A paper card that is used to store information. The information is encoded as a series of holes punched into the card by a keypunch machine. Punched cards were used extensively in early computer systems, but have been replaced with interactive video display terminals.

punch off   An EBCDIC control code designed for control of a card or paper tape punch. This value, when received by the punch, will turn the unit off. The EBCDIC value of this code is 4, and the abbreviation is PF. See also *punch on*.

punch on   An EBCDIC control code designed for control of a card or paper tape punch. This value, when received by the punch, will turn the unit on. The EBCDIC value of this code is 52, and the abbreviation is PN. See also *punch off*.

purge   To delete something from memory or from the disk.

push   To add information to a stack or queue.

push-down list   Synonymous with stack. See also *last in, first out*.

QB Advisor   In the QuickBASIC programming environment, the context-sensitive help system.

QBE   See *query by example*.

Q-bus   The bus architecture used in the DEC PDP-11 and MicroVAX series of computers.

QMF   An acronym for query management facility.

QMS   See *queue management system*.

q-pointer   In the PICK operating system, a type of file pointer that enables alternative means of access to a file. A q-pointer is sometimes called a synonym.

quadword   Four words of memory space; a 64-bit quantity of memory.

quartet   A byte consisting of 4 bits. See also *nibble*.

query   An inquiry, usually issued to a database interface to extract information from a database. A query is typically issued in the form of a sentence or near-English command.

query by example   In database terminology, a method of searching (querying) the database by entering search criteria into a form resembling a template for the database records. The common acronym is QBE.

query language   A database language designed to make optimum use of queries. See also *structured query language*.

queue　A temporary holding place for information. See also *first in, first out* or *last in, first out*.

queue management system　In the NetWare environment, QMS provides a method for storing and prioritizing jobs to be processed. These jobs can later be serviced by an application at a remote node on the network.

QuickBASIC　A variation of the BASIC programming language published by Microsoft Corporation. QuickBASIC provides an integrated development environment including an editor, compiler, and linker.

QuickC　A variation of the C programming language published by Microsoft Corporation. QuickC provides an integrated development environment including an editor, compiler, and linker.

QuickDraw　A graphics language system built into the ROM of Apple Computer Inc.'s Macintosh series of computers. The QuickDraw routines allow a programmer to request the creation of certain graphic shapes and elements on the screen. This relieves the programmer of the necessity of creating low-level graphics routines, and provides a consistent, standardized graphics programming environment.

quick immediate data addressing　Another name for *immediate addressing*.

quick library　In the QuickBASIC, QuickPascal, or QuickC programming environments, a collection of independently compiled procedures that may be used by other programs.

QuickPascal　A variation of the Pascal programming language published by Microsoft Corporation. QuickPascal provides an integrated development environment including an editor, compiler, and linker.

Quicksort　An extremely fast sorting algorithm developed by C.A.R. Hoare in 1962. The following is a string Quicksort algorithm implemented in QuickBASIC:

```
DIM F$(1000)
DIM ST(25)
'*********************************************************
' * Routine to sort F$(?).  Enter with X set to the   *
' * number of active elements in the array.           *
'*********************************************************
QuickSort:
       P = 1
       Q = X
       TO = 0
SI.1: IF P < Q THEN
       I = P
       J = Q + 1
SI.2:    J = J - 1
         IF F$(J) > F$(P) THEN GOTO SI.2
SI.3:    I = I + 1
         IF F$(I) < F$(P) AND I < X THEN GOTO SI.3
         IF J > I THEN SWAP F$(I),F$(J) : GOTO SI.2
         SWAP F$(P),F$(J)
         IF (J-P) < (Q-J) THEN
            ST(TO + 1) = J + 1
            ST(TO + 2) = Q
            Q = J - 1
            GOTO SI.4
         ENDIF
         ST(TO + 1) = P
         ST(TO + 2) = J - 1
         P = J + 1
SI.4:    TO = TO + 2
      ENDIF
      IF TO <> 0 THEN
         Q = ST(TO)
         P = ST(TO - 1)
         TO = TO - 2
         GOTO SI.1
      ENDIF
      RETURN
```

quintet   A byte consisting of 5 bits.

radix   A value of each digit position in a numbering system. Also called the base. In the binary system, the radix is 2; in the decimal system, the radix is 10.

RAM   See *random-access memory*.

RAM disk   See *RAM drive*.

RAM drive   A portion of memory reserved for and configured to act as a logical disk drive. A RAM drive is extremely fast, but its contents are lost if system power is lost.

RAM-resident   See *terminate and stay resident*.

random access   A data storage and retrieval technique in which individual data elements can be accessed directly.

random-access file   A file whose records are accessible in any order.

random-access memory   Memory that can be changed under program control, the contents of which are erased when power to the memory area is removed.

range   The set of all possible values, delineated by a minimum and maximum value or a starting point and ending point.

RAS   An acronym for row address strobe.

raster graphics   A method of representing a graphics image as a series of dots.

raster image processor   A computer device that converts a vector image into a raster image prior to printing on an output device that requires raster technology. A RIP is most commonly used to translate PostScript files for printing on any of a number of typesetting machines.

raw data   Unprocessed information.

raw mode   An input mode in which input is accepted without any processing or translation by the operating system. See also *cooked mode*.

ray tracing   In computer graphics, a method of adding a degree of realism to an image through the use of reflections, refractions, and shadows. Ray tracing requires the definition of a light source, and then algorithms are used to determine the path the light follows from the source and how it reacts with the objects in the image. Ray tracing can produce very good results, but requires an enormous amount of processing power.

RDBMS   An abbreviation for relational database management system.

read   To transfer information from a mass storage device into the computer's memory.

read error   An error that occurs while attempting to read information from memory or a peripheral such as a disk drive.

reader stop   An EBCDIC control code designed for control of a computer input peripheral. This value, when received by the device, will turn the unit off. The EBCDIC value of this code is 53, and the abbreviation is RS.

read-only access   A level of file access that does not allow any change or deletion of information, or that may prohibit execution. See also *permission*.

read-only memory   Nonvolatile memory contained within a PROM or EPROM chip, the contents of which are static—they can be read, but not changed. Abbreviated as ROM.

read-only permission   See *permission; read-only access*.

read/write head   A device that stores and retrieves information from a magnetic recording surface such as a disk drive or tape.

read/write memory   See *random-access memory*.

read/write permission   A level of file access that allows both reading from and writing to a file. See also *permission*.

real   A finite value that can be represented by an integer value along with an associated fractional (decimal) portion.

real address   See *absolute address*.

real-address mode   See *real mode*.

real mode   On certain members of the 80*x*86 (Intel) family, an execution mode that provides emulation of the 8086 CPU. While in real mode, applications may address up to 1MB of memory.

real time   A generic term referring to the ability of hardware or software to acquire, process, and display information immediately, based on availability of the source information.

reboot   See *boot*.

received data   In data communications, a circuit in RS-232 connections used to carry data from data communications equipment to data termination equipment. RXD is defined as line 3 in RS-232 connections.

record *n*   **1.** In database terminology, a collection of related individual data items (fields). A record consists of fields, and a file consists of records. **2.** In the PICK operating system, a record is called an item.

record *v*   To write information to a mass storage device.

record layout   In database terminology, the format of the information stored in a data record.

record length   The size of a database record, usually denoted in bytes.

record locking   A method of data security typically used in multiuser or networked environments. When a user accesses information in a file, the records to be updated are read and then locked to prevent other users from changing data at the same time. When the original user has finished updating the records, they are unlocked so they are available to other users.

record number   In database terminology, an identification number assigned to a record. This number makes it easy to retrieve the record by referring to it by its number.

record pointer   A numeric value maintained by a database system that indicates the record number of the currently selected database record. See also *file pointer*.

record separator   A control character used on some computer systems to indicate logical boundaries between data records. The ASCII value for this character is 30, and the acronym is RS. See also *interchange record separator*.

record size   See *record length*.

recovery   The process followed to return to a normal operational condition after an error condition.

recovery time   The period of time required to return to an operational condition after an error.

recursion   The process of a routine calling itself in order to solve an algorithm.

recursive   See *recursion*.

redirection   Causing input or output to occur through devices other than those set up as the standard devices for such operations. For instance, through redirection it is possible to send output to a file rather than a printer. Such output would be totally transparent to a program, which simply outputs information to an output device. See also *stdout*.

reduced instruction set chip   A type of processor architecture that minimizes the number of instructions performed by the processor. In RISC systems, a heavier burden is placed on software computations. See also *complex instruction set chip*.

redundancy check   See *cyclic redundancy check; longitudinal redundancy check*.

reentrant   The characteristic of a procedure or subprogram that allows it to either (1) call itself (recursive) or (2) be called a second time by an interrupting routine or another process or thread while executing the first time.

reentrant code   Programming logic that can be used multiple times in a simultaneous fashion. For instance, most interrupt routines must be reentrant, because it is possible for the routine to be called a second time before completion of the first pass through the routine; i.e., the interrupts happen in quick succession. Writing reentrant code opens up whole new avenues of thought to programmers who must be concerned with the private use of variables for each iteration of the routine.

reference bar   In the QuickBASIC programming environment, the bottom line of the screen; it shows current function key assignments and brief help information.

refresh   To recharge circuits that lose their contents after a short time without power. Certain types of RAM chips lose their contents if power is turned off. To compensate, the chips are refreshed thousands of times each second. See also *dynamic RAM*.

refresh rate   The rate at which electronic circuits are refreshed. See also *refresh*.

register   High-speed data-storage areas, usually 16, 32, or 64 bits in length, used by the processor in performing operations.

register addressing   A method of assembly language addressing in which the contents of a register are used as the operand. An example of this type of addressing (for the 80*x*86 family of microprocessors) is

```
MOV    AX,BX
```

See also *addressing mode; address register addressing; data register addressing*.

register-based routine   A function or subroutine which requires passing or returning parameters through specific CPU registers instead of through the stack.

register indirect addressing   A method of assembly language addressing in which one of the operands is a register that contains the address of (a pointer to) a memory location whose contents are used in the operation to be performed. An example of this type of addressing (for the 80*x*86 family of microprocessors) is

```
MOV    AX,[BX]
```

See also *addressing mode*.

register indirect with offset addressing   Same as *base relative addressing*.

register window   A technique where a collection of CPU registers is accessed by hardware as a set.

relational database structure   A database model that does not rely upon physical links between individual records in separate databases. Instead, records can be logically related to each other based upon the contents of a shared or associated field. Because there is no "set" relationship between files, the amount of software processing needed to maintain the necessary links can cause slow response times when database traffic is heavy.

relational operator   Any of a series of program operators that determine a relationship between two items and return a value representing that relationship. Typical relational operators include =, >, and <. Specific language implementations may add other relational operators to this set.

relative address   An address that is calculated from a specified base (or starting) address. Contrast with *absolute address*.

relative coordinates   Coordinates given as a series of offsets from some set point other than the origin point for the axis set. If the set point that the coordinates are relative to is the previously plotted point, then the relative coordinates are also known as incremental coordinates.

relative pathname   In operating systems based on a hierarchical file structure system, the full path to a file, beginning at the current directory. For example, the following is a relative pathname from the MS-DOS operating system:

```
..\COMPANY\DATA
```

while the absolute pathname may be:

```
D:\ADAMS\COMPANY\DATA
```

See also *absolute pathname; path*.

relative vector   In computer graphics, a vector with end points designated in relative coordinates.

relocatable code   A series of machine-language instructions (or an entire program) that can reside any place in memory.

relocation dictionary   That portion of relocatable code that details all the addresses that must be modified at load time in order for the program to execute properly.

relocation factor   A numeric value representing the difference between the assembled or compiled address of a program and its runtime address.

remote   In network terminology, any peripheral to which a user has access, but that is not at the same physical location as the user's computer.

removable disk   See *removable media*.

removable media   A storage device in which the recording media can be removed from the drive unit that provides access to the media.

REM statement   In some programming languages, a remark or comment line.

repeater   In data communications, a device that receives information on an incoming data link and immediately transmits the same information on an outgoing data link. Repeaters are used as signal boosters for long-range communications needs.

report generator   A program that is used to create a report from information stored in a database.

requested privilege level   In certain members of the 80x86 (Intel) family, the privilege level applied to a segment selector. Access to a segment takes place at the least privileged of either the RPL or CPL.

request to send   In data communications, a hardware handshaking line from data termination equipment to data communications equipment. The RTS line is secondary in nature to the DTR line, and is defined as line 4 in RS-232 connections. See also *CTS*.

RES   An abbreviation for restore, an EBCDIC control code with a value of 20.

reserved words   In programming languages, a set of words that cannot be used as variable names because they represent the commands and functions used by the language.

reset button   The button or key on a computer that causes a reboot.

resolution   The degree of detail with which an image is displayed or printed.

resource　1. In a network environment, anything that provides a service available on the network. A resource can be an item such as a file server, database server, or printer. 2. Anything that may be assignable to a specific process executing in a computer system. For example, a resource may be a specific CPU or memory area. 3. In the Macintosh environment, a piece of data stored in a resource file. A resource is specially indexed information that can be accessed by its type and ID.

resource attribute　In the Macintosh environment, a set of properties associated with a resource. These properties indicate the characteristics that a resource will possess when it is accessed or loaded into memory. See also *resource*.

resource fork　In the Macintosh environment, the portion of a file that contains properly formatted resources. See also *data fork; resource*.

resource map　In the Macintosh environment, an index to the resources in a resource file. See also *resource*.

response time　The length of time it takes for a computer system, either local or remote, to act upon and respond to user input. As an example, this can be the time between pressing the Enter key and the display of the first character of the response.

result set　The results of an operation, particularly in databases. For example, a result set can be the records that satisfy a specific set of criteria.

result table　See *result set*.

return code　Sometimes called a completion code; the value returned by a function that indicates the result of the operation.

Return key　The keyboard key usually used to signify when user input is completed. On some systems, the Return key is referred to as the Enter key.

reverse engineering　To start with the output (including screen displays) of a finished software or hardware product and create separate software that produces exactly the same results. Reverse engineering requires analyzing how a software system accomplishes a task, and then generating new code to do the same tasks in the same way.

reverse Polish notation   See *postfix notation*.

reverse stroke   Another term for *backslash*.

RFI   An acronym for radio frequency interference.

RGB   An acronym for red green blue, the primary colors of light.

RGBI   An acronym for red green blue intensity.

RGB monitor   A video display screen that requires separate red, green, and blue video signals from the video source.

RI   See *ring indicator*.

right-hand rule   A method of determining the direction of revolution. The rule is based upon extending your right thumb along the positive x axis and pointing your index finger in the positive y direction. When you then curl your fingers, they point in the direction of revolution.

right justification   See *justification*.

ring indicator   In data communications, a hardware line used by a modem to detect an incoming call on a line that is on-hook. The RI line is defined as line 22 in RS-232 connections.

ring network   See *token-ring network*.

ring sequence   In a token-ring network environment, the order in which devices are connected to the network.

ring status   The condition of a local area network that uses a token-ring topology.

ring topology   See *token-ring network*.

RIP   See *raster image processor*.

RISC   See *reduced instruction set chip*.

RJE   An acronym for remote job entry.

RLL   See *run length limited*.

RO   An acronym for receive only.

roll in   In a virtual memory system, the process of loading memory areas previously stored on disk. Roll in may also apply to multitasking operating systems that do not implement virtual memory. See also *roll out*.

roll out   In a virtual memory system, the process of storing memory areas on disk. Roll out may also apply to multitasking operating systems that do not implement virtual memory. See also *roll in*.

ROM   See *read-only memory*.

ROM BASIC   In some members of the IBM PC family, a simple version of BASIC included in read-only memory. ROM BASIC is started automatically if the system cannot find a disk from which to boot.

ROM BIOS   BIOS stored in read-only memory. See also *basic input/ output system*.

root   1. The highest level of a hierarchical system. 2. See *root directory*.

root directory   In hierarchical file systems, the fixed starting point in the hierarchy.

root name   See *base name*.

rotational delay   The amount of time required for a disk to rotate so the desired information is under the read/write head. See also *latency*.

round   To adjust a number so that it is accurate to a certain, specified degree. See also *truncate*.

routine   See *subroutine*.

routing   In a networked environment, the assignment of the path by which a message will reach its final destination.

row   In SQL terminology, a horizontal line of data in a table, containing the values of one or more columns. A row is analogous to a record.

RPG   A programming language developed by IBM in the early 1960s. RPG is an acronym for report program generator, and is used chiefly for specifying reports to be created from information in a database. RPG II was introduced in 1970.

RPL   See *requested privilege level*.

RPN   An acronym for reverse Polish notation. See also *postfix notation*.

RS   See *record separator* or *reader stop*.

RS-232   An acronym for recommended standard-232, the EIA standard for serial communication.

RS-485   An acronym for recommended standard-485, the EIA standard for multidrop communications lines.

RSTS/E   An operating system for the DEC PDP-11 series of computers.

RSX-11   A multiuser, multitasking operating system for the DEC PDP-11 series of computers. RSX-11 is an abbreviation for resource sharing extension — PDP-11.

RT-11   A single-user, multitasking operating system for the DEC PDP-11 series of computers.

RTS   See *request to send*.

rubout key   On some terminal keyboards, the key that deletes the last character that was entered. On other keyboards this function is performed by the Backspace key.

rule In the Prolog programming language, a rule is a statement of relationship between one fact and other facts.

rule-based expert system An expert system based upon a collection of rules. See also *model-based expert system*.

run To begin execution of a program.

run length limited A method of storing information on a disk. RLL is implemented by the hardware in the disk controller.

runtime The point at which a program is executed.

runtime error An error that occurs during the execution of a program.

runtime module In certain compiled languages, a runtime module is required to provide basic language services to the application as it executes. Thus, at least two files are required to run the application: the compiled program and the runtime module.

runtime System A system manager that oversees operation of a language during program execution.

RXD See *received data*.

RZ An abbreviation for return to zero.

S-100   The IEEE 696 bus standard, used extensively in early microcomputers.

SAA   See *system application architecture*.

safety ring   See *file protect ring*.

SAM   See *sequential access method*.

sampling rate   When digitizing information, the speed at which samples are taken. Higher sampling rates result in digitized images, which more closely resemble the original image, but also require more memory and storage space.

SANE   See *Standard Apple Numerics Environment*.

sans serif   Literally, without serifs. See also *serif*.

SAP   See *service advertising protocol*.

scalable fonts   See *outline font*.

scalar   A single item or value.

scalar processor   A computer or peripheral that performs calculations on one number at a time. See also *vector processor*.

scalar variable   In programming, a variable that contains one value.

scan code   A numeric value passed to the computer by the keyboard. The scan code indicates the position of a key that has been pressed; routines in the BIOS or operating system must translate that value into a code usable by the rest of the system. See also *break code; make code.*

scan line   An individual horizontal line of pixels on a video screen.

scanner   A computer input device that accepts paper input and converts the images on the paper into an electronic representation of the image. There are many types of scanners; some save the scanned images as a literal graphic image, others convert scanned information into a different format. An example of this latter type is an OCR system, which converts printed text into ASCII or some other coded format. Scanners can further be differentiated by whether they process color or are limited to shades of gray (a gray-scale scanner).

SCC   See *serial communications controller.*

scheduler   In certain operating systems, the routines that control when programs are executed.

schema   The logical structure or layout of a database.

schematic   A representation of a logical or physical structure, usually in the form of a drawing or diagram.

scientific notation   A display of numbers using a base number (representing the significant digits) followed by a number representing the power of 10 to which the base number is raised. For example, the scientific notation for 128,000 is 128E3 or 1.28E5.

scope   1. A range of information affected by a command. In a database application, the scope may be a range of records or rows. In the dBASE language, the scope is specified by use of the ALL, REST, NEXT, or RECORD arguments. 2. In certain programming languages, the scope of a variable is its availability to functions within the program.

screen buffer   See *video buffer.*

screen dump   A printed copy of exactly what appears on a computer screen.

screen group   In the OS/2 environment, a series of one or more processes that share a logical screen and keyboard.

screen map   See *video buffer*.

script   See *macro*.

scroll   To shift text either up, down, left, or right from its current on-screen position.

scroll arrow   In GUI environments (such as Microsoft Windows, Presentation Manager, or the Macintosh), the arrows at the right side or bottom of a display area that control the scrolling of the image on the screen. (See Figure S-1).

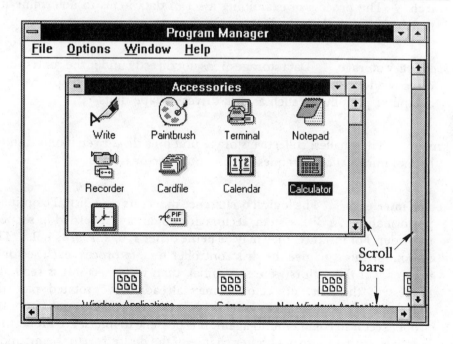

Figure S-1.   Scroll bars in Microsoft Windows

scroll bar   In GUI environments (such as Microsoft Windows, Presentation Manager, or the Macintosh), the vertical bar at the right side or horizontal bar at the bottom of a display area that controls the scrolling of the image on the screen (see Figure S-1).

scrolling   The horizontal or vertical movement of an image on a computer screen.

SCSI   See *small computer system interface*.

SCSI address   A unique numeric value between 0 and 7 used to identify an SCSI device connected to an SCSI controller.

SDLC   An acronym for synchronous data link control, an IBM data communications message protocol for SNA communications networks.

search   The process of examining a set of data items to determine if a match can be made according to specific criteria.

secondary storage   Data storage areas not directly under the control of or directly addressable by the CPU. Secondary storage consists primarily of computer peripherals such as disk drives or tape units.

sector   The smallest collective storage unit on a disk. Even if only a single byte of information is requested, an entire sector is read.

sector interleave   The logical occurrence of sectors on a disk. To optimize performance of a disk system, sectors are not always recorded in sequential order. For instance, they may be in the order 1, 6, 2, 7, 3, 8, 4, 9, 5. The reason for this is to give the disk controller time to process each sector as it is read. If the sectors were sequential, then when sector 1 is read and processed, the start of sector 2 may already have rotated past the read/write heads. This causes a delay while the controller must wait for the proper sector to come around again. It is possible to interleave the sectors, however, so that there is a higher chance of the desired sector being under the read/write heads at the proper time.

seed　A value used initially by an algorithm. For example, a random number generator may use a seed to begin creation of a series of random numbers.

seek　A command or action resulting in the locating of desired information on a disk or in a database.

seek time　The time required to move a disk's read/write head to the desired track.

segment　**1.** In a segmented memory model, a contiguous block of memory, the maximum size of which is determined by the size of the offset address register in use. **2.** A portion of a network.

segmentation　A form of memory management that provides multiple blocks of memory space, each independent from the other. Depending upon the implementation, segments may be consecutive or overlapping.

segment descriptor　In certain members of the 80x86 (Intel) family, a data structure defined by operating system software and used by hardware for implementing a segmentation scheme. It includes the base segment address, as well as the segment size, type, and protection information.

segment mark　In the PICK operating system, a reserved ASCII character used as a delimiter between items. A segment mark has an ASCII value of 255.

segment offset　The value to be added to the result of 16 times the segment value, thereby producing an absolute memory address.

segment register　In the 80x86 (Intel) family, any of the CPU registers designed to contain a segment address. They include the CS, DS, ES, and SS registers.

selection set　A collection of one or more objects to be processed within a program.

selection sort   A sorting algorithm in which the entire list of items to be sorted is scanned repetitively. On each pass, the lowest-value item is selected and placed in its final position. The following is an implementation of a selection sort for character strings in QuickBASIC:

```
Sort.It:
   FOR J = 1 TO Total - 1
       J9 = J
   FOR K = J + 1 TO Total
       IF A$(K) < A$(J9) THEN J9 = K
   NEXT K
   IF J <> J9 THEN SWAP A$(J),A$(J9)
NEXT J
RETURN
```

selector channel   A high-speed I/O channel used to connect a peripheral device such as a disk or tape drive to a computer.

semantics   The logical meaning of a statement, separate from grammatical structure.

semaphore   A flag or indicator used by either hardware or software to control an operation. Semaphores can be set either by hardware or software. See also *flag*.

sensor   A device used to measure or detect conditions in the real world.

separation   In the PICK operating system, the number of frames in a group.

septet   A byte consisting of 7 bits.

sequence check   The testing of a list of items to determine if they are in the proper order.

sequenced packet exchange   In a NetWare environment, an implementation of the Xerox Network Services InterNet Transport Protocols. An SPX packet is an extended form of an IPX packet and is accessed through the network communications services.

sequential access method   In database terminology, a method of data storage that requires all records to be organized and stored in the desired order. SAM tends to be inefficient for large data files, as the only way to locate information is to search the entire database from either the beginning or end of the file. See also *indexed sequential access method*.

serial channel   See *serial port*.

serial communications controller   In the Macintosh environment, a chip used to control the serial communications ports. The SCC used on the Macintosh is the Zilog Z8530.

serial interface   See *serial port*.

serialize   **1.** To convert parallel data to a serial format. **2.** To add or insert a serial number.

serial port   An I/O channel used to connect the computer to computer peripherals that communicate using a serial protocol. Common serial devices include modems, mice, and some printers. Information is transmitted over a serial port one bit at a time.

serif   Flourishes at the end of each line making up the characters in a typeface. A typeface can be either serif or sans serif, as the following examples show:

This text has serifs.
This text is sans serif.

server   In a network, a device that is dedicated to serving other nodes attached to the network. See also *database server; file server; print server*.

service advertising protocol   In the NetWare environment, SAP is used by servers or processes to inform clients of their presence on the network.

service protocol gateway   In the NetWare environment, a program used to translate Apple system calls into a form compatible with the NetWare core protocol.

servo track   See *index track*.

session   1. In data communications, the time during which an active connection exists between a sender and receiver. 2. The time period during which an application program is used. 3. The consecutive time period during which a computer operator is using a terminal.

session layer   In networking terminology, layer 5 of the OSI model. This layer is used to manage a session between two applications. See also *open system interconnection*.

Session Manager   In the OS/2 environment, a system utility that manages screen group switching. If Presentation Manager is functioning, it replaces the Session Manager.

set   A collection of objects or data elements.

sextet   A byte consisting of 6 bits.

SFGet box   In the Macintosh environment, a dialog box that allows a user to select files or programs from a list.

SFPut box   In the Macintosh environment, a dialog box that allows a user to save files to a disk.

SFT   See *system file table*.

SG   See *signal ground*.

shared memory   A portion of memory that can be accessed simultaneously by more than one process.

shared resource   A resource shared by more than one user or computer system.

shareware   Software that is distributed free of charge, but for which a user "donation" is requested. If users like the program, then they send a suggested amount to the author who will then provide service, updates, or enhancements to the shareware version of the product.

sheet feeder   An attachment that feeds noncontinuous forms into a printer.

shell   A user environment that functions under the computer's operating system to provide a meaningful method of working within the OS. See also *Bourne shell; command processor; C shell; DOSSHELL.BAT.*

shell script   In the UNIX environment, a text file containing a series of commands that can be sequentially executed by the shell.

shell sort   A sorting algorithm that is a variation of the insertion sort. The difference is that the shell sort does not do comparisons of adjacent items until the last pass through the list. Instead, it compares items that are a successively smaller distance apart in the list, making insertions as necessary.

shift in   A control character that, on systems that support it, signals that the alternate character set should be replaced with the standard character set. The ASCII and EBCDIC values for shift in are both 15, and the acronym is SI. See also *shift out*.

Shift key   A specialized keyboard key that, when pressed at the same time as other keys, alters their meaning, function, or interpretation. Typically used to produce capital letters when used with an alphabetic letter key.

shift out   A control character that, on systems that support it, signals that the standard character set is to be replaced with an alternate character set. The information following receipt of this signal determines which alternate character set is to be used. The ASCII and EBCDIC values for shift out are both 14, and the acronym is SO. See also *shift in*.

shift register   An internal CPU register used for shifting bits left or right.

short branch   In the 680*x*0 (Motorola) family of microprocessors, a branch requiring a displacement value that can be contained in one byte. Thus, a short jump can be to a point 128 bytes before or 127 bytes after the current program counter location.

short-haul   In data communications, devices capable of transmitting signals about a mile or less.

short integer   An integer format that consists of a two's complement value. The capacity and length of a short integer depends on the programming environment and the computer system. On some systems, a short integer is defined as 16 bits, on others it is 32.

short jump   **1.** In the 80*x*86 (Intel) family of microprocessors, a jump requiring an offset value that can be contained in one byte. Thus, a short jump can be to a point 128 bytes before or 127 bytes after the current instruction pointer location. **2.** In the 680*x*0 (Motorola) family of microprocessors, a jump using a 16-bit address as a destination.

SI   **1.** In the 80*x*86 (Intel) family, the 16-bit source index register. **2.** See *shift in*. **3.** An acronym for systems integration.

SIB   An acronym for secondary input buffer, used in PROCs under the PICK operating system.

sideband   In communications, the upper or lower half of an AM signal envelope.

sieve of Eratosthenes   A benchmark program used to test a computer's calculation speed. The program calculates prime numbers using Eratosthenes' algorithm.

sifting sort   See *bubble sort*.

SIG   An acronym for special interest group.

sign   A symbol that identifies whether a number has a value greater than (+) or less than (−) zero.

signal ground   In data communications, a circuit in RS-232 connections used as a common reference point for other circuits in the protocol. SG is defined as line 7 in RS-232 connections.

signal-to-noise ratio　The relative power levels (expressed in decibels) of a communications signal and noise on a data line.

signature　In the Macintosh environment, a unique four-character string that identifies a particular application program. This signature is included with every file created by the application. See also *creator signature*.

sign bit　In some systems, the high-order bit of a numeric representation. This bit indicates the sign of the number stored in the remaining bits. See also *sign flag*.

sign extension　A method of data conversion to a larger format in which extra bit positions are filled with the value of the sign. This form of conversion preserves the value of signed integers. See also *zero extension*.

sign flag　In certain CPUs, a bit in the flags register that is set equal to the high-order bit of the result of the last operation.

significand　The portion of a floating-point number that contains the most significant non-zero bits of the number. In some implementations this is called a mantissa.

significant digits　The digits within a number that determine its precision.

sign off　See *log off*.

sign on　See *log on*.

SIMM　See *single in-line memory module*.

simple mail transfer protocol　The electronic mail utility that is used with TCP/IP.

simple variable　A non-array variable.

simplex　One-way data transmission.

sine wave　A uniform wave generated by a single pure frequency.

single in-line memory module   A module designed to add memory to a computer system, a SIMM contains in one package all the circuitry needed to add 256K or 1M of memory.

single precision   In number storage, the use of one computer word (usually a 16-bit word) to represent the number.

single quotes   Another name for the prime mark ('), often used inaccurately to distinguish the character from a quote mark (").

single-sided disk   A floppy disk that uses only one side of the disk to store information.

skew   A deviation from the normal alignment along a specific axis.

slot   **1.** A bus connection in a computer into which an integrated circuit board can be inserted. **2.** In data communications, a unit of time in a multiplexed channel.

SLSI   An acronym for super-large-scale integration.

SM   An acronym for set mode, an EBCDIC control code that has a value of 42.

small computer system interface   A parallel interface format that offers the capability of connecting, in a series, up to seven computer peripherals. The common abbreviation is SCSI, often pronounced "scuzzy."

small memory model   In the C programming language in the 80x86 (Intel) environment, a type of program in which the program and data each reside in less than 64K of memory.

SmallTalk   A combination operating system and object-oriented programming language developed by Alan Kay at Xerox's Palo Alto Research Center (PARC). SmallTalk has served as the forerunner of various computer languages and environments in use today. Versions of Small-Talk are still used on several different hardware platforms.

Smart Editor   The program editor in the QuickBASIC programming environment.

smart terminal   A computer terminal possessing a limited degree of processing power, independent of the host computer.

SMDR   An acronym for station message detail reporting.

SMM   An acronym for start of manual message, an EBCDIC control code with a value of 10.

smoothed data   Statistical information that has been averaged or processed using curve-fitting algorithms. When smoothed data is plotted, the resulting curves are free from irregularities.

SMT   An acronym for surface mount technology.

SMTP   See *simple mail transfer protocol*.

SNA   See *systems network architecture*.

SNOBOL   A high-level programming language developed in 1962 at Bell Laboratories. SNOBOL is a contraction for string-oriented symbolic language, and was one of the first list-processing languages. As such, it was the forerunner of languages such as LISP. It is designed to be adept at manipulating text instead of numbers, and is procedural in nature.

SO   See *shift out*.

SOB   An acronym for secondary output buffer, used in PROCs under the PICK operating system.

soft font   A font or series of typefaces contained in software that can be downloaded to the printer to enable it to use the characters defined by the font. See also *cartridge font; internal font*.

soft return   In some word processing software (such as WordStar), a carriage return that may be automatically inserted or removed as part of special formatting by a word processor.

soft-sectored   A floppy disk organization method in which the information marking the beginning and end of sectors is recorded on the magnetic media itself. See also *hard-sectored*.

software   The logical sequence of commands making up a computer program. See also *firmware; hardware*.

software development tools   Special programs used to develop, analyze, debug, and perfect software. These tools can drastically reduce the amount of time a programmer spends coding algorithms. Software development tools include prototyping software, editors, compilers, linkers, debuggers, optimizers, and libraries.

software interrupt   See *interrupt*.

SOH   See *start-of-heading character*.

solids modeling   A technique for depicting solid objects in CAD systems. Solids modeling is very calculation-intensive, but presents a degree of realism not available with traditional wire-frame or surface modeling.

sort   The procedure of ordering records (either physically or logically) in a database file based on the contents of specified fields or columns.

sort algorithm   The series of programming instructions used to sort information.

sort key   The database field that indicates the order in which the database records should be sorted.

SOS   **1.** An acronym for start of significance, an EBCDIC control code with a value of 33. **2.** An acronym for silicon on sapphire.

source code   The programming instructions, written by humans, that cause a computer to execute a series of functions in an organized manner. Source code is a program. An assembler or compiler translates source code into object code.

source file   A file containing source code.

source operand   In assembly language instructions, the first operand immediately following the instruction.

SP   **1.** In the 80x86 (Intel) family, the 16-bit stack pointer register. **2.** See *space (1)*.

space   **1.** A blank character; the ASCII value 32 or the EBCDIC value 64. The abbreviation for this character is SP. **2.** A parity technique in which the parity bit is always clear (0).

space parity   See *parity*.

spaghetti code   A program written with poor structure and very little discernable logic flow.

SPARC   A 32-bit chip system from Sun Microsystems. SPARC is an abbreviation for scalable processor architecture, and is based on RISC technology. It implements an extendable architecture featuring register windows.

special file   See *device file*.

speech synthesis   The computer generation of sound that resembles human speech. The synthesis is accomplished through the use of algorithms and stored sounds.

SPG   See *service protocol gateway*.

spike   A sudden, unexpected, and dramatic increase in line current. Spikes can result in damaged equipment if not compensated for by special filtering equipment.

SPL   An acronym for systems programming language, an assembly language for the Hewlett-Packard 3000 series of minicomputers.

splitter   A device that causes one electrical signal to be propagated on two physical paths.

spool folder   In the Macintosh environment, a folder used to store print files waiting to be printed.

spooling   The process of storing information in a special area of memory or a disk in preparation for being sent to the printer. A spooler is typically used to speed up the apparent throughput of a computer system. The spooling area (memory or disk) accepts the information at a fast rate and then feeds it to the printer at a slower rate (which may be required by the printer). While the spooler is feeding information to the printer in the background, the process in the foreground is free to continue processing. The term spool is actually an acronym for simultaneous peripheral operation on-line.

spreadsheet   A classification of application software that allows for the processing of information arranged in rectangular arrays. There are many types of spreadsheets available, Lotus 1-2-3 being the most popular.

sprite   A moving cursor in a graphics display.

SPX   See *sequenced packet exchange*.

SQL   See *structured query language*.

SR   See *status register*.

SRAM   See *static RAM*.

SS   In the 80x86 (Intel) family, the 16-bit stack segment register.

SSDD   An acronym for single-sided, double-density. See also *single-sided disk; double-density disk*.

SSI   An acronym for small scale integration.

SSP   An acronym for system support program, an operating system from IBM for their minicomputers.

stack   1. An area of memory set aside for the temporary storage of values in a computing environment. The stack operates in a LIFO fashion.

Perhaps the most important use of the stack is to track the return addresses of calling programs. This enables the modularity of programs and ensures the orderly execution of instructions. **2.** A HyperCard file.

stack-based routine   A function or subroutine that requires passing or returning parameters through the stack.

stack frame   The portion of a stack containing a procedure's local variables and parameters.

stack pointer   An internal CPU register that contains a pointer to the stack address at which the next stack operation will occur.

stack segment   In the 80x86 (Intel) family, a data segment used to hold the stack.

stand alone   A system (hardware or software) that is able to function without additional support from other hardware or software.

Standard Apple Numerics Environment   A set of floating-point arithmetic features and capabilities provided on Macintosh computers. SANE conforms to the IEEE 754 standard.

standard file box   In the Macintosh environment, a collective name for the SFGet and SFPut boxes.

standard file package   A standard Macintosh package used to format filenames for I/O operations in a standard manner. This package is provided in the system resource file. See also *package (2)*.

standard input device   See *stdin*.

standard output device   See *stdout*.

star-dot-star   In the MS-DOS environment, the pronunciation of the *.* wildcard specification.

start bit   In asynchronous data communications, a bit that precedes the data bits and signals to the receiving computer that data is to follow.

start line   In the MS-DOS environment, the scan line at which the cursor begins. See also *stop line*.

start-of-heading character   In data communications, a control character that signifies that the data immediately following is to be treated as the header for the message that will follow the header. The ASCII and EBCDIC values for this character are both 1, and the acronym is SOH.

start-of-text character   In data communications, a control character used to signal the start of the transmission of a block of text. The block is ended with an ETX (end-of-text character). The ASCII and EBCDIC values for the start-of-text character are both 2, and the abbreviation is STX.

star topology   A network configuration in which a central computer, or hub, serves as an intermediate for communication with all nodes attached to the network. A possible star topology for a network is shown here:

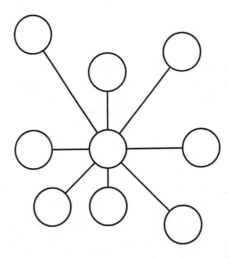

STARTUP.CMD   In an OS/2 environment, a file containing commands to be executed by the system when it is first started.

startup disk   In the Macintosh environment, the disk used to boot the computer. See also *boot disk*.

statement   In programming, a statement is typically analogous to a single line of program code. Statements are broken down into lower-level instructions by the compiler or an interpreter.

static array   An explicitly declared array.

static RAM   A type of random-access memory that maintains its contents as long as power is maintained. Compare with dynamic RAM, a type of RAM that must be refreshed many times each second.

statistical multiplexer   In data communications, a device used to combine several low-speed communications channels into a single high-speed channel. The multiplexing is done dynamically, based upon the load and use patterns of the channels being combined. Sometimes referred to as stat mux.

stat mux   See *statistical multiplexer*.

status register   In the 680x0 (Motorola) family of microprocessors, a CPU register made up of the condition codes register and various status information about the 68000. Status register is abbreviated SR.

status word   In the 80x87 (Intel) family, a 16-bit register used to indicate the status or result of certain operations.

stderr   Abbreviation for standard error. This is the device name assigned to the error reporting device in the MS-DOS, OS/2, and UNIX operating systems.

stdin   Abbreviation for standard input. This is the device name assigned to the input device in the MS-DOS, OS/2, and UNIX operating systems.

stdout   Abbreviation for standard output. This is the device name assigned to the output device in the MS-DOS, OS/2, and UNIX operating systems.

stop bit   In asynchronous data communications, a bit that follows the data and parity bits, and signals to the receiving computer that the character is complete.

stop line   In the MS-DOS environment, the scan line at which the cursor ends. See also *start line*.

storage class   In the C programming language, an attribute of a variable that defines its scope and the length of time it remains in memory.

stored program concept   See *von Neumann architecture*.

streaming tape   A high-speed magnetic tape drive used to make backup copies of a hard disk's information.

string   A series of alphanumeric characters. A string's contents are treated as though they were text, even if the string contains numbers.

structured programming   A programming technique that relies on a set of formal rules. If the rules are followed, programming should be easier and the program should be more readable, understandable, and easier to maintain.

structured query language   A database language that allows users to present near-English queries to the database manager in order to view the database in a variety of different ways. SQL was originally developed by IBM for use with their relational database systems.

STX   See *start-of-text character*.

style sheet   In word processing or desktop publishing, a file that specifies how the text in the document is to be formatted.

stylus   A hand-held pointing device resembling a fancy pen with a spring-loaded or electronic tip. Used in conjunction with a digitizing tablet to enter information into a program.

SUB   See *substitute*.

subdirectory   In an operating system that uses a hierarchical directory structure, a directory branching off of another directory. The terms subdirectory and directory are virtually interchangeable.

subprogram   A self-contained coding segment designed to do a specific task, sometimes referred to as a subroutine, procedure, or function.

subroutine   A self-contained coding segment designed to do a specific task, sometimes referred to as a procedure.

subscript   In programming, a value that identifies which element or elements of an array are to be operated upon.

substitute   A control character that indicates that the original character normally occupying this position could not be transmitted, represented, or displayed for some reason. The ASCII value for the substitute character is 26, the EBCDIC value is 63, and the abbreviation is SUB. In some ASCII systems, the ASCII value 26 is also used to signal the end of a file. See also *end of file*.

substring   A string contained within another string; a contiguous portion or segment of a larger string. For example, "ABC" is a substring of the string "ABCDEFGH." See also *string*.

subvalue   In the PICK operating system, a portion of a value.

subvalue mark   In the PICK operating system, a reserved ASCII character used as a delimiter between subvalues. A subvalue mark has an ASCII value of 252.

supercomputer   The largest classification of computers available today. Supercomputers are capable of doing a phenomenal number of computations per second. They are very expensive (several million dollars) and are typically used for the toughest computational tasks.

superuser   In the UNIX environment, a system access level granted to the system administrator. As a superuser, the administrator can access anything and everything on the system.

supervisor   An operating system or portion thereof that controls the overall function of a computer system.

supervisor state   The operational mode of a computer when it is executing privileged operating system instructions.

surface modeling   A technique used in CAD systems to represent solid objects by calculating the appearance of the surface of each object in an image.

surge supressor   An electrical device designed to limit power spikes within a certain frequency range. Surge supressors are used to filter line current and protect equipment connected to them. See also *spike*.

swap file   A disk file used to hold the contents of a memory area temporarily until it can be loaded back into memory.

swapping   See *paging*.

switch   An optional command parameter that modifies how the command will function.

Switcher   In the Macintosh environment, a forerunner of MultiFinder. Switcher was developed by Andy Hertzfeld.

SYLK file   A file format used with Microsoft products such as Multiplan and Excel. A SYLK file is used for exchange of spreadsheet information with other programs. SYLK is a contraction for symbolic link.

symbolic address   A mnemonic label that represents an address. When the program is compiled or assembled, the symbolic address can be translated to either a relative or absolute address. If it is changed to a relative address, then a final conversion to an absolute address occurs when the program is loaded.

SYN   See *synchronous idle*.

sync character   A special character used to synchronize timing between devices utilizing a synchronous communications link.

synchronization services   In the NetWare environment, a collection of services that control file and record sharing.

synchronous communication   The transmission of information between two devices (including two modems) in which intercharacter timing between the two devices is strictly synchronized. A sync character is periodically transmitted across the communications link to ensure that both devices are in step with each other. Synchronous communications can have a much faster throughput than asynchronous communications because there is no need to send start and stop bits between data packets. See also *asynchronous communication*.

synchronous idle   In synchronous data communications, a control code that is transmitted while no other character is being transmitted. It is used to allow both transmitter and receiver to stay in sync. The ASCII value for the synchronous idle character is 22, the EBCDIC value is 50, and the abbreviation is SYN.

synonym   See *q-pointer*.

syntactic analysis   A method of analyzing text in terms of sentence syntax. This method is usually accomplished by parsing the individual words within the sentence.

syntax   **1.** The correct way of writing a command or series of commands, including all the proper options, switches, and command-line statements. **2.** A set of rules that govern how a programming language can be used.

syntax error   An error that occurs when a computer language interpreter or compiler cannot understand a command entered by the programmer.

sysgen   A contraction for system generation, the process of installing or transferring an operating system.

sysop   A contraction for systems operator; the person who runs a bulletin board system.

SYSPROG   In the PICK operating system, analogous to a superuser under UNIX. See also *superuser*.

system application architecture   IBM's set of standards for their entire product line. SAA defines user interfaces, program interfaces, and communications protocols for their mainframes, minis, and microcomputers.

system board   See *motherboard*.

system disk   A disk that is bootable. A system disk contains the operating system files necessary to start the computer and load the operating system. Sometimes referred to as a master disk.

system failure   A malfunction of the hardware or systems software within a computer system.

system fault tolerant   See *fault-tolerant system*.

system file table   In the OS/2 environment, a table maintained by the operating system that tracks every currently open file on the system.

system folder   The folder (subdirectory) within the Macintosh environment that contains the system files. This includes the operating system, Finder, and any cdev programs the user may have added.

system generation   See *sysgen*.

system prompt   See *DOS prompt; prompt*.

systems analyst   A person who is responsible for the overall design and development of a computer system or project. A systems analyst typically does not do actual programming, but works with end users, programmers, and hardware vendors to provide a computing solution to a user's need.

systems disk   The disk that contains the operating system and other systems software that must be available at all times.

systems engineer   Typically, a person who does tasks related to either the operating system or the overall function of a computer system.

systems network architecture   IBM's network architecture for its mainframe environments. Abbreviated SNA.

systems programmer   A programmer who specializes in writing, analyzing, and maintaining systems software.

systems software   Software that controls the operation of a computer system. Examples of systems software include operating systems, user interface programs, and network control programs.

T1   In data communications, a long-haul transmission medium capable of transmitting information at 1.544Mbps. Information on a T1 medium is typically multiplexed into 56Kbps or 64Kbps channels.

tab   Either of two control codes that cause the display or printer cursor to move to the next predefined horizontal or vertical tab stop. Horizontal tabs are used more frequently. See also *horizontal tab* or *vertical tab*.

tab character   A cursor-control character available on most keyboards. It typically causes the cursor to move to the next predefined horizontal tab stop or column. See also *horizontal tab*.

tab-delimited   A data file in which the individual fields are separated by tab characters. See also *comma-delimited*.

table   **1.** In SQL terminology, a database file; a structure, consisting of a two-dimensional arrangement of columns and rows, in which data is stored. **2.** Any array of equal-sized records in computer memory.

table look-up   The process of searching for data in a table.

tagged image file format   A common file format used to store bit-mapped graphic images. The TIFF format will handle gray-scale shading and images with a resolution up to 300 dpi. The common acronym is TIFF; the common file extension for this type of file is .TIF.

tag word   In certain members of the 80x87 (Intel) family of numeric coprocessors, a 16-bit FPU/NPX register that indicates, for each space in the FPU/NPX stack, whether the space is occupied by a number. If so, the register also indicates the type of number contained there.

tap   In local area network terminology, a connection onto the LAN.

tape drive   A computer peripheral that allows access to information stored on magnetic tape.

task   A program or procedure running (or waiting to run) in a multitasking system.

task switch   In a multitasking operating system, a change between the tasks processed by the CPU. Task switching involves overhead operations such as setting up data areas, loading information from disk, and entering different operating modes.

TCL   See *terminal control language*.

TCP/IP   See *transmission control protocol/InterNet protocol*.

TDM   An acronym for time-division multiplexing.

telecommunications   A term describing the communication of information over long distances.

Telenet   A public wide-area packet-switched network service, used to connect to remote computing services across the world.

teleprinter   A computer I/O terminal consisting of a keyboard and a printer (no video display monitor).

template   A pattern; a guide used in creating another form in the shape or format of the original.

tera   A prefix meaning one trillion. See also *trillion*.

termcap   In the UNIX environment, a file that describes the capabilities of each terminal connected to the system. In System V and later versions, this file is replaced with the file terminfo.

terminal   An I/O station for a computer system. A terminal typically consists of a video display screen and a keyboard.

terminal control language   In the PICK operating system, the language used to communicate with and issue commands to the operating system. TCL is used from the system prompt.

terminal emulation   The capability of a computer, through software, to mimic the behavior of a different type of computer terminal.

terminate and stay resident   A program that remains in memory after it is executed. TSR programs are used extensively in computers that run the MS-DOS operating system. They are used to simulate multitasking, as they stay in memory and only become active when the user presses the keystrokes necessary to access the program and make it active.

terminator   In cabling connecting devices, either in a network or a daisy-chained series of devices, a device used to signify the end of the series.

terminfo   See *termcap*.

ternary   A choice or condition that has three (and only three) possible solutions.

test data   Information used to test software or hardware systems prior to field testing or beta testing.

text   **1.** In data communications or networking, the part of a message between the header and the trace section or tail that constitutes the information to be processed or delivered to a specific receiver. **2.** Another name for alphanumeric data.

text editing   The process of changing alphanumeric text by adding, deleting, and rearranging letters, words, sentences, and paragraphs.

text editor   A software program used to create, edit, save, and manage text files. Text editors differ from word processors in that text editors are usually more limited in their abilities, particularly in formatting and printing.

text file   See *file*.

text graphics   Graphic images created by combining special characters assigned to the ASCII character set of some computer systems.

texture mapping   In computer graphics, the application of graphic representations of surface textures to objects.

thermal printer   A printer that produces an image by bringing heated pins in close proximity to special heat-sensitive paper.

thimble   A print head used in some printers that consists of individual typeface characters attached to the end of prongs, which make up the sides of a thimble-shaped cup, as shown here:

thrashing   A condition characterized by excessive paging in an operating system that employs virtual memory.

thread   A portion of a single program that can be executed simultaneously with other threads in the same program. In this way, a single program can accomplish several tasks at the same time. See also *multithreading*.

throughput   The effective speed at which a computer can process data. Throughput is not measured by CPU speed or commercial specifications, but by a collective measure of how fast the CPU, memory, storage devices, and peripherals can process information. Instead of being just a measure of speed, throughput can also be a measure of the amount of work a system can effectively perform in a given time period.

TIFF   See *tagged image file format*.

tiling   **1.** The arrangement of on-screen windows so that there is no overlapping. **2.** In computer graphics, the filling of an object with a pattern instead of a solid color.

time-out   In data communications, an error condition that occurs if no response is received within a given time.

time-sharing   A processing technique in which multiple users have the ability to share computer resources simultaneously.

time slice   In a multitasking or multiuser environment, the amount of time allotted to each process or user operating on the system.

tiny memory model   In the C programming language in the 80x86 (Intel) environment, a type of program in which programming code and data together reside in less than 64K of memory. Sometimes referred to as the 8088 or 8080 memory model.

title bar   In GUI environments, the line of text at the top of a window that indicates the name of the application or file in that window.

TLB   An acronym for translation lookaside buffer.

TOF   **1.** An acronym for top of file; see also *beginning of file*. **2.** An acronym for top of form.

toggle   An on/off switch (either hardware or software). The state of the switch changes between on and off each time it is selected.

token   **1.** A symbol or representation of a value. For instance, in an interpretive language like BASIC, each program keyword is replaced with a token that represents the keyword, but requires less memory for storage. **2.** In network environments (particularly those following the token-ring model), a sequence of bits passed from node to node along the network. A token consists of a starting and ending delimiter surrounding a frame control field that contains a token indicator bit. This bit indicates if the token is able to accept information. If a receiving station has data to send along the network, it attaches the data to the token. The token then becomes a frame.

token ring   See *token-ring network*.

token-ring network   A network topology characterized by a series of devices connected so that the first node is connected to the last, resulting in a closed ring. Messages are passed around the network in one direction as a series of tokens and frames.

toner cartridge   In a laser printer, the portion that holds the electrically charged dry ink and drum used in creating an image on the paper.

toolbox   In the Macintosh environment, the routines and functions contained in ROM, which may be tapped by programmers to ease their programming burdens.

toolkit   A collection of program modules designed to aid a programmer in the development of software.

tools   See *software development tools*.

top of file   See *beginning of file*.

topology   In network terminology, the layout scheme for the network. Typical topologies include star, ring, and bus topologies.

TOPS   **1.** An acronym for transparent operating system, an operating system for several DEC (Digital Equipment Corporation) computer systems. **2.** A local area network from TOPS (a subsidiary of Sun Microsystems) that allows the connection of Apple, IBM, and Sun microcomputers. TOPS features peer-to-peer communications; therefore, it requires no dedicated file server.

TOUCH   In programming, a utility that changes the date and time stored with a file so that it will be recompiled and linked when using a MAKE utility. See also *MAKE*.

touch screen   A combination video display screen and overlay that allows the input of information by touching areas of the screen.

TPA   See *transient program area*.

tpi   See *tracks per inch*.

track   A series of sectors on a disk at the same horizontal distance from the edge of the data recording area. When the disk's read/write head is stationary, a track is all the sectors that spin past the head in one rotation of the disk.

trackball   An input device that is nothing more than a large, upside-down mouse. A typical trackball is shown here:

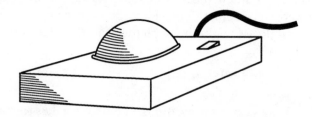

It allows the user to rest his or her palm on the surface of a rotating sphere. As the sphere is rotated, sensors detect the movement and feed information to the computer, which allows it to update the position of the on-screen cursor.

track density   See *tracks per inch*.

track pitch   The distance between adjacent tracks on a recording surface.

tracks per inch   The number of tracks stored in a linear inch of a storage medium, such as a disk or magnetic tape. The acronym is tpi.

tractor feed   A paper-handling device used in printers that print on continuous paper or forms. The tractor ensures that the paper does not drift horizontally or vertically over time as it is fed into the printer. A tractor feed uses sprockets to interlace with the holes at the sides of the continuous paper.

trailer   In data communications, the last part of a packet. It follows the user text and contains end-of-packet control information as well as any error-correction information.

trailing decision   In logical programming loop structures, the conditional statement following the body of the loop that determines if the loop is to be repeated. See also *leading decision*.

transaction   In database terminology, a series of consecutive interactions with a database.

transcendental functions package   A standard Macintosh package used to calculate certain mathematical values such as logarithms, exponentials, and trigonometric functions. This package is provided in the system resource file, or in ROM beginning with the Mac Plus. See also *package (2)*.

transfer rate   See *data rate*.

transfer time   In data communications, the time it takes to transmit data from the sender to the receiver.

transient   A malfunction or program bug that occurs at random intervals with no readily apparent cause for the problem.

transient program area   An area of memory used to hold programs while they are running.

transmission   The communication of information over a communications channel.

transmission channel   See *channel*.

transmission control protocol/InterNet protocol   A communications protocol used widely under the UNIX operating system. TCP/IP was originally developed by ARPA, an agency of the Department of Defense.

transmit   To send or output information on a communications channel.

transmitted data   In data communications, a circuit in RS-232 connections used to carry data from data termination equipment to data communications equipment. TXD is defined as line 2 in RS-232 connections.

transparent   The opposite of opaque; a device or software program that has no effect on raw data. A system that is transparent passes through all data exactly as it received it.

transport layer   In networking terminology, layer 4 of the OSI model. This layer is used to transfer information between endpoints. See also *open system interconnection*.

transpose   To switch the positions of two adjacent elements.

transverse parity check   In a series of bits arranged in a matrix, a parity check performed on the bits in a single column.

trap   In the 680*x*0 (Motorola) family of microprocessors, an error or abnormal condition that causes the CPU to suspend normal program execution temporarily and execute a trap handler routine to respond to the condition. See also *exception*.

trap flag   The bit in an 80*x*86 (Intel) family of microprocessors' flags register that indicates a single-step instruction execution mode. If the trap flag is set, a single-step interrupt occurs. The flag is then cleared after the CPU executes the next instruction.

trap handler   See *exception handler*.

trapping   1. During program development, testing for a particular condition. Once the condition is detected, then the programmer can devise a method of having the software deal with it. 2. When running a program, error trapping is the interception and handling of errors as they occur.

trap vector   See *exception vector*.

tree   A nonlinear data structure where individual data elements in the tree, called nodes, are connected to other nodes through a series of links, usually implemented as pointers. These links are called branches. A tree is a hierarchical representation of data.

trillion   One thousand times one billion (1,000,000,000,000). This is roughly equivalent to a tera; thus a terabyte is approximately one trillion bytes.

triplet   A byte consisting of 3 bits.

troff   In the UNIX environment, a text formatting program used with files destined for laser printers or phototypesetters. See also *nroff*.

Trojan horse   See *virus*.

True BASIC   An updated version of the BASIC language. True BASIC was developed by the original authors Kemeny and Kurtz in response to criticisms of the earlier language. See also *BASIC*.

truncate   To drop the fractional portion of a number (or that portion to the right of the decimal point). This is done without rounding. Sometimes used interchangeably with chop. See also *round*.

truth table   A method of detailing the outcome of Boolean operations. For two variables, there are three columns in a truth table. The first column indicates possible values for the first variable, and the second shows the same for the second variable. The number of rows in the table is determined by the total number of combinations of the two variables. The third column shows the outcome of the operation using the values in the first two columns. For instance, the following illustration shows a truth table for the AND and OR operations with two variables, A and B.

AND				OR		
A	B	result		A	B	result
0	0	0		0	0	0
0	1	0		0	1	1
1	0	0		1	0	1
1	1	1		1	1	1

See also *Karnaugh map*, a simpler method of showing the same information.

TSI An acronym for time slice interval.

TSO An acronym for time sharing option.

TSR See *terminate and stay resident*.

TTL An acronym for transister-to-transister logic.

TTS An acronym for transaction tracking system.

TTY An abbreviation for teletypewriter.

tuple A group of related fields in a database system.

Turbo Pascal A variation of the Pascal programming language published by Borland International. Turbo Pascal provides an integrated development environment including an editor, compiler, and linker. The latest versions of the language include object-oriented language extensions to the original Pascal language.

turnaround time See *response time*.

turnkey system   A complete, ready-to-run hardware and software system. Ideally, when a turnkey system is installed, the only thing that needs to be done is to plug it in and turn it on.

turtle graphics   The graphics system in the Logo programming language. The turtle, which is the graphics cursor and appears as a triangle on-screen, responds to drawing commands from the user such as "go forward" or "turn right."

tutorial   Written or computer-based information that is instructional in nature.

tweak   To make a series of minor adjustments.

twinaxial cable   Often called simply twinax, a cable similar in use to coaxial cable, except that the conductors do not share the same axis, as there are two internal conductors.

twisted pair   A cabling methodology used in networking or data communications that is implemented by a pair of small insulated wires twisted in a spiral fashion around each other. In this way, each wire is subject to a like amount of environmental interference.

two's complement   A number derived by reversing all the binary digits in a number and adding 1. The resulting number is used in mathematic operations.

TXD   See *transmitted data*.

Tymnet   A public wide-area packet-switched network service, used to connect to remote computing services around the world.

type *n*   1. Short for *data type*. 2. The product produced by a typesetting system.

type *v*   To press keys on a keyboard to produce input for a computer system.

typeahead   The ability to type or send characters, which are stored in the typeahead buffer, while the system is busy doing something else.

typeahead buffer   A storage area in memory used to store keystrokes while the computer is busy performing other tasks.

type checking   In compiled languages, a stage in which the compiler verifies that procedure and function calls are passing, receiving, and returning the proper data types or operands.

typeface   The design of a set of printed characters or a family of fonts. Common typefaces include Courier, Helvetica, Times Roman, and Palatino.

type font   See *font*.

typematic rate   The speed at which a keyboard will repeat a key when it is held down for an extended period.

typeover mode   An input condition in which what you type overwrites the characters currently on the screen.

UART   See *universal asynchronous receiver/transmitter*.

UC   See *uppercase*.

UCS   See *user coordinate system*.

UCSD p-system   A programming system that allows programs to be run on a variety of differing hardware platforms without changes to the source code. UCSD is an acronym for University of California at San Diego, the place where the p-system was developed. The system is implemented by translating the source code (which may be written in traditional programming languages) into an intermediate language called p-code. This intermediate language is then run on the target system by the use of an interpreter designed for that system.

UDF   An acronym for user-defined function.

ULA   An acronym for uncommitted logic array.

ULSI   An acronym for ultra-large-scale integration.

unary operation   See *monadic operation*.

unconditional branch   See *branch*.

unconditional jump   See *jump*.

undelete   To undo a previously performed deletion.

underflow   An exception or error condition that occurs when the result of an operation is smaller than can be accurately represented by the computer.

undo   To erase the effects of a command or series of commands. Sophisticated software generally provides an undo capability; how it is implemented or executed varies depending on the software.

Unibus   A bus architecture from DEC (Digital Equipment Corporation) introduced in the early 1970s and used on their PDP-11 and VAX computers.

unification   In Prolog, a process that attempts to match a goal with a clause.

uninterruptable power supply   A device that provides backup power for a computer system when the primary power source fails. Usually a UPS provides power for only a short time, allowing either the original power source to be restored or the system to be safely powered-down.

unit   In the QuickPascal programming language, a collection of predefined, related declarations and subprograms. This collection is stored in a library and any unit may be invoked by declaring the unit by name without explicit declarations for the included elements.

unit separator   A control character used on some computer systems to indicate logical boundaries between data records. The ASCII value for this character is 31, and the acronym is US. See also *interchange unit separator*.

universal asynchronous receiver/transmitter   A hardware device, typically implemented on a chip, that converts information from a parallel to a serial format and vice versa. UARTs are used extensively in data communications where information must be sent in a serial format. See also *universal synchronous/asynchronous receiver/transmitter*.

universal product code   A standardized bar code format used in the retail industries. The code represents the vendor's ID and product numbers, which are read by a scanner at a check-out stand and cross-checked for price in a computer system. The common acronym is UPC.

universal synchronous/asynchronous receiver/transmitter   Similar in function to a UART, except that synchronous communication is also supported. See also *universal asynchronous receiver/transmitter*.

UNIX   A multiuser, multitasking operating system that runs on a wide variety of hardware platforms. There are two primary variants of UNIX, one available from AT&T (System V), and the other based on Berkeley extensions. UNIX was first developed at AT&T's Bell Laboratories in the early 1970s. It is currently written in the C programming language.

unpack   To convert information from a coded, compressed format to its original condition.

unrecoverable error   See *fatal error*.

untyped file   See *binary file*.

UPC   See *universal product code*.

update *n*   A later generation of a program or data.

update *v*   **1.** To modify or make more current the information in a database. **2.** To upgrade a computer system or operating system.

upload   To move a file from your computer to a remote computer over a communications channel; the opposite of download.

uppercase   An EBCDIC control code that enables uppercase characters on a perhiperal. The EBCDIC value for uppercase is 54, and the acronym is UC. See also *lowercase*.

UPS   See *uninterruptable power supply*.

upstream   In network terminology, an area further along the network in the direction opposite the data flow.

uptime   The normal operating time of a computer system; the opposite of downtime.

upward-compatible   A quality of software that enables it to run without modification on larger or later models of a computer system; the opposite of downward-compatible.

USART   See *universal synchronous/asynchronous receiver/transmitter*.

USENET   The news, information, and bulletin board channel of UUCP, a wide-area network for UNIX systems.

user   A person who uses, or operates, a computer or software system.

user coordinate system   In CAD programs, a custom coordinate system defined by the user.

user-defined data type   In certain programming languages, a complex data structure composed of simpler data types.

user-friendly   An overused term meaning that hardware or software is easy to learn and use.

user group   An organization composed of the end users of a particular hardware or software product.

user interface   The portion of a program that handles interaction with the user.

user interface toolbox   See *toolbox*.

utility   A classification of programs that perform "housekeeping" or diagnostic tasks on computer systems.

UUCP   A wide-area network for UNIX systems. UUCP offers many services to installations around the world. UUCP is an abbreviation for UNIX to UNIX copy program.

V

V.21   An ISO recommendation, through the CCITT, for 300-bps modem operation over phone lines in Europe and Japan.

V.22   An ISO recommendation, through the CCITT, for 2400-bps modem operation.

V.24   An ISO recommendation, through the CCITT, for serial communications. V.24 is essentially the same as the RS-232 standard.

V.26   An ISO recommendation, through the CCITT, for 2400-bps modem operation; the successor to V.22.

V.29   An ISO recommendation, through the CCITT, for half-duplex 4800- and 9600-bps modem operation.

V.32   An ISO recommendation, through the CCITT, for full-duplex 4800- and 9600-bps modem operation over normal telephone lines.

VAB   An acronym for voice answer-back.

vaccine   A program designed to counter the effects of a virus program.

VAD   An acronym for value-added dealer, the same as a *value-added reseller*.

validity checking   The process of verifying that data is correct. Validity checking can either be manual (performed by humans) or automatic (performed by software).

value   1. Another name for data, either numeric or alphanumeric. 2. In the PICK operating system, a subdivision of an attribute. Values may be further subdivided into subvalues. See also *subvalue*.

value-added process   In the NetWare environment, a program that resides on the same node as the file server or bridge. VAPs, along with other network functions, manage a file server's resources and offer additional network services.

value-added reseller   A company that sells complete turnkey systems composed of both hardware and software. A VAR typically purchases the hardware, loads the software, installs the unit in a client's business, and provides after-sale training and support.

value mark   In the PICK operating system, a reserved ASCII character used as a delimiter between values. A value mark has an ASCII value of 253.

VAP   See *value-added process*.

vaporware   A term referring to software that does not yet exist.

VAR   See *value-added reseller*.

variable   A storage location in memory whose value can change during program execution.

variable-length record   A database record that has no set length. Variable-length records are typically used in flat files, or files designed for sequential access. See also *fixed-length record*.

VAX   An abbreviation for virtual address extension, a family of 32-bit computers from Digital Equipment Corporation (DEC).

VAX/VMS   An operating system used for the VAX series of computers from Digital Equipment Corporation (DEC).

VCPI   See *virtual control program interface*.

VDI   An acronym for virtual device interface, an ANSI standard for creating device drivers.

VDT   An acronym for video display terminal.

VDU   An acronym for video display unit or visual display unit.

vector   **1.** In computer graphics, a line designated by its endpoints. Vectors can be calculated in either a two- or three-dimensional space. In vector graphics, all objects are composed of a series of vectors. **2.** A pointer. **3.** An array or matrix of numbers; see also *vector processor*.

vector graphics   A method of representing a graphics image as a series of straight lines.

vector processor   A computer or peripheral that performs simultaneous high-speed calculations on numerical elements. Vector processors are used extensively in systems that require intensive graphics operations, such as CAD systems. Sometimes referred to as an array processor.

vector table   A data structure consisting of addresss pointers to other memory locations.

Veitch diagram   See *Karnaugh map*.

Venn diagram   A graphic representation of Boolean operations. A Venn diagram of the Boolean operation A AND B is shown here:

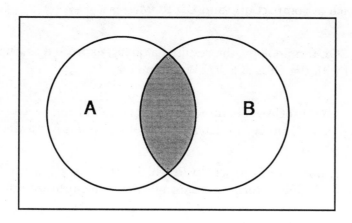

See also *Karnaugh map; truth table*.

vertical recording   A recording method that magnetically records bits vertically instead of horizontally, thereby requiring less space and providing greater storage capacity. Sometimes called vertical magnetic recording or perpendicular magnetic recording.

vertical tab   A control code that causes the cursor on the display or a printer to move to the next line that is predefined as a vertical tab stop. The ASCII and EBCDIC values of a vertical tab are both 11, and the acronym is VT.

VGA   An acronym for video graphics array, a type of display adapter for IBM-compatible microcomputers.

VHSIC   An acronym for very-high-speed integrated circuit.

video   Computer output or other information presented on a display screen and intended for human consumption.

video buffer   An area of memory set aside to store information as it appears on the video screen.

videodisc   A storage medium for digital video data that is later read by means of a laser beam. The videodisc is related to other forms of similar storage such as compact disc and CD-ROM.

view   In SQL terminology, the result of a query, expressed as a table and preserved with the CREATE VIEW statement.

viewpoint   In AutoCAD, the direction and elevation from which you view a drawing; your location in relation to the object you are drawing.

viewport   A portion of the screen to which activity is currently limited. Viewport is a less-used term that is roughly equivalent to window.

virtual control program interface   A memory-management technique used under the MS-DOS operating system running on 80386 and 80486 systems. VCPI allows EMS emulators and DOS extenders to peacefully coexist on the same system.

virtual disk   See *RAM drive*.

virtual file   A logical database file that does not physically exist. A data set is extracted from a physical file and manipulated in the form of a new (virtual) data file.

virtual memory   A memory management technique that allows a program to access more memory than is physically available in a computer system. Memory is divided into pages; some of these pages are stored in RAM while the rest reside on disk. When information from the disk-based pages is needed, then some of the memory-based pages are stored to disk and the required disk-based pages are brought into RAM so the desired operation can occur.

virus   A program that attaches itself to other programs or data. A virus' typical purpose is to disrupt the processing of information on an infected system. When an infected program is executed, the virus reproduces and spreads by searching for other software that is not infected, and then attaching itself to previously "clean" software. A virus is similar to a worm. The difference is that a virus always attaches itself to other programs, whereas a worm may not. Both typically have the same destructive purpose. A Trojan horse is a type of virus that does its damage right away without attaching itself to any other programs in the system.

VLSI   An acronym for very-large-scale integration.

VM   An acronym for virtual machine.

VMS   An operating system that runs on Digital Equipment Corporation's family of VAX computers. VMS is an acronym for virtual memory system, and provides a multiuser, multitasking, virtual memory environment.

VM/SP   An acronym for virtual machine/system product, an operating system for large IBM mainframe computers.

voice recognition   The ability of hardware or software to recognize and respond to spoken commands.

volatile memory   Memory that is only temporary and does not maintain its contents once power is removed.

volume label   In certain operating systems, a user-defined name that identifies a disk or magnetic tape.

von Neumann architecture   A model for computer design developed by John von Neumann. It calls for programs and data sharing the same memory space. Often referred to as the stored program concept.

VRC   An acronym for vertical redundancy check, a method of character parity checking.

VRX   The operating system used on NCR's V8500 and V8600 mainframes.

VSAM   An acronym for virtual storage access method, a data storage method used in large IBM mainframes.

VSOS   An acronym for virtual-storage operating system.

VT   See *vertical tab*.

VT-100   A popular and widely used type of terminal developed by Digital Equipment Corporation (DEC).

VTAM   An acronym for virtual telecommunications access method, an IBM SNA communications program.

VTOC   An acronym for volume table of contents.

waiting time   See *latency*.

wait state   A dormant state during which a computer simply "marks time," waiting for an operation to occur. Wait states are often used for synchronization purposes—for example, when a fast CPU must wait for information from a memory area that cannot operate as quickly.

WAN   An acronym for wide-area network.

Wangnet   A type of broadband LAN from Wang Laboratories.

warm boot   The process of starting a computer from a warm, or powered-on condition. See also *boot*.

watch variable   In the QuickBASIC, QuickC, or QuickPascal programming environments, a variable that the programmer selects to be displayed in the watch window. The contents of the selected variable are then displayed at all times.

watch window   In the QuickBASIC, QuickC, or QuickPascal programming environments, or in the CodeView debugging software, a window used to display the value of selected expressions and variables during program execution. The watch window is used primarily during testing and debugging programs.

WCS   See *world coordinate system*.

Weitek coprocessor   A numeric processor extension for computers using the Intel 80286 or 80386 CPUs.

Whetstone   A benchmark program implemented by testing how a computing system fares at performing floating-point operations. Test results are expressed in Whetstones per second.

whitespace   Any character that does not result in a printed letter, number, or symbol. Whitespace includes spaces, tabs, and blank lines.

wide-area network   A network in which the computers and other equipment connected to the network are separated by wide distances.

wideband   See *broadband*.

widow   In word processing and publishing, the last line of a paragraph that appears as the first line of a printed page. Special software routines are commonly used to make sure there are no widows when a document is printed.

wildcard character   A symbol used in filenames and extensions to represent another character or string of characters. In the MS-DOS operating system, the asterisk (*) and question mark (?) are the wildcard characters. In the NetWare environment, compound wildcards such as ^., ^?, and ^* are allowed. These represent the indicated ASCII characters with the high-order bit set. In the UNIX environment, wildcard characters are often referred to as metacharacters.

Winchester disk   A sealed, fixed-disk technology developed by IBM and made popular on hard-disk systems included with microcomputers.

window   A portion of the screen to which activity is currently limited.

windowing software   Software that uses windowing techniques to display information or get input.

windows environment   A computing environment characterized by an operating system that allows multiple windows on the display screen. Examples of such environments include DESQview, Microsoft Windows, Presentation Manager, and X Window for the IBM, and Finder or MultiFinder for the Macintosh.

Windows program   A program written to run under Microsoft Windows.

wire-frame modeling   In CAD systems, a display technique that shows three-dimensional images in outline form. Wire-frame modeling does not attempt to suppress hidden lines.

wire wrapped   Electrical connections formed by wrapping bare wire around a metal prong.

WK1 file   A file with the extension .WK1. Usually used to designate a worksheet file compatible with Lotus 1-2-3 version 2.0 or later. See also *WKS file*.

WKS file   A file with the extension .WKS. Usually used to designate a worksheet file compatible with Lotus 1-2-3 version 1A. See also *WK1 file*.

word   A basic unit of data storage and manipulation. Typically, a word is equivalent to 2 bytes, or 16 bits. Thus, a word can contain values ranging from 0 to 65,536. On some computer systems, a word is more properly defined as the number of bits that can be processed at a single time. Using this method of definition, it is possible to have 32- or 64-bit words.

word addressable   A condition that exists when the smallest unit of memory that a computer can independently address is a word.

word length   The number of bits that make up the basic word unit on a given system. See also *word*.

word processor   A classification of application software that allows for the entry, manipulation, formatting, and printing of textual information. There are many types of word processors available, WordPerfect being the most popular.

work area   A memory area designated for use by the program currently running.

working directory   See *current directory*.

workspace   See *work area*.

workstation   A computer or terminal connected to a local area network, or a terminal connected to a multiuser computer.

world coordinate system   In graphics programs, a device-independent Cartesian coordinate system that defines the location of every entity in a drawing.

WORM   See *write once, read many*.

worm   A destructive routine in a program that is designed to corrupt information on a disk. A worm differs from a virus in that it cannot replicate itself or attach itself to other programs.

worst case   During testing, a set of conditions and data that will provide the least-favorable operating situation for a hardware or software system. By using a worst-case scenario, developers attempt to anticipate the worst possible conditions under which their systems can run, and to make sure they do so.

wpm   An acronym for words per minute.

write   To transfer information to a mass storage device from the computer's memory.

write-enable notch   See *write-protect notch*.

write error   An error that occurs while attempting to write information to memory or a peripheral such as a disk drive.

write once, read many   A mass storage device (such as an optical disk) on which information can only be recorded once in any given location. WORM devices are typically used for high-capacity archiving of data.

write permission   A level of file access that only allows writing information to the file. See also *permission*.

write protect   A level of protection applied to files or an entire disk that prohibits the altering of the information contained within the file or disk.

write-protect notch   On a diskette, the small notch on the side of the disk that controls whether the diskette can be written to or not. On 5.25″ disks, if the notch is covered with something, then the disk cannot be written on. On 8″ disks, if the notch is uncovered the disk cannot be written on.

write-protect tab   See *write-protect notch*.

write ring   See *file protect ring*.

write through   A technique where all information written to a buffer or cache is immediately written to memory or other storage. This ensures that the storage area is always up to date, but obviates the benefits of the cache or buffer.

WXmodem   A variation of the Xmodem communications protocol that allows the sending system to transmit data before receiving acknowledgment that the last block was correctly received.

WYSIWYG   An acronym for "what you see is what you get." It refers to software that displays, on-screen, your information as it will appear when printed.

X Y Z

X.25 A standard format for data packets used in public switched networks. X.25 defines synchronous communications protocols. This standard was formalized by the Consultative Committee for International Telephony and Telegraphy.

X.3 A standard protocol for the packet assembly/disassembly facilities of a public data network. This standard was formalized by the Consultative Committee for International Telephony and Telegraphy.

X.400 A set of standard protocols for electronic mail systems. This standard was formalized by the Consultative Committee for International Telephony and Telegraphy.

XCFN In the Macintosh environment, a program function written in a high-level programming language designed to be used with the Hyper-Talk programming language. An XCFN (external function) is designed to return a value that can be accessed, interpreted, and acted upon by HyperTalk.

XCMD   In the Macintosh environment, a user-defined command developed for use with the HyperCard system. XCMD is short for external command.

XENIX   An enhanced version of AT&T System V UNIX from Microsoft Corporation that runs on IBM PC systems.

Xerox network services   A collection of services used to access the capabilities of a network. In the NetWare environment, XNS are implemented through SPX and IPX protocols.

Xerox network systems/InterNet transport   A communications protocol used in early EtherNet networks. XNS/ITP is now obsolete, and replaced with TCP/IP.

XFCN   An abbreviation for external function.

XLS file   A file with the extension .XLS. Usually used to designate a worksheet file compatible with Microsoft Excel.

Xmodem   One of the oldest asynchronous communications protocols for personal computers. Xmodem was originally developed by Ward Christensen, and has served as the basis for many other communications protocols such as Ymodem and Zmodem. It is used for error-checking and correction of files transmitted across a communications link. Xmodem transmits information in 128-byte blocks.

Xmodem-CRC   A second-generation version of the Xmodem communications protocol that uses cyclic redundancy checking to detect errors. Xmodem-CRC is also very closely related to the Ymodem protocol.

XMT   An abbreviation for transmit.

XNS   See *Xerox network services*.

XNS/ITP   See *Xerox network systems/InterNet transport*.

XON/XOFF   In asynchronous data communications, a rudimentary handshaking protocol that is used to control the flow of information.

When the receiving device cannot process any more information, an XOFF signal is sent to the transmitting device, indicating that transmission should be halted temporarily. When the receiving device is again ready to accept data, an XON signal is transmitted, indicating that transmission should be resumed.

XOR   A Boolean operation meaning exclusive-or. It compares corresponding bit positions of two sets of equal-length data and sets the resulting bits based on the condition of the tested bits. If one of the corresponding bits is on, then the resulting bit is on. The resulting bit is off if both of the original bits are off, or if both of the original bits are on. Sometimes referred to as the exclusive operation. The following illustration shows the K-map for the XOR operation using two variables:

	0	1
0	0	1
1	1	0

X.PC   An asynchronous version of the X.25 standard.

XQL   In the NetWare environment, an RDBMS that understands SQL statements.

X Window   A windowing environment for graphics workstations, commonly used under the UNIX operating system. X was developed at MIT in conjunction with Digital Equipment Corporation (DEC) and IBM.

Ymodem   An asynchronous communications protocol that allows for the transmission of multiple files with a single file specification (using wildcard characters). The transmission method and error detection are identical to the Xmodem-CRC protocol, except that Ymodem generally transfers 1K blocks of data.

Z8530   See *serial communications controller*.

zap   To delete information, usually within a database.

zero extension   A method of data conversion to a larger format in which extra bit positions are filled with zeros. See also *sign extension*.

zero flag   In the 80x86 (Intel) family, the bit in the flags register that indicates whether the result of the preceding operation is zero. If the result was zero, the flag is set; if the result was not zero, the flag is clear.

zero page   In systems based on the 6502 microprocessor, the first 256 bytes of memory.

Zmodem   An error-free communications protocol typically used to transfer large files. Zmodem, along with its Xmodem and Ymodem predecessors, uses a CRC for error detection.